NO REGRETS

The Life of an American Martial Artist

Jerry E. Fisher

Note for Librarians: A cataloguing record for this book is available from Library
and Archives Canada at www.collectionscanada.ca/amicus/index-e.html

Printed in Victoria, BC, Canada.

ISBN: 978-1-4251-9239-6

*We at Trafford believe that it is the responsibility of us all, as both individuals
and corporations, to make choices that are environmentally and socially sound.
You, in turn, are supporting this responsible conduct each time you purchase a
Trafford book, or make use of our publishing services. To find out how you are
helping, please visit www.trafford.com/responsiblepublishing.html*

*Our mission is to efficiently provide the world's finest, most comprehensive
book publishing service, enabling every author to experience success.
To find out how to publish your book, your way, and have it available
worldwide, visit us online at www.trafford.com*

Trafford rev. 6/8/2009

North America & international
toll-free: 1 888 232 4444 (USA & Canada)
phone: 250 383 6864 ♦ fax: 250 383 6804 ♦ email: info@trafford.com

The United Kingdom & Europe
phone: +44 (0)1865 487 395 ♦ local rate: 0845 230 9601
facsimile: +44 (0)1865 481 507 ♦ email: info.uk@trafford.com

10 9 8 7 6 5 4 3 2 1

THE LIFE AND TIMES OF AN AMERICAN MARTIAL ARTIST

1936: THE MIDDLE of the Great Depression. Rapid City, South Dakota. A small town in the American Midwest. June 19th, one of the hottest days of that summer. My mother, Lucille Mayfield, was a pretty, twenty year old, blue-eyed blonde with a wonderful sense of humor. She gave birth to me in the local hospital.

My father was a twenty-one-year-old ex-college football player and member of the boxing team at the School of Mines, a local college. He was working, and lucky to be working at all in those terrible times, at the Fairmont Creamery. It was part dairy and part slaughterhouse.

Ed Fisher was a cold and distant man, one of those individuals who was conceited without any justifiable reason to be. Perhaps, in part, it was because he was a spoiled only child, and in part to compensate in some way for growing up in a time of so little opportunity. After the Depression ended, and for the rest of his life, he was scarred by the experience. He always "played it safe," afraid to take a chance on anything new for fear of losing whatever he had, however little it might be.

My paternal grandparents, Park and Hazel Fisher, were good, simple, hardworking people. Park owned a four-chair barbershop, the only one in town. It was located in the lobby of the Alex Johnson Hotel on Main Street, the tallest building in Rapid City, about seven or eight stories. Hazel was a "housewife" of the old school. Cooking, cleaning, washing, and canning occupied her days to the fullest. She kept a modest, clean and decent home. They were keepers of what could be called simple Midwestern values and ethics. I spent a great part of my first five years under their care and tutelage. Honesty, fairness and good work ethics were ingrained into me there.

My maternal grandparents, Vivian "Jack" Mayfield and Alma Cook Mayfield, also lived in Rapid City. They had six children. My mother was the middle of their three daughters.

Jack was the deep end of my gene pool. He was a fighter. I always wondered how much of that was the result of his parents naming him "Vivian," like "A Boy Named Sue" of Johnny Cash fame.

Jack referred to himself as a "wrassler." Born in 1888, he had grown up in Kansas, Nebraska and Colorado. He had worked at many jobs and owned several businesses, from farming and chicken ranching to owning a radio station.

During the first five years of my life and for a few years before that, he had owned a tire shop and automobile wrecking yard on the outskirts of Rapid City. He managed to make a decent living from them even during that awful period of American history.

In one of the outbuildings of his business he had dug a circular "pit" about four feet deep and perhaps twenty feet wide and in it he continued, even though he was well into his fifties, to fight any and all comers for money. He rarely lost a fight. As a little boy I loved to play in the pit, pretend fights that I always won and in which I never got hurt.

He had to have been my genetic and environmental role model who started me towards my life-long love for the challenge and art of personal combat.

As a little boy growing up in Rapid City South Dakota, I naturally became fascinated by the Sioux Indians.

My Grandfather Fisher had his barbershop located directly across the street from a store called Duhamel's Trading Post. Duhamel's specialized in Sioux artifacts and products.

The Lakota and Ogallala Sioux tribes brought their hand made items for sale into Duhamel's, and on the weekends, weather permitting, they would put on a show, wearing full costume, and dance in front of the store.

My grandfather was always very friendly and kind to the Indians, providing them with water and whatever else they needed during the long, frequently very hot or cold days.

My grandmother donated two days a week working at the Tuberculosis Hospital for the Sioux that had been established on the reservation. She was one of the only white women that did so. She was well known and very much loved and respected by the Sioux.

From the time I was three or so, I used to love to mingle with the Sioux during the days that they were putting on a show. Eventually I learned the dances. It must have been a strange sight, seeing this four- or five-year-old, blue-eyed, blond little boy dancing with those fierce warriors. They made authentic clothes for me just for the dances, complete with deerskin breechcloth, moccasins, tomahawk, and feathers. I think they must have thought it was very funny.

Once in a while they would take me home with them at the end of the day. I am told that at first it caused a great deal of consternation with my grandparents, but after a few times they were okay with it.

One day when I was not quite yet five years old, the family that had "adopted" me the most, their last name was Twotrees, had taken me home with them. (They really lived in teepees.)

They had a big surprise for me.

After a lengthy and formal ceremony, I was inducted into the Sioux nation. The family was Ogallala but the event was held on the Lakota reservation ground, making me both an Ogallala and Lakota Sioux.

I have never forgotten that honor! They made me a warrior, officially.

At the end of the summer of 1941, my father lost his job at the creamery. There were no more jobs in town. A year or so earlier my maternal Aunt Lillian had moved to San Francisco with her husband and my two cousins, Bill and Tom, who were my age. My aunt and uncle had found work there; it was decided that we would do the same. So we made the long trip in a 1936 Oldsmobile. It was exciting, not like travel today. It was a big adventure. The car broke down at regular intervals. Usually we were on some two-lane road in the middle of nowhere. I remember once being pulled into the next little hamlet by a farmer and his horse. There we waited a day or two for a part to arrive and be installed.

I have a clear memory of watching my grandmother Fisher sewing some spare cash into the lining of my father's jacket to hide it from potential bandits we might encounter on the road.

When we finally arrived in San Francisco in the summer of 1941, we stayed with our relatives for a few weeks until my father found work in the shipyards of

Oakland, California. It turned out to be a very important factor in our future. When the war broke out a few months later, his work was immediately classified as "essential to the war effort," and he was deferred from having to serve in the military. When he was earning enough money, we rented a small apartment at 1260 Broadway. The building was built right after the great earthquake and fire of 1906 and still stands in use today. We lived there for four years, on the third and top floor in the southwest corner facing Broadway.

When my aunt had married her husband, Bill Irvin, she had converted to his Catholic faith and had raised my cousins, Bill Jr. and Tom as Catholics. Although my parents remained staunch supporters of their own systems, he a Methodist and she a Presbyterian, they made a decision that I believe further influenced my evolution as a fighter. They enrolled me in Saint Bridget's, a Catholic school.

As far as I know I was the only Protestant child at Saint Bridget's. When that was discovered, I became "that Protestant kid." The bullying and fighting soon started. It followed me throughout the four years that I attended school there.

I'm sure that those early experiences, with the resulting conflict, were primarily responsible for my resulting confusion and life-long pursuit of a religious answer.

Throughout a large portion of my life I experimented with everything including Atheism, Agnosticism, Buddhism, Catholicism, various forms of Protestantism, until finally, in 1980, I became a staunch Christian, basing my beliefs on my own reading, study and interpretation of the New Testament.

For some reason, it never occurred to my parents to take me out of that environment and send me to a public school. Instead when I would come home at night with the perennial black eye, cut lip or bloody nose, they would tell me that I shouldn't give in to either the pressure to become a Catholic or to let them "run me off." Instead, my father taught me all he could about boxing and then enrolled me in a YMCA boxing program when I was seven years old.

I found a home there at the "Y." Soon Jack Mayfield's genes took over. I loved it: the training, the acceptance, and the challenge. Those were the things that gave me a different outlook on life. Instead of being the outcast, I became a part of the whole thing. I trained almost every night. I started participating in the intramural and extracurricular matches and tournaments. I began to win consistently, and at the "Y," I became a well-liked and popular figure for the first time in my life. Although I was so young, from seven to ten years old, some of the boxing matches remain clearly etched in my memory. By the time I was starting the fourth grade at Saint Bridget's, I was no more liked or accepted than before but the bullying stopped. Even the older, bigger boys learned not to fight with me. Certainly I didn't always win, but I gave too good of an account of myself for them to want to try it again.

Our apartment, close to the top of Broadway, was only three or four blocks from Chinatown, located on and around Grant Avenue. I learned to escape from the local Catholic boy peer pressure by walking down the hill to Chinatown. There I found a new world full of strange smells, sounds, sights and people. I felt oddly at home there even though I was still obviously out of place. I spent a lot of time wandering the streets of Chinatown. It was like a secret, special world. I kept it to myself; my parents had no idea how much of the time I was living in my Chinese world.

Then, suddenly, in one of life's unexpected turns, my parents decided to move to the Mission District of San Francisco. It was a little step up for them, out of an apartment and into a tiny little house in a poor, mostly Italian neighborhood. It was 1945; World War Two was coming to an end. For the first time I was allowed to attend a public school. I finished the fourth, fifth and sixth grades there at Monroe Elementary School.

After a few encounters with the tough Italian kids of the neighborhood, and after soundly beating a few of them, again I earned acceptance. It was my fighting ability that made it happen. Boys, even more so then than today, lived in a violent and "survival of the fittest" world.

I liked school and I went on to be the captain of the "traffic squad," made up of the older boys who made sure the younger kids got to and from school safely.

In the sixth and highest grade I was elected student body president. That was a major, confidence-building event in my young life. I had to preside over the monthly meetings of the assembled students. I learned then to organize my thoughts and plans and to speak to large groups.

We were still very poor; my father never kept a job for very long. I was badly neglected. During those grammar school years I never knew when I came home if they were going to be there or not. Frequently they would disappear somewhere for days at a time.

I soon learned, by the fifth grade, that it was up to me to take care of myself. I set up various after school jobs. I sold newspapers at the corner of Mission and Excelsior streets, and shined shoes there as well. After I had sold my papers I usually went to a movie to see the latest films, then I would stop at the Floralee restaurant for a sandwich before heading home.

I continued with my boxing. I found the PAL (Police Athletic League) program and the Boys Club. Both had good boxing programs. I tried to go after school every afternoon to box for an hour and then go to my paper corner until about nine at night. I had to fight and win a few vicious street fights to hold onto my "corner."

Occasionally I would be allowed to work out at a professional gym on Mission Street. That was exciting stuff. Although I was only 12, and I'm sure they really took it easy on me, nevertheless I was training and interacting and learning from the "real guys." These were the high points of my life during those years.

That period of my life in San Francisco was hard and lonely. We were very poor. I was always ashamed of my old clothes and my shoes always had holes in the soles, which I tried to patch in various ways. I was very sensitive about my condition and after a while everyone learned never to tease me about it. I seldom had a coat or jacket and remember being cold most of the time.

I suppose at this time I could easily have become a bully. I was certainly the best fighter in the school and the neighborhood. However, my troubles became my salvation in that regard.

When I would finish selling my papers, and I knew no one was going to be at home, I would hide my shoeshine box and go to the movies. The Granada Theater on Mission Street was my sanctuary. It was a beautiful, warm refuge, full of magic, and a wondrous place for me to escape from my worries and fears

There I met and discovered John Wayne.

John Wayne became my hero, friend, role model and mentor. I didn't want to be like John Wayne: I wanted to be John Wayne. I would sit through his movies as many times as I could during the week or so they would play. Captain York, Nathan Brittles, John Striker and Sean Thornton became my alter egos. No matter whom he portrayed, he was always brave, honest to a fault, and a defender of womanhood and the weak. A contemporary Knight Errant. His screen persona, which I believe to this day was a reflection of his true character, became my sought-after ideal.

Without John Wayne, who knows what path I may have followed? Many of the kids from that neighborhood went on to become criminals of the worst sort.

My conscience and behavior was molded by the consideration of "what would HE do?" Thank you, John Wayne!

Much later in my life I was fortunate to have a real life mentor and father in the form of a man named Jim Marcus, but that comes later.

Those first twelve years of my life were the foundation of everything that I was to become. Over the rest of my life, of course, I was subjected to many strong influences. We never stop growing and changing until we die. However, those early years are the base of the pyramid, holding everything that comes later, and helping it in its climb to the heights.

World War Two came to an end. It had been a time like no other in the history of this great country. Following upon the heels of the Great Depression, a time of fear, uncertainty and despair, the war years reunited this country. For the first time in many years, the people of the United States were working as one for a common cause. True Evil existed in the world and it had to be stopped. We got past the myopic focus on our own existence and made sacrifices for the common good. Men went to war and died for their beliefs. Those who stayed home worked together as one to further the unified goals of all. "Don't you know there's a war on?" was a phrase you heard daily.

As a boy, I did what I could, all of us did. We collected tin and rubber for "scrap drives." Every week we had "meatless Tuesdays," where no one ate meat. We kept our eyes out for spies and saboteurs. I belonged to the "clean your plate club;" nothing was wasted. We learned to eat margarine as the butter all went somehow towards the war effort. My father escaped military service because his work at the shipyards was classified as "essential to the war effort." He worked 60 or more hours a week, repairing damaged Navy ships and getting them back into the fight. He was also an air raid warden. Living on the West Coast, there was the constant fear of a Japanese raid. We had made raids from our aircraft carriers on Tokyo itself, and felt there was a good chance of reprisal. At one point during the war there was a Japanese submarine that did make it into San Francisco Bay, but no damage was done. An air raid drill was sounded by sirens that could be heard throughout the City and was accompanied by a "blackout" wherein every light in the City had to be hidden until the "all clear" was heard. As a warden, my father had to go out wearing a special white helmet and patrol several assigned blocks and make sure no lights of any kind were visible from the air.

We saw little red, white and blue flags on more and more windows that indicated that the family living there had a loved one in the war. If the star in the flag was gold, that indicated a loved one killed in the fighting. Practically every man you saw between the ages of 18 and 30 was in uniform. When you did see a man of that age in civilian clothes he was usually on crutches, or perhaps missing a limb or an eye. A grim reminder that not all of the servicemen hit by the enemy died outright.

I remember as if it was yesterday the wild, tumultuous celebrations of both VE Day and VJ Day, marking our victory and the end of the war. People were dancing in the streets, hugging, kissing and screaming. My uncle Bob Mayfield was home on leave from fighting with the Marines in the Pacific and was standing in the middle of Mission Street playing his saxophone. All of this signaled the beginning of another new chapter in our history, and in my life: from Depression, to War, to Recovery.

Then another, wrenching change. My parents decided to move across the Bay to Richmond, California. This, during my transition from elementary school to the seventh grade and junior high school.

Richmond, then as now, was a rough, tough place, predominantly populated by black people living in tenement like "projects" that were erected during the war as "temporary housing." I was in for another cultural shock. Again a minority, living first with Catholics, then Italians and now blacks, I couldn't understand it when I heard people refer to white, Protestant Americans as the "majority." I had never experienced that.

Because of my years in boxing, I had a few black friends in San Francisco and had no racial bias whatsoever. It wasn't a problem for me to live in a black majority. I soon found out, however, that it was a problem for some of them.

My parents had borrowed the down payment from my paternal grandparents to buy a house in Richmond, on Ohio Street. It was a little square house, 2 bedrooms and one bathroom, probably 900 square feet in all. No garage. The back fence was about ten feet from a single railroad track. When a train came by, about once or twice per hour, the house would shake. It was like the scene in the "Blues Brothers." However, like Jake and Elwood, we learned to sleep though the noise.

The good thing for me was that I had my own room as I turned thirteen and Harry Ells Junior High was directly on the other side of the railroad tracks.

My father had a new job with Carnation Milk and was earning a regular paycheck. My mother worked in various coffee shops as a waitress and cook. In my mind at the time I felt "normal," almost affluent. Within a few months my mother gave birth to a second child, my sister Sherry.

It was necessary for my mother to get right back to work, so I became the baby sitter. I learned at an early age all of the duties that came with raising a baby. She was born in December of 1948, and by summer I was as well trained in "baby" as any new mother. It became my full-time job. It was training that paid off well for me later in raising my own children and a niece and a grandchild or so.

In between the baby-sitting and school I began to look for a place to continue my boxing. By then, after six years of it, I couldn't imagine not fighting.

There is a Chinese proverb that says, " That which does not kill us strengthens us." Richmond pushed it to the limit.

Harry Ells was a big junior high full of a cross section of 7th, 8th and 9th grade kids: wealthy white kids who lived "on the hill," middle class kids from the nicer neighborhoods to the north, and the rest of us. Mostly black, south of the railroad track and in the apartments.

There was a definite class distinction. As one of the few white kids in the last group as well as being a newcomer from across the Bay, I had to prove myself early.

Within the first week I had three fights at school, and earned an instant reputation as someone not to bother. Six years of devoted training and study in boxing plus my time on the street corner in San Francisco had created in me a formidable street fighter.

We didn't have "gangs" per se. However there was a group, nameless, but who were referred to as the "hard guys." It was a mixed ethnic group of 20 or so. They dressed in the height of local fashion: Levis, dark shirts, big hair, and distinctive shoes. The shoes were an important part of the "uniform." Black leather, highly polished, and with a solid wedge across the bottom between the sole and heel so that the entire bottom of the shoe was then all one piece. The final touch was the application of metal "taps" that covered most of the walking surface. The purpose was twofold, as a badge of membership in the group, (no "geeks" were allowed to wear them), and more importantly as weapons.

Interestingly, at some point, earlier members had developed a style of fighting that included kicking. I'm positive that none of these kids in Richmond in 1949 had ever heard of such a thing as an Asian martial art, yet they had created an effective kicking system. We spent a great deal of our time either fighting with or preparing to fight with the other Junior High in Richmond, Longfellow Junior High. For no reason whatsoever that I can recall, the two junior highs had been mortal enemies for many years. Sometimes the altercations were minor, a fistfight in the park. On a few occasions during my three years, they reached epic proportions with 50 or so kids on each side with the employment of nasty weapons.

Tire irons, chains, bats, homemade clubs and knives were the most common. I preferred the knife. I'm ashamed to say that I did actually cut a few people. Thank God, never seriously.

I owned a couple of good knives; one was a long, 3-½ inch blade, Italian switchblade that I had acquired in San Francisco. I practiced with it constantly. I earned a reputation as being the guy with whom you wouldn't want to knife fight.

I quickly earned a place in the Hard Guys and became very good friends with several members. I bought my shoes and soon learned the techniques involved in using them. Combined with my hand skill and natural ferocity (thank you, Jack Mayfield), I became one of the leaders even though I was one of the lowly seventh graders.

The Junior High experience was life changing. I retained most of my "John Wayne" values but for the first time I became a member of the ruling group in the school hierarchy. It was a new experience.

By the end of the seventh grade I had found a place to continue my boxing training. The city had a system of recreational centers, each one identified by its geographic location. One of them, the "Cutting Rec," so called because it was located on Cutting Blvd in the black neighborhood, had a loose semi-official boxing program. It was run by two black ex-professional fighters, who gave their time when they could. It was good enough that I continued to learn and hone my skills. Interspersed with the occasional street fight, I continued to practice my warrior ways.

I managed to get through junior high with decent grades and a reputation of being a tough, funny, very fair guy without any serious enemies. I also fell in love for the first time with a beautiful, half-Cherokee girl named Jane Melton. Jane had to take the bus to and from school. She lived about 5 miles from Harry Ells. I used to walk to see her 4 or 5 nights a week. Our romance lasted through the 9th grade; when we started high school we attended different schools and were forced apart.

By the start of 1952 I was going into the 10th grade at Richmond Union High School. I had continued to work throughout junior high. There was never enough money at home and I was expected to provide my own clothes, shoes and spending money. I worked at many jobs: for the Acme Fence Company, a number of used car lots, as a bag boy in grocery stores. I even sold apples door to door. When I was 15, I had an opportunity to take a job at a small market called the Vista Drive-in Market. They wanted me to stock shelves and deliver groceries to the wealthy customers on "the hill." I needed a driver's license. My parents, always eager to receive part of my money, agreed to go to the DMV with me and lie about my age. In those days before computers, you could do that. So they appeared with me and signed a document stating that I had been born in 1935. And I was instantly a 16 year old with a driver's license.

The Vista Drive-in Market job was a good one and lasted me through high school. I went from bag boy and delivery boy, to cashier, to night manager. It was a great job for me, in a small market, with 6 or 7 full time employees. I made a man's wages and did a man's work. I came to work at 4 or 4:30, after school and boxing. I worked until 10:00 at night Monday through Friday and put in 8 hours on Saturday. It gave me close to 40 hours a week with a little overtime here and there. I had to pay room and board to my parents. The good thing about that was that they really didn't care what I did or where and when I went as long as I gave them money. I was making plenty of money and could therefore come and go as I pleased.

I didn't sleep a lot. It was my habit to go out after work with a few of my older friends, mostly in their early twenties. We drank and gambled and chased girls. I would get to sleep about 2:00 AM, up at 7:00 and to school, nap during lunch and study hall and somehow make it through the day.

My high school years were 1952, '53 and '54. It was a different world. Drugs were very rare. I only knew one guy who shot heroin, and a meager handful who smoked pot. Alcohol was the drug of choice and everyone drank a lot!

One of the reasons that my job as night manager (I was there alone from 8 till 10 PM) was so great was that I could and did sell beer and wine to my friends. Needless to say, I was very popular. My boss looked the other way; it was nice extra business for him.

One of my good friends, Rene Neville, lived up on the hill in a mansion. His father was an executive with Standard Oil. They were the big employer in Richmond. Rene was 20 or 21, attended UC Berkeley and drove a Mercedes convertible. He used to host poker parties at his house one night a week. The games became well known for some big time action. Gamblers came from San Francisco and farther to sit in. I did quite well and at 17 years old I would frequently double my week's income by playing cards.

I did well enough that I owned two cars, paid for in cash during my senior high school year. In 1954 I had a beautiful, midnight blue 1950 Chevrolet convertible with a white top. Also I had a 1932 Ford coupe with 1948 Mercury V8 engine. It was a drag racer and rarely lost a race.

Girls were my favorite preoccupation, along with boxing. I had many girlfriends. Fell in love a couple of times. My main girlfriend was Sally Cortez, a gorgeous Mexican girl from a wealthy family. She was the head cheerleader and well-liked in school. We were together throughout my junior year. She graduated a year before me and that was the end of that.

Richmond High was a large school serving the entire city of about 80,000 people. The enrollment was over 3500 students. Classes graduated every 6 months in those times. It was 10th, 11th and 12th grades. So every 6 months there was a Senior Ball, the social event of the season. I went to every one except for my first year in the low 10th. I always had a beautiful girl to escort.

High School was a fabulous time for me. Work and all, it was beautiful!

I continued to box and fought a lot of amateur fights in various venues and with several different affiliations. My reputation kept me out of some bad situations.

Having " made my bones" in junior high and with a well-known reputation as a ferocious fighter, I had to prove it far less often than in Junior High. I continued to train at the "Rec" less frequently, but also started working with my friends and schoolmates teaching them boxing at various friends' houses. I finally reached about 5 ft 10 with a consistent weight of 150 lbs. That was where I kept my fighting weight.

One event that stands out clearly in my memory was the "Coach Bagnes" episode.

Bagnes was a Physical Education coach of the old school: rough, thick, 220 lbs, 40 years old and mean. He bullied the students mercilessly.

He particularly disliked me. I was going to school, out by 3:00, boxing till 4:30 then working every night at the Vista Drive-in until 10:00. It didn't make sense to me to then have to spend an hour every day playing badminton or volleyball in the school P.E. class. So I was very unenthusiastic about it. He hated that!

In my senior year, when I was 17 years old, Bagnes and I had reached the point of an explosion. One day he decided to instruct the class in the fine art of self-defense and brought boxing gloves to class. I think he had me in mind from the beginning. Towards the end of class after showing and telling everyone his version of "the Manly Art of Self Defense," he asked if any one would like to take a go with him. "How about you, Fisher?"

I tried to demur but he insisted. He said it would be OK: "I won't hurt you, much." Finally I put on the gloves. He was big, strong and mean, but slow and not very skilled. The fight lasted about 4 or 5 minutes, and he was given the beating of his life, I'm sure, by a 150 lb, 17-year-old boy. I split his lips, broke his nose and knocked him down twice. I was pretty sure I cracked one or two of his ribs as well. He had asked, insisted, in front of the entire class so he had nowhere to go with it. The story was told and retold for a long time at Richmond High.

I met the girl who was to become my first wife in my senior year: Louise Peacock. Although we had gone to school together since the seventh grade, we had hardly spoken. She was from "The Hill" and therefore in a different socio-economic group altogether. We went to our senior prom together, and even though we were only 17, we soon decided to marry. I think both of us were anxious to get out of our respective houses and embark upon "true adulthood." Graduating from high school in June of 1954, we married soon after in 1955, at the tender age of 18. Way too young. These were different times.

The first year before and after being married I managed to attend a year of college, work full time, and fathered a son, Scott, born on January 20th, 1956. My boxing suffered, other than an occasional workout with friends I had little time. I had previously taken a couple of club fights at local clubs, like "The Pheasant Club" in El Sobrante. At the third of these, I sustained a serious injury to my right temple from an elbow and had to stop boxing for an indefinite period.

KARATE, IS IT SOMETHING TO EAT?

IT WAS DURING this period of abstinence from boxing that I first encountered an Asian Martial Art. It was late 1956 or early 1957. A friend of mine from High school, Jerry Finney, had been in the military and was stationed in Okinawa. There he had trained with Tatsuo Shimabuku in Isshinryu Karate.

Upon his return from Asia I met Jerry for a drink at a local Mexican restaurant. We hadn't seen each other for a couple of years and were doing a lot of catching up. He had been a famous street fighter, as had I. So naturally the conversation got around to fighting.

When he first mentioned karate, I didn't know what he was talking about, having never heard the word before. I thought he was talking about a food dish. After correcting my misunderstanding, he went on to explain that it was a method of fighting where you learned to toughen your body and make the entire thing a weapon. He told me what he knew of its history, etc. We ended up in the parking lot and spent a long time with him showing me things he had learned in the year or so he had trained with the Grandmaster.

I was fascinated by it. Over the next year or so I worked out with Jerry whenever possible, combining my boxing skill, and street fighting experience with what I could learn of karate. I built striking boards the way it was explained to me that it was done in Okinawa. I tried to perfect my kicks. It was still almost totally unheard of in most of the Mainland US. I suspect that Ed Parker and we were some of the only people in North America practicing the Asian fighting arts.

I had started another career at the same time. I went to work for a large, wholesale carpet distributor, the Murray B. Marsh Company, working on their order desk in Emeryville, California in 1957. I did well there and in 1959 I was promoted to an outside sales position in Sacramento, California. My family and

I moved there, I began the life of a "traveling salesman," and on January 5th 1961 my second son Kirk Fisher was born.

We remained in Sacramento for almost eight years. I worked hard and was very successful in my business. I traveled every week from Sacramento up to the Oregon border and into Reno, Nevada. Lots of driving and some great experience.

My martial arts studies continued, but it was difficult. There was no school in that part of California at that time that I was ever aware of. However, my interest, my passion for fighting still continued unabated. So I trained myself alone. Books were starting to appear that I could read and learn from, some of which I still have. Probably the earliest was a book by Bruce Tegner. I absorbed them and continued to practice and train and toughen (injure) my hands on my homemade *makiwara* boards.

One of my most memorable experiences occurred while I was traveling up and down Northern and Central California calling on floor covering stores.

I was about 26 years old. It was a presidential election year: Kennedy vs. Nixon. I had become a pretty staunch Republican and so of course was a great admirer and supporter of Richard Nixon.

Every other week my travels took me from Sacramento, north as far as Yreka at the Oregon border. Sometimes I drove all the way up and worked my way back down, all while attending college courses at Sacramento and American River colleges at night. It was a whole week of travel, school and work.

This particular week I was on my way back down. I had spent the night in Redding, California. I had heard on the news and seen in the papers that Richard Nixon was giving a speech in Redding the night I was there. There was no way that I could attend, it was a sell out and I had to work late.

The next morning, I finished my obligations in Redding, packed, checked out of the Casa Blanca Motel and started to drive south to the even smaller town of Red Bluff. It was a little country town of perhaps 6000 people, supported mostly by cattle and agriculture.

I had only a couple of accounts to see. I usually only spent an hour or two in Red Bluff before going on farther south to Chico.

I was in my car, about half way through the 45-minute trip from Redding to Red Bluff. I was listening to the radio and heard that Nixon was also leaving

Redding shortly and would make a stop over in Red Bluff before leaving Northern California for San Francisco.

I didn't think much about it. It was about 11:00 AM, I hadn't had time for a real breakfast so I decided to have an early lunch. One of my favorite places to eat there was the coffee shop of the Red Bluff Hotel. That's where I went.

As I entered the lobby I realized something was up. It looked as if all the leading citizens of Red Bluff had assembled there. There were perhaps 200 people in the hotel lobby; they were surprisingly well dressed for this little cow town.

I was wearing a suit and a tie and carrying my briefcase. This set me apart.

As I walked farther into the lobby a couple of older people came up to me and nervously asked.

"Are you with the Republican Party"?

Since I was a Republican, I answered affirmatively: "Yes, I am."

Before I could say any thing else they started telling me how glad they were that I had shown up. They believed me to be Nixon's advance man.

"Mr. Nixon is going to be here in about 30 minutes and we don't know how to set up the lobby or what to do," was what I heard. Always the organizer and never shy, I decided, why disappoint them? I told them, "Okay, let's get ready for him."

We leaped into action. I started directing the event.

"Let's put the tables over here, the Mayor and City Council members should be here at the front of the greeting line. Put the head of the local Republican Party over here. Move the coffee and food back here to this area. Let's move the signs back to this spot."

In 20 minutes or so we had reorganized the lobby. Just as we finished, a young crew-cut man, about ten years older than me, strode into the lobby of the Hotel. His name was H. R. Haldeman.

Haldeman was there to organize the reception. He was, however, very pleased to see that it was well organized already and he needed to make only one minor change. He said, "My compliments to you for doing such a good job of setting this up."

The locals quickly told him, "Oh it wasn't us, it was the young man you sent ahead from your party."

Puzzled, he asked where this man was. They pointed me out. As he walked towards me I was a little apprehensive. Perhaps there were laws against impersonating an aide to a presidential candidate.

He introduced himself and asked me what was going on. I told him it was a case of mistaken identity. When they asked me for help, I thought, why not give them a hand. "I hope it's okay?"

He looked at me for a few seconds then started to laugh. All he said was "Ballsy," and shook my hand.

He asked me to stick around and went out in front of the Hotel to meet the Nixon motorcade.

The reception went smoothly. Mr. Nixon gave a short speech, shook hands and chatted with the local notables. In less than an hour he was ready to go. I hadn't spoken with him, just watched the proceedings.

Things were wrapping up, the Nixon entourage was moving towards the bus and their cars. Just then Haldeman came up to me and said, "If you have time, Mr. Nixon would like you to ride in the bus with him to the airport."

I was more than ready for that and said, "I would be honored."

As I boarded the bus, Nixon was sitting alone in the first few rows; there were various assistants in the back. Haldeman introduced us and went to the back. Nixon motioned for me to sit across from him.

He said "I didn't take time to eat, would you like a sandwich?" Of course I took one, I don't remember whether or not I ate it.

It was about a 30-minute bus ride to the airport. He told me that he had heard what I did and wanted to thank me personally for my help. I was extremely affected that he would take that much time with me. I certainly hadn't expected it.

He talked, and other than answer a few questions about my life, I listened. He was very friendly and down to Earth and talked about his family and his cocker spaniel. I believe his name was "Checkers."

As we pulled onto the airport tarmac, it got busy again. Haldeman told me that he had arranged transportation back to the hotel for me. I left the bus and walked towards the car. I was standing there watching the party board the airplane.

Just as I thought they were leaving and I was about to get into the waiting car, I saw Nixon walking towards me. He came up to me put his hand out to shake.

He said "Thank you again for your help. Is there anything I can do for you?" I couldn't think of anything so I asked for his autograph: one of the only times in my life I have ever done that.

He took one of his cards and a pen; he asked," What do you want it to say?"

All I could think of is what he wrote:

"Best wishes to Scott and Kirk   Richard M. Nixon"

Then he was gone. Scott and I just talked about that today, 45 years later. It's still a vivid memory for me. The card, the ink badly faded, is displayed in a little frame.

I had reached a sufficient level of maturity and spent all my time working or with my family, so street fighting became a thing of the past.

I had a couple of experiences in the very early Sixties at a boxing gym on Front Street in Sacramento, the name is lost to me. I went in and worked out several times combining boxing and kicks on the heavy bags. I think they thought I was insane. No one there had ever seen anything like that before. Looking back on it now I think it was perhaps the earliest ever "Mixed Martial Art." Who knew then?

I continued in this manner until in 1966, at which time I was offered and accepted a sales position with the largest commercial carpet manufacturer in the industry: Commercial Carpet Corporation, or as it was customarily called,"CCC." I worked for a little over a year in the Northern California and Reno, Nevada area. I was successful in selling one of the biggest orders that the company had received up until then. We carpeted the northern campus of the University of Nevada, about 15,000 square yards of carpet in all. A huge order in those days. As a result I was transferred to their Salt Lake City territory. It was a virgin area and they wanted me to open it up for them.

We spent a year in Utah, during which time very little new happened with my martial arts training, I continued working out and practicing on my own but I now had my sons to start teaching.

The year in Utah was a year of regrouping and growing; the cost of living was much less than that in California. Since I had also been given a raise to help compensate for the move, we were able to get a little stronger financially. It was not an unpleasant time. We made a few friends and my business was very successful.

My efforts at the business paid off and I was able to develop some large continuous business with the LDS Church and the schools.

Then in late 1967, as a result of the big sales increase in Utah, I was promoted by CCC to sales manager for California and transferred to Los Angeles. I bought a nice house in Tarzana, California and worked for CCC in the carpet business out of beautiful offices at 8899 Beverly Blvd. in Beverly Hills. I traveled with my salesmen 2 or 3 days a week.

Then the world changed! I discovered that there were people actually teaching martial arts in professional schools!

After looking at a number of schools that were convenient for myself and Scott and Kirk, I chose to enroll us at Bob Ozman's dojo, headquartered in Van Nuys, California. Mr. Ozman held a 5th degree black Belt ranking in Isshinryu karate from Grandmaster Tatsuo Shimabuku, the first person I had ever heard of in martial arts. But also, and this appealed to me, he had boxed and had incorporated another system, Shotokan, into his "Ozman Ryu" System.

Bob Ozman was then, and still is at the time of this writing, a big, strong man. An athlete all his life and a formidable fighter, he owned and operated two schools: the Van Nuys school and another in Tarzana, Calif. The Tarzana school was run by his second degree black belt, John Atkinson.

Atkinson was an enigmatic figure. At that time only 17 years old, he had already trained with Ozman for 6 years. He was small, about 5 ft 4 inches and 120 lbs, one of the fastest young men I have ever seen and an incredible kicker.

John Atkinson was a contradiction. He was a regular tournament competitor. His record, however, was checkered to say the least.

On one weekend he would be "ON" and beat someone like Bill Wallace or Skipper Mullins. On the next weekend, usually from partying too much the night before, he would lose his first match to a frightened, first time, tournament competitor.

John needed thick, black-rimmed glasses and wore them when he fought. About every other tournament he would either have them broken or sustain a cut over his eye where a kick or punch forced the rim deeply into his face.

These were the bare-knuckle, barefoot days of so-called "control" sparring. I have lost track of how many injuries, broken ribs, nose, hands and feet that I sustained during those years of "control."

The idea of going full speed, with perfect, accurate techniques and coming a half an inch away from your opponent, was a strange one anyway. "Moderate" contact to the body was allowed. That moderate contact cost me a great many broken ribs in the years that I was competing. The head contact, though mostly unintentional, was ferocious when it did occur. Bare-knuckle punches to the head and face delivered by a good black belt at full speed were frequently disastrous.

John held wins over the great fighters of the era such as Benny Urquidez, John Natividad, Bill Wallace, Skipper Mullins, Darnell Garcia and many more. Yet he could never repeat his performance in the ensuing weeks. His lifestyle constantly interfered.

Shortly after starting with Ozman at the Van Nuys School, I made the decision to change to the Tarzana School on Ventura Blvd. We were living in Tarzana at the time so the dojo was only 5 min from our house. I was very impressed with Atkinson's ability, not only as a fighter but as a superb technique and forms expert as well, and thought he would be a great person from whom my sons and I could learn the system.

That proved to be true. John was, although young, a very good teacher and his techniques were flawless. We absorbed like sponges.

In about three years, we were all very quick studies because of lives devoted to study and practice and because of our 5 times per week schedule at the school, we were awarded our first degree black belts in Ozman Ryu. As mentioned earlier, the style was made up of Isshinryu plus Shotokan.

This was in the early 1970s, at the same time that my career at CCC had exploded. I had moved upwards from sales manager to regional manager to Western Area vice president for the 17 western states. With about 20 salesmen and many millions of dollars under my control, I continued to travel every week.

With the motivation of keeping my own hours and coming and going as I pleased plus as an investment, I bought the Tarzana school from Ozman.

Atkinson, Scott, Kirk and I did all the teaching, six days per week.

It was during those years that we began experimenting with tournament competition. I was, in 1972, already 36 years old. I too was hit and miss; frequently I would take first in my age division only to lose for Grand Champion, to a quick, well known 23 year old. Nevertheless I loved the combat, win or lose.

Although we continued to teach the system pretty much unchanged, a few new developments occurred. For one thing, we introduced more boxing-style hand techniques in our school.

The younger Shimabuku, Ezu, came to the US for a visit and was impressed with the school and promoted me to Sandan , 3rd degree black belt, in Isshinryu. About that same time I met and befriended Master Mike Slaney who was a 5th degree master of Hapkido . After an evening of sparring at his school, when I soundly defeated him and all of his black belts, he asked me to come in and teach his sparring classes. I agreed in exchange for his teaching me hapkido. The plan resulted in his fighters getting much better, and I earned a first degree Black Belt in Hapkido. This was also incorporated into our system.

Mike died from cancer before actually finishing my certificate. However in an example of the kind of honor that I have learned to know and respect in the martial arts, actually on his deathbed, he signed my certificate and asked his wife to find me and give it to me. I received it a few weeks after his passing. In the pages to come there will be many more examples of this "Code of Honor" that I believe exists in the martial arts community. This code reminds me of my childhood "John Wayne" code, and I believe it was a tremendously beneficial force in the development of the character and strength of my children, Scott, Kirk, and later, my daughter Xian and son John.

It was during the early '70s that we really became involved in tournament production. Partly because I was older, and also because I had a reputation of being totally "color blind" and scrupulously fair, I became a constant and well-known referee. I held my first tournament in 1972 at the Culver City Auditorium. It was a great venue. Over the next 25 or so years I personally promoted over 45 of my own tournaments at that location. Combined with the fact that David Torres and I ran or greatly helped run the other promoters' TPA tournaments almost EVERY weekend during this time, we presided over close to 1000. I can't help but believe that is a record that may never be broken. David and I finally burned out in the late '90s; we just couldn't do it any more.

In the early days of Karate Tournaments, they were generally each held and sponsored by one major style. There were Japanese tournaments, Korean, Chinese, etc. A good example were the great tournaments held at the Japanese Deer Park, an attraction in southern California. They were straight shotokan and woe betide the fighter who came from any other style. They were hard fought and bloody. It was close to impossible for practitioners of any other styles to prevail. It wasn't "cheating," or maybe not always even favoritism. It was mostly that the judges of a specific style would always tend to recognize points first and mostly from techniques that they were familiar with.

By the same token the Tae Kwon Do Tournaments, although billed as "Open" tournaments, were almost never won by any one other than a Tae Kwon Do practitioner. That was just the way it was. The black fighters, mostly Kenpo people, felt, with some good reason, that they couldn't get a fair deal at the tournaments and so formed the Black Karate Federation, or BKF, to put on their own tournaments and go to other tournaments as a group in able to demand fair treatment. To further add to the chaos that was the tournament scene in the late '60s and early '70s, every tournament was governed by different rules. At most the rules were not written or discussed until just beforehand. It was not unusual for there to be a 4-hour debate prior to the beginning of the event over what the rules should be for the day!

Needless to say it was a chaotic mess. Fights were a common occurrence, as were boycotts, even riots. It was totally out of control. I have seen, for example, instances where a fighter was dropped for the count with a perfect reverse punch to the solar plexus, only to see the victor be denied the point because 2 of the 3 judges didn't like the way the punchers fist was turned.

Then a respected, high-ranking, martial artist, Mr. Ed Hamile, a Shotokan Master from Hawaii, stepped forward. His original idea was to form an association, which he called the Referee and Judges Association, or RAJA, and *standardize* the rules. At first the idea met with a great deal of opposition. Then little by little people started to come over to it. Ed held meetings at the schools of anyone who was interested, and worked tirelessly to make it work. He received no financial remuneration for it; it was a labor of love for him. I joined forces with him early on and supported him fully. A standard set of rules began to emerge, rules that would be the same every weekend. These were not only rules of conduct, but also rules governing what is a point, how do you call a point? Clinics were held at various schools; instructors and any black belts who wanted to participate were invited to come and take part. The attendees were issued RAJA ID cards upon completion of training. Actual matches were held to help the attendees with their learning process. RAJA caught on and for the first time, throughout Southern California tournaments were starting earlier, ending earlier and proceeding with a minimum of strife. The confusion over the rules slowly abated.

Ed's hard work was paying off greatly. Then, calamity, he allowed some of the members to talk him into what turned out to be a huge mistake. They wanted uniforms. After great deal of arguing and debate they decided on black pants and black and white striped referee shirts like the NFL. No traditional uniforms and no belts or rank insignias. It was a major disaster! The majority of the referees and judges hated the uniforms and dropped out of the organization rather than wear them. They wanted to wear their own school uniforms with their well-earned black belts. The unhappy ex-members did a good job of turning many others against RAJA and the organization died with a whimper.

However, the most important result of RAJA survived: the standardized rules. We owe that to Ed Hamile and his good-hearted, tireless efforts.

Having had a taste of what changes standardized rules could bring about in tournament organization, a handful of promoters, myself included, decided to try to bring more order to the scene.

To that end, Dave Torres, a well-known and popular Kenpo instructor and tournament regular, agreed to host a meeting at his school in Pico Rivera. The exact date eludes me but I believe it was in 1980 sometime. I have a photo on the wall of my office of the original attendees. First and foremost was " the Father of American Karate" himself, Grandmaster Ed Parker. Without his support the idea of a tournament organization would have been stillborn. Also in attendance were, Dave Torres, Bob White, Steve Fisher, Solomon Kaihewalu, the Pacheco brothers, Rose Cassamassa, Ed Hamile, John Conway, Frank Trejo, Art Ruiz and myself, and perhaps others. If I have unintentionally omitted anyone from this first meeting, I apologize.

Those of us who were there were the producers of the biggest and best tournaments in Southern California, the number one of course being Ed Parker's "Internationals." Unquestionably it was the largest and most prestigious, at least in the west if not in the entire country.

There was great chemistry in the air at this meeting. An atmosphere of mutual respect and honor pervaded. It was decided then to form an organization to be called simply the Tournament Promoters Association, or the TPA. David Torres was elected as our President. I was elected Secretary. (A lot of work accompanied that position.)

The first action was to publish a booklet of the new Standardized Rules. The second order of business was to create a master tournament calendar. This was a huge breakthrough! Prior to this first meeting it was not uncommon to work for weeks, rent a venue, buy trophies, only to find that one or more other tournaments were being held on the same day. A recipe for disaster. The calendar eliminated date duplications.

The fledgling TPA quickly earned respect and an excellent reputation for standard rules, good organization, starting and ending on time (a major innovation), and fair judging.

One of the biggest reasons for the great success of the TPA tournaments was the fact that the TPA promoters had also pledged to help one another at their events. When I gave a tournament I was assured of the attendance of the other members and their students. Also, and very important, none of the other members would schedule a Tournament for the same date. Each of us had certain strengths that the others could rely on to help them at their tournament.

For some reason I gravitated towards coordinating the event through the microphone; Dave Torres was excellent directing on the floor. David and I became a great team and brothers. Some other member would do the line ups, an important part of the success on the floor. Yet another TPA member might handle security and so on.

More promoters joined. The Pacheco brothers, although young, had the help and support of their parents. Frank Trejo, Ron Chapel (although not a promoter himself, this fine martial artist and tireless man represented Mr. Parker at the TPA), Danny Rodarte, Steve Torres, Muhammed Jahan Vash, Steve Muhammed (Sanders), Art Ruiz, and more.

The TPA was a ground-breaking organization, widely emulated even to this present day. Like many such coalitions throughout history it came about from the diligent, honest efforts of people who came together at the right place and the right time with the necessary talents to make it all happen. Much more about tournaments later.

It was sometime in 1976 or so that a pair of (husband and wife) promoters named Don and Judy Quine created one of, if not the, first Full Contact karate leagues.

They invited the best fighters in the world to compete in a huge event in Los Angeles to determine who would be the world champion in each weight division.

My son Scott and I were asked to do the television commercial to be shown all over the country to advertise the event.

We met at 3:00 AM on Venice Beach for the filming. The time was selected, as that was when the beach was most deserted.

A famous martial artist and swordsman, Hidey Ochiai, was filmed doing a katana form. It was beautiful. I performed part of an Isshin Ryu form. It was Scott, however, who got the short straw. He had the job of doing a short fighting set with the indomitable Ralph Alegria, ending with Ralph doing a spinning back hook kick to Scott's head. The camera crew had trouble getting the shot and Scott ended up getting kicked in the head about a dozen times before it was a wrap!

The week leading up to the event, I was in Hawaii on business and flew back that day to act as one of the judges.

As I recall the winners were, in descending order by weight: Mike Stone, Jeff Smith, Chuck Norris, Cecil Peoples, and Benny Urquidez – all of whom I gladly count as old friends.

THE PUMA SYSTEM

DURING THE TPA times mentioned earlier, my own training and learning was constantly evolving. At the risk of having to insert a lot of "I"s into the narrative, it is necessary to digress to a brief history of the development of PUMA.

Sometime in 1978 it became expedient to divest myself of the Tarzana school on Ventura Boulevard. My older sons Scott and Kirk, along with John Atkinson, had been the reason I could continue the school. My other career had continued to rise. I was now the Vice President of sales at CCC, and still traveling, now all over the world, at least 2 nights every week.

Scott had graduated from UCLA and Kirk was following 5 years behind him at CSUN. Atkinson was still pursued by his own personal devils.

A buyer came forward and it seemed to be a good time to get out, so I did.

Prior to the sale of the school, my sons and I had continued to look outside for more techniques and theories to absorb into our growing repertoire. It now included boxing, kick boxing, Isshin Ryu , Shotokan and Hapkido. My oldest son, Scott, had trained for quite a while with my life long friend and another of my true martial arts brothers, Bobby Burbidge. Scott brought a lot of Tang Soo Do back into our system with him.

At the same time I had developed a very close and personal relationship with Mr. Parker and he and his disciple Ron Chapelle had begun to introduce me to the wonderful intricacies of Parker Kenpo. I ultimately was awarded a 3rd degree, *sandan*, rank in Parker Kenpo which occupies a place of honor on my dojo wall along with the other previously mentioned certificates.

At this point in time we realized, my sons and I, that we now had developed and created a very unique and different "mixed martial art", one of the first! In

1978, most schools were still teaching very traditional arts. I remember once that some traditional stylist referred to our system in an insulting tone as a "mish-mash" system. Implying that traditional arts should never be mixed. Forgetting that they all had to be mixed at some point in their history.

We decided we needed a name for what we were doing. After casting about for a while, I think it was Scott who said,"How about, "Pacific Unified Martial Arts" Perfect! It says it all. Unified, for the different Pacific Rim countries that are represented in the style and its combination with American boxing. Martial Arts, as opposed to naming a specific style. Last but not least the initials spell PUMA, a Native American Lion! That was it. The logo became a puma leaping through a yin and yang. The old and the new combined.

Over the intervening years we have trained and developed many outstanding students, including about 100 black belts. We are very proud of all of them. The PUMA system is now being taught all over the country. It continues to evolve.

In 2007, for example, Mr. Joe Stevenson, the number-one-ranked lightweight in the UFC, and a Puma black belt, who does his prefight training at our Big Bear Lake headquarters is adding his great talent as a black belt in Brazilian ju jitsu to the system. We never want to stop growing and evolving!

Just to name a few of the PUMA Black Belts of whom I am so proud, there are 8th degrees Scott and Kirk Fisher, Ron Pohnel, and Ken Firestone. 7th degrees: Leslie Fisher (my wife, with 27 years under her belt and my partner for 27 years in life and at the Big Bear lake school), Greg Zem and Johnny Gyro, a famous tournament competitor. (I just recently promoted Johnny to 8th degree). 6th degrees: Burnis White who is the ex-Middle weight champion of the world, and Ed Anders, a well-known fight and stunt coordinator for films. 5th degrees: Mark Zacharatos, Gates Foss, Todd Whetsel, Greg Megowan, Lester Salvatierra, and many more.

I must mention two other later supporters and contributors to the PUMA system: my daughter Xian and my youngest son John.

Xian, whom I adopted from Korea when she was 4 ½ years old in 1976, was one of the reasons that early in my Tournament career, all the races accepted me as a fair and impartial "color blind" official. Xian became a very fine black belt and presently lives in Hawaii with her husband, Adam Chapman. She will next reach the rank of 4th degree.

John (born in 1974) began his Martial Arts training at the age of 5. In his pre-teens and teens he was a well-known figure at the tournaments and was a regular winner in the junior brown and black belt sparring events. He too is working towards his 4th degree Black Belt. He presently owns his own business in the drug and rehabilitation field and is working for his master's degree in psychology.

I have always encouraged my children and students to look outwards and try and experiment with different styles and disciplines. Our system is never closed or secret. We are interested in pragmatism. If it works, use it and find a counter for it.

One of the opportunities that I am very happy to have had was the experience as a martial arts consultant for the Los Angeles Police Department, adding so much more to the PUMA system.

Burnis White was an LAPD officer assigned to the training academy, then located at a large facility in a Korean church on Beverly Blvd. in Los Angeles. He was also a 6th degree black belt in the PUMA system. He invited me to join the LAPD team as a defensive tactic consultant. Some of the other members at that time were Benny Urquidez, Cliff Stewart, Gene LaBelle, the Machado Brothers, Art Hopkins, Al Thomas, and Gokor, to name just a few.

The purpose of assembling this panel of experts was for them to devise new and more effective techniques to be taught to rank and file police officers for their use in hand to hand combat and arrest and control situations.

Usually each month or so the panel would be given a specific assignment based on records of reports from the street. We might be told, for example, "Last month there were over 400 reports of   officers being attacked by multiple assailants," or perhaps it would be "sharpened screwdrivers." These are only two actual examples. It would then become the work of the panel to meet and work together to find solutions.

Although the subject matter was indeed serious and the panel devised many techniques and methods in common use today, it was an enjoyable process filled with a great deal of good natured camaraderie.

Gene LaBelle was a particular pleasure to work with. The great fighter, teacher, film consultant, stunt man, speaker and writer was always a source of both good ideas and humor.

Working with the panel there was always a group of young, strong athletic police officers assigned to the training force. Each month there would be a few new ones. When Gene would stand on the large blue workout mat to discuss and illustrate a technique, he would ask for a volunteer. Those who had been there before would suddenly find an interest in their fingernails or shoelaces to keep from making eye contact with Gene. Eventually one of the new men would volunteer to act as his assistant for the purpose of showing the assemblage Gene's latest response. The group would gleefully then watch Gene proceed to strangle, stretch and otherwise contort the newcomer into positions that human beings were never made to experience.

Then there was Art Hopkins. Art had been the first hand-to-hand combat instructor to the United States Marines during World War Two. One of the world's greatest Jujitsu exponents, now in his mid Eighties and with hearing aids in both ears, Art was about 5 ft 5 inches tall and maybe weighed 130 lbs.

He would sit quietly but intently listening to the ideas and suggestions of the assembly, and then perhaps once in each meeting he would raise his hand. When that happened there would be a respectful silence while he slowly made his way to the mat. He might say, "What if you tried it this way?" And then, with a seemingly effortless movement on Art's part, one of the 225 lb, 27-year-old officers would fly through the air and land in a heap a few feet away.

Another frequent contributor was my old friend Cliff Stewart. A big man, and a formidable martial artist, Cliff was at that time, and still may be, the instructor and head of security for actor Wesley Snipes.

I remember working with Cliff one day after the panel had moved to the new facility on Manchester. That day we were working on ways to turn the tables on someone who had you pinned against a wall.

Before going on the mat we would meet each morning, first for coffee and donuts in an adjacent room. This is where we would assemble and be given our "problem of the day." I recall an incident that typifies the frequent humor that pervaded the atmosphere.

Cell phones were just then becoming commonly used. The ring tones were being improved all the time. New ones, previously unheard, were coming into use.

Just as the meeting was breaking up to move to the mat, everyone was standing and moving toward the door. When the cell phone belonging to Gokor, one of the greatest grapplers of all time, went off. The new ring was a loud Latin melody. Upon hearing it this assembly of serious world famous martial artists and police sergeants, simultaneously broke into dance! Imagine if you can, Gokor, Gene LaBelle, Burnis White, and the rest, dancing around the room at the police training facility to the beat of a Rumba.

Although I believe we all enjoyed our time together very much, some excellent, constructive ideas came out of the group and systems were implemented that are still in use today not only with the LA Police Department, but with many other organizations across the country. The arrest and control techniques that resulted from this group are in use in many other departments and State and Federal Agencies across the world.

During that time the tournament scene became a more and more demanding responsibility. David Torres and I were unable to say no to any promoter who needed us to help them with their tournament. We felt a responsibility to be there and contribute. We worked together almost every Sunday! One year alone we went to 50 tournaments. That was not uncommon after a while. We became friends for life and became more like unidentical twin brothers; we were almost able to read each other's thoughts.

David would control the floor, supervise the lineups, and take the competitors to the rings. I would, from the microphone, call the divisions to the line up areas, assign referees and judges to specific rings to call points, solve problems and keep the event running at a fast, steady pace. The inevitable problems, squabbles, disagreements, angry parents, missed assignments, etc. were handled by which ever of us got it first. Our equal understanding of the rules and our close working relationship kept us always in agreement on any issue.

Tournaments themselves began to change. In the '70s there was a marked, highly visible difference between the competitors. An experienced tournament official could immediately identify the style, school and often even the instructor of every competitor. It wasn't only the difference in their uniforms, but their stances, guard, and techniques were unique to each style.

If they had all been dressed identically, in 30 seconds or less you could see; this was a Shotokan stylist, or a Tang Soo Do or Kenpo or Kung Fu practitioner. The antecedents of each competitor's style were obvious to a trained observer.

As the eighties developed, the differences began to fade. Regular tournament competitors began to pick up techniques that worked from their interaction with students of other disciplines. If a fighter from one system got hit a few times with a technique used commonly in another system he would assimilate that technique into his own arsenal. What developed during the 80's was a pragmatic, realistic, tournament style of fighting. As the decade progressed the tournament fighting style became a thing of its own.

I continued to referee at most events, mostly the black belts and finals, my favorite job.

Just this last July 2008, at Stan Witz's prestigious International World Championships in Las Vegas, I refereed all of the black belt continuous sparring, the "West Coast" black belt sparring (where the groin IS a target), the mixed martial arts fighting and the black belt finals. I hope to be doing it for many years to come!

David and I had many funny and memorable experiences together.

I recall the time that Frank Trejo, one of Ed Parker's top black belts and a ferocious fighter in his own right, decided to hold a tournament. Frank was the head instructor and manager of Mr. Parker's Pasadena School on Walnut Street. Although Mr. Parker made frequent appearances there, his traveling and seminar schedule required him to be gone a great part each month, therefore Frank was left to his own devices much of the time.

Frank notified the TPA of his choice for a tournament date and it was placed on the calendar. He specifically asked Dave and me if we would be sure and come to do our "thing" for his tournament. Being good friends of Frank's, we of course assured him we would.

I had, by 1980, assembled my "tournament in a box." I had purchased a large, red footlocker. In it was everything needed to stage an event. Most tournaments had eight rings taped out ahead of time. To be safe I had twelve of everything: stop watches, clipboards, tape for the rings, and the sponges for the timekeepers to throw into the ring when time were called. In addition, it included a first aid kit and six walkie talkies, plus the necessary papers: sign up sheets, releases, and elimination brackets. If someone had the venue, they could do an entire tournament with my "box." I of course, encouraged each promoter to supply his own materials, but I always could provide any inevitable missing items.

In the case of Frank's tournament, the day arrived. He had rented a good-sized area in the Pasadena Hilton. Close to the school and Mr. Parker's home. Ed Parker himself was on one of his very frequent trips out of the country that weekend.

The tournament was scheduled to open its doors, as usual, at 9:00 AM and begin at 10:00 AM. Dave Torres and I arrived at about 8:00 AM or so, fortunately. Nothing was ready. We commandeered some of Frank's students and had them start taping the rings with tape from my box. By 9:00, still no Frank, so we set up a table in the front and had a couple of his students begin the sign ups, again using my materials. By 9:45 we had the tournament set up and ready to roll. We held our black belt meeting and began the line-ups. About then Frank appeared, wearing a beautiful, white, rented tuxedo. David and I were very impressed that Frank had dressed in such a way for his tournament.

Frank then proceeded to tell us that he had to go to a wedding and would be back as soon as possible. As, I'm sure, our jaws hung to the floor, he gave us a typical, jaunty Trejo wave and left the hotel.

We went to work. The Tournament was large and successful and ran until about 6 or 7 PM. At the end we had concluded the finals and had students removing tape and finishing the clean up.

I had just finished packing my box and was talking with David when in strolled Frank, still looking dapper in his white tuxedo. We handed him a paper bag full of money, he thanked us and took his leave.

David and I couldn't do anything but laugh. We will never forget Frank's way of putting on a tournament. All you need is the idea!

Another of the hundreds of memorable incidents occurred at a Tournament somewhere in East LA.

As a young man, David had learned sign language. He was very proficient at it.

I was at my usual place, on the microphone, in the front of the gymnasium. When three young men, all brown belts, came to stand in front of me. When I looked up to see what they wanted, they indicated that they all could neither hear or speak.

I motioned for them to wait and called David to come to the microphone. He conversed with them by signing for a few minutes, and told me he would see that they were taken to the proper ring for their events and keep an eye on them.

Some time later, two of them came running up to me gesticulating rapidly; obviously very upset about something that must have occurred at the ring. Again I motioned for them to wait and called David.

When he arrived, it was clear that they were very upset, as their hand motions were being delivered very rapidly and with great gusto, accompanied by excited facial expressions. After a few moments David replied with sign of his own. They stared at him for a few seconds then broke into smiles and started laughing silently. Impressed by the sudden change in their demeanor, I asked David "What did you say to them"?

He replied, "I said, 'Don't yell at me!'"

The problem was soon solved and calm was restored.

Another time David and I were working together at a tournament in Indio, Calif. David had been asked to step in and take center for the black belt weapons division finals. The last competitor was doing a difficult nunchaku form at great speed. He was executing a move where the stick comes over his shoulder from behind him when it struck him with full force in the back of the head and he fell to the floor unconscious. After an initial gasp, a silence fell over the crowd for a few moments. Then David calmly looked at the other four judges and said, "Call for points." Five zeroes!

So many of the great stories involving David and me occurred at the Internationals in Long Beach, Ed Parker's never rivaled or equaled tournament. I will recount many more of them later on when we reach that chapter.

The TPA was and continues to be an unusual success story in the history of the martial arts. In spite of the individualism and the fierce independence of martial artists as a whole. The organization has survived and has been emulated throughout the country. I am proud to have been there from the beginning. In 2004 I was inducted into the Black Belt Hall of Fame at Stan Witz's United States World Championships in Las Vegas. The inscription on the plaque reads:

USA
World Championships
Hall of Fame
Grandmaster Jerry Fisher

Jerry, you have done so much to aid in the development of Martial Arts and sport karate in America. Your unselfish contribution to our youth can only be described as incredible. As one of the TPA founding fathers, we, the promoters and competitors, owe you a world of gratitude. I, for one, owe you a sincere Thank You for the success of the USA World Championships. Thank You and God Bless.

Master Stan and Christina Witz.

Over the years I am fortunate to have accumulated a great many plaques and trophies but this one, along with my Internationals trophies, means the most to me.

At the 2004 World Championships, at the presentation ceremony were many old friends. Some of them, now promoters in their own right, were only children when I first saw them attending my tournaments.

Jose Pacheco and his brother, Junior, first did their famous "blind man" defense routine at one of my tournaments in Culver City, when they were perhaps 10 or 11 years old.

Leilagi "Butch" Togisala, I remember first seeing as a 5 or 6 year old, holding his fathers hand and walking into a ring to do a *kama* form.

Mohammed Jahan Vash, although not a child, was a young Red Dragon black belt, introduced to me by my dear old friend, Grandmaster Lou Cassamassa, who asked me to come down and run Mohammed's first tournament for him and show him "how to do it."

It meant very much to me to have these men and so many others, including Ray Wizard, a dear friend, Rick Kenji, Drew "Booie" Christianson, and Art Ruiz at this presentation.

One other instance that occurred at the USA World Championships that I shall always remember was on June 19th of 2005. I had been terribly busy all day running from ring to ring, 16 of them, all full, acting as Tournament Director for Stan Witz. There were also events being judged up on the elevated stage at the end of the hall. Stan got on the microphone and said, "Master Fisher report to ring 17 on stage at once." Thinking it was a problem I hurried to the stage. When I got there everything had stopped. From the other end of the auditorium, Stan's voice came over the sound system: "Stop all matches!

"It is Master Fisher's birthday today!" He then led the voices of 5000 martial artists and their families in singing HAPPY BIRTHDAY! Quite an unforgettable experience.

ED PARKER'S INTERNATIONALS

"ED PARKER'S LONG Beach Internationals." Never has, or in my opinion, never will, a martial arts tournament equal this huge, incredible, prestigious event.

First, no one in living memory has equaled Mr. Parker himself. Born in Hawaii in 1931, this legend began his martial arts training under William S. Chow in Chinese Kenpo in Honolulu.

Having been raised and committed for life to the tenets of the Church of Latter Day Saints, or Mormon, or LDS church, he migrated to Utah after high school. He attended Brigham Young University where he earned a bachelors degree in Psychology.

He started teaching in Utah, but soon moved with his wife Leilani to Los Angeles, where he opened his first commercial Kenpo School in 1956. It was the first martial arts school in the contiguous 48 states. Coincidentally, it was the same year that I heard the word "karate" for the first time.

His reputation spread. He began to teach many students, including among them a large number of those connected with the film industry. Soon he was doing consulting and fight choreography and making a name for himself.

As his fame spread his art began to evolve. He never resisted change; "if it works, it works" was how he thought. He began to apply all of his marvelous intelligence to the task of updating and improving his soundly based art. He did so in a way that I have never seen before or since. His moves were concise, economical and yet they displayed pure genius in their complexity.

It is no wonder that he ultimately became known by all as "the father of American Karate."

After some wrangling with various other kenpo leaders, Mr. Parker put together the IKKA and held his first "Internationals" in 1964. At that tournament he introduced America to a young Chinese martial artist named Bruce Lee. Many other martial arts greats such as Chuck Norris, Benny Urquidez, Steve Sanders, Alvin Prouder, Barry Gordon, Johnny Gyro and Mike Stone followed over the years, experiencing their first recognition by winning the "most prestigious tournament in the world."

My Internationals experiences began in about 1973.

I was first introduced to the event as a competitor in that year. It seems to me that I placed second in a large 35 and over age group. I was happy with that, being my first time at the International and already 37 years old.

These were in the "bare knuckle" days.

To digress a little, any reader who competed in those times will tell you that "controlled, bare knuckle" competition was a much, much different thing than tournament fighting was after the advent of what Bobby Burbidge christened as "bunny hands and bunny feet." That's really what the first pads looked like.

Before the pads were introduced, the art had a much different look. The black belt divisions were really beautiful to behold. It must be very difficult for today's martial artists to envision a fight between two highly trained martial artists moving at FULL speed but pulling their head shots an inch or less from touching, relying on the instant judgment of the officials as to whether or not it was "in."

The body shots were a different matter. I have seen some of the toughest and best fighters in the world go down from a well placed and timed reverse punch, front kick or round kick to the body. In my years of competition I received 18 or 19 broken ribs from solid bare-knuckle, barefoot, body shots.

For every year thereafter as long as Mr. Parker lived, I continued to attend the Long Beach tournament as a competitor, a judge, and a referee. Finally, during the last several years as the Tournament Producer I worked, as always, with Dave Torres, the Tournament Director.

During the late '70s, as mentioned previously, I was immersed in the TPA. Becoming very well known as a tournament director and producer, I would see Mr. Parker and Ron Chapel, frequently at TPA meetings and all of the tournaments. We started to become quite friendly. They seemed mostly interested in how David Torres and I could get even the most apparently unorganized, difficult situations under control and end them at a reasonable hour. That was always the challenge facing the Internationals. With 4 or 5 thousand competitors and 27 rings, held over 3 days, the logistics were almost insurmountable.

At Mr. Parker's instructions, David and I were approached by Ron Chapel in time for the 1980 Tournament and asked to "do what it is you do."

David and I had worked together so long and so well that we were undaunted by the challenge, even though a "big" tournament by normal standards for us were perhaps 500 competitors with 8 to 10 rings. That year the Internationals, the biggest in the world, boasted 27 rings and over 4000 competitors in 3 days time.

With a little preparation and planning we accepted the challenge. I will never forget, and neither did Mr. Parker during his lifetime, the results of that first effort.

It was customary for the Internationals to begin on Friday afternoon and run until about 4:00 AM Saturday. Saturday then would go from 8:00 AM until about 4:00 AM Sunday. The Finals were scheduled to begin at 7:00 PM on Sunday. Usually they would get started about 10 or 11 that night and maybe conclude at 3:00 AM Monday. Those who competed prior to 1980 can vouch for this as fact!

David and I had the events scheduled for Friday over by 10:00 PM. Saturday we started at 8:00 AM and were finished by 5:30 PM. The Parkers were in shock, they kept thinking something was wrong or that we had made some horrible mistake and forgotten some divisions. The clincher was on Sunday. We finished the competition about 5:00 and had time to eat, set up and start the Finals, on time, at 7:00 PM. They were over and people were on their way home, happy, at about 10:00 PM.

We were hired!   From that time on, David Torres ultimately was named Director of the Tournament, and I was named Producer. (Mr. Parker preferred "Executive Producer" as his own designation.) We were the managers of every Tournament, up to and including the last one in 1990.

That last one boasted just barely more than 5000 competitors who were taken through 29 rings in two and half days. A monumental feat.

There were so many other people involved in the success of the venture. Beth Parker and her sisters started a few weeks after each event working on the next one. Edmund Junior was unflagging in his hard work and support of the family effort. Son in law Nalu, Ron Chapel, and of course my wife Leslie who was the chief statistician, a Herculean job, keeping track of the all of the winners and next three places for all those hundreds of divisions.

Mostly it was the masterminding and guidance of Mr. Parker himself. He called a meeting the weekend after each tournament at his home in Pasadena, and those mentioned above would sit all day and critique the recent event and make plans for improvements for the following year, 51 weeks away.

Ed Parker and I became very close, personal friends. I never lost any of the respect I had for him as a teacher but our friendship became one of the best of my life. We shared many interests and became frequent partners in interesting business ventures. We shared an entrepreneurial nature and restless minds. We were close to the same age, had similar educations (psychology), martial arts of course and similar senses of humor. We spent a great deal of our time together laughing! One of us was always coming up with some kind of an idea. We would get it started and run with it to see if it had merit. Of course we intended for our schemes to make money, but it was largely a "game" with us too.

Our first effort was to become "Herbalife" dealers. It was a "down line" sales system of good food products. We thought that it was a decent, healthy, plan that we could perhaps place through a "down line" of dealers through our martial arts schools, students and friends. We went to meetings together and learned the ins and outs of the program. We held meetings of our own and set up "distributors." Although we had a lot of fun and laughs, we soon realized that it was just a little too boring for us and we abandoned it.

At one meeting, we wanted to emphasize the significance of losing 10 lbs. We went to the butcher shop of a Gelsons Market in Encino and between us convinced a butcher to grind up 10 lbs of just fat and wrap it in clear plastic for us. I believe he thought we were madmen but he finally agreed. Later, at the meeting the effect of seeing 10 lbs of fat, about the size of three footballs, was very dramatic. I don't remember what we did with the fat afterwards but I would bet it was something funny.

Our best and most successful effort came about during the Los Angeles hosting of the World Olympics in 1984. It was also the time of one of our more significant failures.

Both Ed and I had, ourselves and through our students, done some "body guarding" work over the years.

We felt that there were major business opportunities to be capitalized upon with all those people coming to LA for the Olympics.

The Press was full of hype every day about the hundreds of thousands of visitors that were coming, the hotels would be overflowing, the transit systems (such as they were in LA then, practically nonexistent) would be unable to move that many people, crime would be rampant!

We saw Opportunity!

We held brainstorming sessions from time to time, frequently they would be at my home in Encino. I had purchased a house in the mid '70s at the top of Gable drive. It was on an acre, behind iron gates and had a full 180-degree view of the San Fernando Valley, from Glendale to Calabasas. It held a parking lot behind the pool that was big enough to accommodate up to 30 cars. The house was built into the side of the hill; all of the rooms on the northern side had huge picture windows and outside sitting decks to take full advantage of the view. Ed and I loved to sit out and make our plans while looking out for miles across the valley.

It was while sitting there that we conceived, what was to become PARKER/FISHER Security, a California corporation.

We felt that there would be a demand for both transportation, to and from the scattered Olympic events and security for many of the wealthier visitors in attendance. We began work on it immediately.

We leased a white stretch limousine, then set up a photo shoot in a nice neighborhood of Pasadena. Choosing a location in front of a stately home on a beautiful, tree lined street, we put a chauffeurs cap on either Ron Chapel or Frank Trejo (don't remember which) and asked a pretty friend of my wife's, Gail Zooker, to portray a wealthy client getting into the limo, and from that we had a brochure made.

Our next step was to select and train black belt students of ours to do the "security" jobs, protecting the clients.

It was here that we met our first real obstacle.

We both had black belt students who came from many walks of life and that we knew were qualified to protect a client. Their fighting abilities were more than adequate. After meeting and discussing the needs and requirements of the job with several, we decided to administer a test to the candidates.

I recall the question that was the major stumbling block on the test. It went something like this:

You are walking with your client, you turn onto a narrow street, it is dusk and the street lamps are not yet lit. After walking a few yards, you see first, a man lurking in the shadows about 15 paces ahead of you on your right. Farther ahead, about another 25 paces on your left you see 2 men crossing the street diagonally from your left. They will all meet and intersect with you at the same time 15 paces ahead. What should you do?

The answers varied in detail but were mostly very much like this:

"If the man on the right attacked, I would meet him with a strong side kick to the knee to take him out of the action. I would then turn my attention to the two men in front and to the left; I would place the client behind me, to my right. I would then disable the attacker closest to me, probably with another low kick, and finish off the remaining assailant any way I needed to."

However the answer that Ed and I were looking for was. "As soon as I perceived the danger, I would turn around and take the client back the way we came and to safety."

We realized that most of our students were well trained in fighting but not in avoidance. We were not looking for confrontation, what we preferred was more like a tactical retreat. We decided that we didn't have time to train all the Black Belts to always react in the way we wanted. A change was needed.

Our next step was to employ students who were off duty police officers instead. Not only were they trained in avoidance techniques but could legally carry weapons as well.

That worked well, but the Olympics were a disappointment to many.

We probably broke even. However, we continued with Parker /Fisher security for a year or two after. We did do some security work for some well-known movie and music personalities before letting it die. We did, however enjoy the process and had a good time doing it.

The "failed project" referred to earlier wasn't actually our idea. Someone else introduced it to me and I got Ed interested in it. The premise was that according to all the press, the hotels would not be able to handle the volume and people would have no where to sleep. The deal was that we would hold "block meetings." We would invite local homeowners to meet and discuss the idea of signing an agreement to do short term, 2 to 6 week leases on their homes to bonded Olympic visitors, at prices similar to a top class hotel. It seemed like a win/win situation for everyone. We took only a small, fair percentage. To make a long story short, we signed a lot of people on contracts, we had plenty of homes, but we didn't find one person to lease one of them It was a total flop! It still seems like a good idea to me.

Ed and I continued to work on projects, besides the Internationals, right up to the time of his death in 1990.

One of our pet projects, that I am sorry that we never undertook to complete, was a book about the history of the Internationals with an emphasis on the funny, strange stories that came out of the experience. Stranger than fiction in most cases.

What turned out to be our last plan never reached fruition. It could have been the best of all.

In typical Ed Parker fashion, about midnight one night in early 1989 he awakened me with a phone call. He always started our conversations at full speed, as if it was a continuation of one that just been interrupted, even though it might have been a month since we last spoke.

"What about this?" were the first words out of his mouth. "I'm in Saudi Arabia doing some work with" (King or Prince someone.) "He is interested in financing the Shrimp Thing."

As I recall, my response was, "I hesitate to ask, but what in the heck is the Shrimp Thing?"

Ed launched into an explanation, which I will shorten and clarify here in the interest of time. Our phone conversations could get quite complicated and lengthy, this was before E-mail and instant messaging.

Ed Parker was a descendant of THE Parkers of Hawaii. An old family, part Hawaiian, part missionary, they were best known for owning the vast, sprawling Parker Ranch on the big island.

He explained to me that on the ranch property were huge pools perfect for raising and growing shrimp as a food source. The plan was that we would obtain a refrigerated Boeing 747 with the Sheik's money, grow the shrimp in Hawaii on Parker Ranch property, and then market them and fly them all over the world in the refrigerated plane.

We became excited and started making plans. This project was still on the table and moving forward in 1990. We had only put it on a back burner, as we got busy with the Internationals. After the tournament Ed didn't seem to feel his usual self and we slowed it down a lot.

He and I were so very close, he was a brother, best friend, and partner to me. I knew him so well. Many nights we sat up to the wee hours discussing, religion, the spirit world, and premonitions, etc. He had some great Hawaiian ghost stories, stories of things that had occurred to him personally.

One thing he was adamant about: he told me on several occasions that he would not live to see his 60th birthday. I was concerned about it but hoped he was wrong. He had a strong premonition early in his life and remained convinced of it.

Although a pillar of the Mormon Church throughout his life, Ed was also a believer, as am I, in ghosts and could tell some amazing true stories of the ghosts of Hawaii that he had met in his youth. His knowledge and belief in some aspects of the supernatural were well known to me.

As I understand the events that led up to his death as told to me by his wife Leilani, it went like this. Sometime on December 14th, he told Leilani, "We have to go to Hawaii as soon as possible." He was desperate about it; they threw things in suitcases and made arrangements to take the very first available flight. When they landed at Honolulu airport, he hurried off the plane. No sooner were his feet on the Hawaiian ground than he suffered a massive heart attack and died. It was December 15th, just over three months short of his 60th birthday.

The last time I saw my friend was at his funeral in Pasadena. I was one of the handful of those who were allowed into the private viewing room to say a personal goodbye before the services.

He was wearing all white, Mormon, burial clothes and lying in a white casket. I said "Goodbye my old friend, I will see you again soon enough."

I did "see" him once more after that. As I said, Ed and I had many conversations about the afterlife and spiritual things.

On the third night after his passing, I had one of the most unusually vivid dreams of my life. In it I saw Ed and he was walking away from me clad in the white clothing I had last seen him wearing. Those who knew him well will recall the little grin he had when he was very pleased by something. He was looking back at me over his shoulder wearing that smile; he nodded to me, waved and walked away. That dream brought me a peaceful acceptance of his death. I still miss him these fifteen plus years later. I will never have another friend like Ed Parker!

The Internationals and the times we had there remind me a little of "Camelot." I have so many memories of the incredible things that happened there.

David Torres and I have remained great friends. Although distance prevents us from being together as much as we would both like, we speak on the phone fairly often. He and his beautiful wife Hilda have, at the time of this writing, a three-year-old son David Aaron Torres. David Senior, like me, continues to do what we love most, teach.

When we do speak the conversation usually ends with reminiscence of some of the great stories of the Internationals.

The tournament was held at the Long Beach Arena close to the beach and the Queen Mary. It was a perfect venue for such a complex and gigantic event.

It was Mr. Parker's habit to remain in the office behind the T-shirt concession that was manned by his family members throughout most of the tournament. He was such a charismatic and legendary figure, that if he spent any time at all on the floor he would be swamped by well-wishers and fans.

David, Mr. Parker and I were in constant communication by a closed band radio handset. I was ensconced in the very center of the auditorium on a dais raised about 12 feet above the auditorium floor. This gave me an unobstructed view of the entire arena, the line up area and all the levels of viewer's stands. From there I controlled and directed the flow and momentum of the event.

It was part of my job to keep the next divisions always ready in the line up area, keep all 28 rings (plus one more in the evenings) manned with officials at all times, and to keep every ring moving so there was no down time. My position also helped me to spot trouble early and dispatch either the director, David , or one of the several Arbitrators to quickly solve any problems. I made all the announcements, called the divisions, and made frequent introductions during the day as famous competitors and celebrities arrived: Benny Urquidez, Chuck Norris, Eric lee, Bill Wallace, past winners etc.

David was constantly roaming the floor, watching the rings, the judging and the competitors. He was first on the scene if a problem did arise. Both of us consulted with Mr. Parker by radio on any matters we felt might require his personal touch.

Several times during each day Mr. Parker would climb unnoticed with or without David or Ron Chapelle to an isolated balcony seat to observe the proceedings from there. At those times we would have discussions on our radios about how the overall tournament was moving or about specific incidents occurring on the arena floor.

Some of those incidents bear repeating here.

In one such incident, Mr. Parker called David and me on the radio, "Meet me at ring 22 right away." Fearing a serious problem, we arrived quickly. It was a kata event. There were probably 20 some Competitors involved. One was in the middle of executing his form when we arrived. Looking around the ring we perceived nothing out of the ordinary. Mr. Parker said, "Look at the judges." There, one of the five officials, seated just to the right of the center judge, was leaning on a cane. "Look closer," Mr. Parker said. We realized then that the judge leaning on his cane was blind. He had his head turned slightly to one side and was listening to the competitors do their forms. The "blind kata judge" became a famous story of the Internationals.

In another case, during musical forms competition, I noticed some unusual activity around one of the far corner rings. I asked David to investigate. In a few minutes he radioed for Mr. Parker and me to meet him at the ringside. There was a large woman, in her late twenties, wearing a very loose fitting, floor length gown, singing an operatic aria while she performed a kata using a small hand spade in one hand and a garden trowel in the other. We were dumbfounded. Each time as she turned to strike or block with one of the gardening weapons, her breasts would fall out of the top of her gown, fully exposed. After a few moments, David stopped the action and with his usual calm demeanor, quietly notified the contestant that her kata was "inappropriate," and that she could not continue. We returned to our posts incredulous.

It is said that life imitates art. In many cases rules were instituted as a result of events that occurred at the tournament.

David remembers the incident that led to our making a "5-minute limit" on all forms.

The center referee in one of the rings appeared to be highly agitated; I had seen him frantically waving at me for attention. I quickly dispatched David to ringside. When he arrived, as usual, he unobtrusively approached and knelt behind the judges, the center told him, "Look at this, it's been going on for over 10 minutes." A contestant in musical forms had made his own music tape and, wearing his martial arts uniform, had been doing nothing but jumping rope to music for the entire time. David waited another minute or two; the man continued to jump rope. Finally David walked into the ring, put up his hand, thanked him and said, "Your time is up." We never knew how long he had planned to continue. The following year the "5-minute limit" was in the rulebook.

In a forms ring one year my attention was attracted by crowd noises in one of the rings, David was already there. A contestant had incorporated a large number of jumping, flying sidekicks into his form. Obviously he was quite good at them and did them well. The problem was that he was executing them, over the heads of the panel. He would run straight at the center judge and, with a loud *kiai*, leap over his head landing in the next ring where they were trying to run an event of their own. Of course a stop was put to that immediately.

Another time my old friend Steve Fisher (I have a number of great anecdotes concerning Steve) was sitting in the center of a women's black belt forms ring. One of the judges had asked to bow out for a few minutes and David had sat next to Steve to act as a temporary replacement. Towards the end of her hard style form she drew near Steve and with a loud *kiai* punched him directly in the middle of his forehead. Without a pause she turned and continued her kata. A few seconds past in silence then Steve said to David, "She punched me in the head." David said quietly, without turning, "I saw that, Steve." Needless to say, her score was very low.

I have to depart from the Internationals to tell two more Steve Fisher stories.

One occurred in the mid 80's at one of the many Red Dragon Tournaments that I attended. Lou Cassamasa the Red Dragon Grandmaster is an old friend and when ever he asked me to come and help I was there.

At this particular tournament a very rare situation prevented me from being on the microphone as I almost always was. I was going to center referee the black belt fighting and finals. Steve and I had arrived early; the event was just getting started when Lou came to where we were standing and asked if we would mind running just one kids divisions for him. Of course we agreed and went to an empty ring and seated ourselves. Then they brought the contestants. About 100 or more 5 and 6-year-old white, yellow and orange belts, each with a set of Plastic nunchaku!

They proceeded to come up one at a time and each do the SAME form. We were shattered! The scoring is set between parameters for each tournament event. In the case of this one the rules stated the scores were to be between 5 and 8, with decimals.

About half way through, well over an hour had elapsed, we had been handing out a lot of 6.1 to 6.9s with an occasional score of 7 or 7.1 when one of the 5-year-old competitors dropped his weapon, forgot his form and left the ring. I gave him a 5.3, I looked over at Steve's card and saw a 5.0. I said to him, "Are you sure that's a 5.0?" He said, "How can it get any worse than that?"

About a half a dozen contestants later another little boy dropped his weapon, forgot his form and left the ring, but before that, during his form he had wet his pants! I told Steve, "Now THAT'S a 5.0."

The other Steve Fisher story also involves the awarding of the worst scores possible in an event.

We were sitting together again on the Weapons and Forms finals at a Flores Brothers Tournament in Ventura, Calif. The last contestant, Fairborz, a well known competitor, was just finishing his Sickle form when one of the flying blades hit him in the head and made a deep cut across his scalp, splashing blood all over Steve and me. At the end we gave him the lowest score allowed for the event. After he came up to us, highly incensed, and demanded to know why we gave him such a low score. One of us said, "When you hit yourself in the head with your weapon, that's a fail. You are lucky you weren't doing gun kata."

There are so many stories from the Internationals that they could just about make a separate book. I can't possibly relate them all here.

There was the dangerous situation at the pre-tournament meeting of scores of black belts from all over the country at the Aladdin Motel in Long Beach. Word reached Frank Trejo that a specific man in attendance had told others that he planned to rob Mr. Parker after the Tournament. When Frank heard he looked for and found the man at poolside, and after delivering some crushing blows leaped into the pool with him and tried to drown him. It took the combined efforts of several of us to keep Frank from carrying out his strategy. The police were subsequently called and the "would be" robber taken away.

The stories are almost endless. But for now I would like to spend a little more time on Frank Trejo.

Frank was absolutely loyal to Mr. Parker. As mentioned earlier, Frank ran the Walnut Street School in Pasadena, California. He was big and strong, a knowledgeable Kenpo Black belt and a ferocious fighter.

About 1980-81, one night every week there were four of us who would meet, after classes, at the Walnut Street School and fight for two hours. It was Frank, Ron Chapel, his Black Belt, Tommy Chavies and I.

I remember vividly what a great time we had. We were such good friends. There is a bond that is formed between martial artists who train and fight together that is different than anything else I have ever experienced. This was during the transition period between "bare knuckles" and "pads." Although we still preferred the increased reality, speed and accuracy of technique of bare knuckles, still we recognized that the pads were the wave of the future. We would therefore spend time doing each.

Frank had a collection mounted on the wall behind the desk in his office. People seeing it for the first time were usually nonplussed. It would appear to be a collection of totally unrelated objects: knives, bandanas, vests, a leather jacket, a wooden stick, a tire iron. He didn't offer an explanation. One might think it was an eclectic art form.

However, to those of us that knew the story behind this mélange it was hilarious. They were all items that Frank had, at one time or another, taken away from southern California "bikers" and "gangsters." It was his hobby. "Hey man, some people collect stamps," he would say.

One day, I was meeting Ed Parker at the Walnut Street School to work on one of our projects. At that time Frank was competing in some "full contact" kick boxing matches. As I walked into the mat area, I immediately became aware of Frank, working out alone on the dojo floor, kicking the heavy bag. Then I realized it wasn't a heavy bag at all.

To prepare himself for the leg kicks that were being allowed in his forthcoming matches, Frank had hung an inflated truck tire, rim and all, from a chain and was kicking it with full power shin and instep kicks! His shins were a mess. Black and blue, scarred and bloody. Ah, what sacrifices we make for Art.

Over many years, Frank Trejo and I were together many times. I learned to always expect the unexpected from him.

For now, we will leave the Internationals and Frank Trejo.

The way my first very tournament came about was a kind of a fluke.

I was living in Tarzana, California; it was 1975. We were between schools, having just sold the Ventura Blvd. School and not yet opened the Encino school.

My sons and I had noticed a Tae Kwon Do school on Ventura Blvd. next door to a movie theater. One day I stopped in and introduced myself to the owner, a nice, young, Korean black belt. His name was Chong Lee. I was impressed by the fact that at his young age, maybe mid twenties, he was already a well-known "kicker," having published two books on the subject. The title of the first, and best known was *Dynamic Kicks*.

We hit it off at once, and before long the idea of our training at his school came up. I believe he wanted to check us out first, so we arranged a work out for my son, Scott, and me at his school for a few days later. Scott was 19 at the time. The three of us met alone at the school. We spent an hour or so doing techniques and forms and then decided to spar a little, we were using no pads then.

Chong Lee sparred with Scott first, although only 19, Scott was a strong fighter and weighed about 175 lbs. He gave a good account of himself but suffered a bad bloody nose in the process. (*Editor's note: it was my own fault. I knew Chong Lee was famous for his jumping kicks, so when he leapt into the air and threw a spinning back kick, I stepped back to avoid it easily. As he continued his spin in the air, without having touched the ground, he threw a second kick, a right roundhouse, which I also dodged, and which left Chong Lee with his back to me. Thinking I could counter before he recovered, I moved in preparing to reverse-punch as he touched down, and walked directly into his third consecutive kick, a spinning back-crescent with his left foot: the third kick delivered from the same jumping spin without landing. My nose still bends slightly to the right...--Scott*)

My filial emotions must have surged a little because when it was my turn to spar with Lee we took it up to a pretty high level and before a minute had passed we were going very hard. I believe I won the contest because of my superior hands but he was a better kicker and dropped an ax kick on my right shoulder, which I remember still today when the weather turns cold. He must have cracked something.

It turned out very well. When we were all through fighting, we all shook hands and ultimately became very close friends! He invited us not only to train at his school until we were ready to open a new one of our own but to teach his sparring classes.

Chong Lee was a highly respected member of the Korean community in Los Angeles. His father was a very well known Tae Kwon Do Master.

We had been training and helping teach at the Chong Lee School for some months when he suggested that we do our own tournament together. I was more than agreeable so put it together and held it at the Culver City Auditorium in April of 1976. Over the years that became my favorite tournament location. It was my first solely owned and produced tournament, and it really went quite well. At that time there was still a lot of insularism and separatism of the styles. Since Chong Lee was very well known in the Tae Kwon Do community and

I elsewhere it resulted in a good cohesive mix. The fact that I had a Korean daughter was not lost on the Korean community.

We did more tournaments together after that. Because of them I became very friendly with many Tae Kwon Do Masters such as Hee Il Cho, Jun Chong, Bong Soo Han, Simon and Phillip Rhee, and many more. I would mostly announce and organize the tournaments for them. I spent most of my time on the microphone because of my English. Periodically one of them would come to the Mike and make announcements in Korean. After the Tournaments we would all adjourn to the Woo Lae Oak restaurant in Korea town for a *bul gogi* party.

During that period I met and became friends with Johnny Vaneck. He was an interesting man. Born in Korea, of pure Korean stock, his family had all been killed during the Korean War. He had been taken in and cared for by a group of American GIs when they discovered that he was an orphan. They had actually smuggled him into the country with them when they came home. He was adopted then by Mr. Vaneck. One day when I was teaching classes for Chong Lee, Johnny came in and signed up. He was very strong, he owned a large framing company in the construction business. His pretty wife, Sherry, who was Japanese, owned a successful restaurant in Sherman Oaks, California, called The Rickshaw. Their son and daughter had been students of mine previously, as had Johnny himself for a while.

In time, Johnny Vaneck became a very good black belt. He will be the subject of more future tournament stories later.

It was sometime about then that a funny incident occurred at a demonstration.

Somehow we had managed to secure a karate demonstration at a very large Boy Scout gathering. There were about 300 Scouts in attendance.

As part of the demonstration, we were showing a self-defense technique wherein, Scott and I were holding Kirk, who was about 12 at the time. One of us had each of Kirk's wrists and were puling him in each direction. I was explaining the defense move as we were doing it.

Kirk was supposed to first sidekick me in the ribs with his right leg, then when I released, turn and round kick Scott in the head with the same leg and stop.

Instead he decided to add another sidekick to my ribs for good measure. I was totally unprepared for the 3rd and last kick and he broke my rib in front of

300 boy scouts. I tried my best to not let on and finished the demonstration in considerable pain.

The most important event that occurred for me during that period was the advent of my daughter Xian. It relates closely to the role that was developing for me in the martial arts of Southern California. Her introduction into my family followed a long and circuitous route and requires some lengthy background explanation.

My sons, Scott and Kirk, were and are very close to me. However, all my life I had wanted a daughter as well. It didn't happen and by the time they were 15 and 20, I realized it wasn't going to.

I had strong feelings then and now do more than ever, that the major problem facing the world was, and certainly still is, overpopulation. Global warming is no longer the threat that it was then. It is a reality! Our planet is facing the greatest threat since the Big One hit us and wiped out the dinosaurs. Our species may not survive as the dominant life form on Earth. There are just too many people! In the 1940's, I recall when the population of Earth was approaching a billion. It seemed incredible, now it is passing six billion and we continue to multiply like lemmings. Greenland and the polar ice caps are disappearing . New species of animals are becoming extinct at a rapidly increasing rate. This direction of thinking leads to a very negative, dismal state of mind and it is not my intention to pursue it any longer at this time.

Suffice to say, that my beliefs about population control, combined with my fervent desire for a daughter brought me to the decision to adopt a little girl.

In the 1970's this was no easy task. I understand it is better now, but at the time it was extremely hard to find children who could be adopted without the constant fear of a long lost relative stepping forward at some future date and reclaiming them. I had heard so many horror stories of people who had adopted and after many months, even years, had the child torn away from them. I was positive I didn't want to risk that.

So this was the state of my mind in 1975. It needs to be further explained what was going on at that time.

My carpet business was doing better than great; CCC had become the largest exclusive manufacturer of commercial carpeting in the world! We were famous, doing most of the huge jobs in the US. We were the major or exclusive supplier to such users as the U.S. government, Boeing Airplane Co. Disney, Arco, and the World Trade Center, just to name a few. Our list of corporate users read like the top 100 companies in the Stock Market; we were doing universities, huge buildings, major commercial centers and projects everywhere. I had become Vice President. We had a dozen offices and scores of highly paid sales engineers each selling millions of dollars of commercial carpet. We had trouble getting the carpet installed to our satisfaction, so we employed technical experts whom we would send out to the big multi thousand-yard jobs to supervise the installation. Where we couldn't find a good installation workroom to do the work we set up our own.

The owner of CCC, my boss, James L. Marcus was the real genius behind it all. He was born in 1904 in New York City. He had risen from abject poverty in the "Hells Kitchen" area of the city. He was a legend in the carpet business and was loved and respected by thousands. He was my other mentor, along with John Wayne.

Jim was a liberal, Jewish New Yorker, and would deny any commonality with John Wayne, my other hero. However, Jim possessed so many of the same qualities: honesty, fairness, strength, a basic good nature and a loving kindness with consideration for all. I learned so much from Jim. He is my Father in spirit. At the time of this writing he just passed away after celebrating, last November 1st, his birthday of 103 years! Who said the good die young?

My role at CCC kept me very busy and I was traveling all over the world about 2 or 3 nights every week. I kept my headquarters and office in Los Angeles while Jim was in New York. We shared the workload; it worked quite well for us that way.

In spite of my extreme involvement in CCC, I always found the time to pursue my love for the Martial Arts. With a few short periods of time excepted, I always owned a school, taught, fought and did the tournaments. Many of my business acquaintances had a passion for golf or tennis. Mine happened to be different.

This was the environment in which I found myself as I started my search for my daughter. It was a long, sometimes emotionally tortuous road that covered a great many miles and a long span of time.

I did adopt my daughter, she was 4 and half years old when she arrived in America on May 27th 1976 at 5:10 PM, at Los Angeles International Airport .She came in with another adoptee and a Korean lady sent to accompany them. It was on Northwest Orient Airlines, flight #22 . Someone had dressed her in pink overalls, white shoes and a white T-shirt with an American Flag on the front. That is all she had in the world when she came to me. That and a note pinned to the front of her pink overalls. I still have it; I've editorialized somewhat to make it more cogent, but it read:

"This is Seon Sun Soon Kim. She is a bright and happy little girl, we guessed her birth date as October 5th. We also gave her the name. She was found abandoned, wandering the streets. She was suffering from malnutrition, pneumonia and rat bites. No one knows how long she had been out there. We have brought her back to health. She loves to run errands, sing, is negative with her friends and has a big nose! Koreans don't like Cheese."

Later I will relate more about what had led up to this event.

In order to complete the story of her adoption and how she affected and changed my role in martial arts, I need to relate other events that had to occur first. This may take a while but I will come back to it.

About 1974, I had an invitation and an opportunity to attend a Charity Fashion Show, in Newport Beach California. My reason for attending, and donating money to the Charity as that the master of Ceremonies was none other than my hero and lifelong role model, John Wayne.

I finally had an opportunity to actually see in person, perhaps even meet my legendary hero.

My seats were good and the show lasted about 3 hours. I was about 4 rows back from the dais where himself and his son Patrick held forth. Try to imagine the "Duke," probably the greatest man's man of all time, reading, as a model approaches the stage to show her gown, "The next gown is made entirely of taffeta with a tulle bodice and empire waist line. The color is a muted mauve with overtones of puce."

Horrors! What I wanted to hear him say was, "Ya better circle them wagons, pilgrim, if you don't want to get your scalp lifted."

Nevertheless he gave it his best shot, with a good-natured humor that eventually won over even the most liberal and effete member of the audience.

I made sure to donate enough money to the Charity that it earned me a trip to the "Sponsors Party" held in a small room of the venue after the conclusion of the show. He was there. I was able to meet him and actually spend quite a long time in conversation with him while we shared a couple of "bourbon and branch waters." My most vivid memory is of shaking hand with him when we met and when we parted. His hand was huge, callused and strong. It was like having your hand enveloped by a tight leather saddle and squeezed till the blood stopped flowing temporarily.

I have always had a very strong handshake, the only other man whom I felt was equally strong was my good friend and later partner in the Four Seasons tournaments, Mike Stone. I have to say John Wayne put us both to shame.

Other than my realization of a lifelong dream in meeting my hero, another very important and life-changing meeting occurred at the show.

INTERNATIONAL ORPHANS INC. 101

At the sponsors party afterwards I was introduced to two women who had an affect on me that actually, in many ways, altered the course of my life.

Yvonne Phederson and Sarah Omeara were intelligent, fashionable and very pretty women, about my age or a little younger. I was introduced to them by someone as the "Orphan" ladies. Very intriguing. I was then in the early stages of looking for a child to adopt.

We spoke for a long time and had a subsequent meeting at my karate school, since we all lived in the San Fernando Valley where the school was located on Ventura Blvd in Tarzana.

Their story was fascinating. They had met several years before, both of them were actresses; they were on a tour in Japan when a major earthquake and flood occurred. It was a bad one, devastating a large part of the country. Many people were killed. Yvonne and Sarah were touched by the plight of the many orphaned children.

They came to the aid of the orphans, staying over in Japan to help find shelters and caregivers. They managed to get a start on the situation before returning to Los Angeles. Once back in the United States, they raised a significant amount of money to send back to Japan to provide for the needs of the orphaned children.

Being the wonderful people that they are, they decided, "Why stop now?" They had met with and received the aid of many well-off Southern Californians who had expressed their willingness to continue to provide, money, goods and services for orphaned children.

Yvonne was married to a very well known and successful movie and TV producer, Don Phederson; Sarah was married to the national sales manager of a large, country-wide manufacturing company.

With their husbands' blessings they began what became their life's work. Soon they felt the call to care for the thousands of orphans being created by the situation in Vietnam.

Although to me it has been and always will be "The Vietnam War," the truth is that war was never declared by the United States. Nevertheless we lost just under 59,000 killed and many more thousands wounded during the eleven year course of what is generally termed the "Vietnam Conflict." It is estimated that a total of 3,000,000 people on all sides lost their lives. Imagine how many orphans were produced.

Sarah and Yvonne began to raise serious money, primarily in Southern California. With it they found and secured, buildings, people, bedding, clothes, food and medicine to care for the many hundreds and thousands of starving and destitute children, orphaned by the "Conflict."

With tireless effort and sometimes at serious personal risk they continued to care for these kids for years.

The War ended, officially, on January 27th, 1973. For months prior to that date, South Vietnam was in total chaos! The northern forces were winning and driving the Southern armies back steadily towards the capitol of Saigon. In the path of the cruel and relentless invaders stood, among so many other things, several orphanages set up, cared for and funded by the Organization that Yvonne and Sarah had christened International Orphans Inc., or as it was better known, IOI.

By that time I had been a member of the board of directors for a few years. We met on an as-needed basis usually at the Phedersons home in Encino. I was involved in overall planning, and working on various fund raising projects and charitable functions whenever called upon. I loved those two ladies very much and would have done just about anything for them.

One particular fundraiser stands out in my mind over the others. It was a full, ornate, formal costume ball, held at the Beverly Hilton Hotel, on October 18th, 1975. I had rented my costume from Western Costumers, the supplier of most of the costumes to the studios. It was a complete, Napoleonic-era French cavalry officers uniform, from boots and jodhpurs to a steel breastplate, plumed helmet and sword. I felt dashing, but as the evening wore on I gained a great deal of respect for the men who wore these heavy, bulky accoutrements on a regular basis. Try dancing like that. I felt and probably looked like, the "Tin Woodman" From Frank Baum's *Wizard of Oz*. The ballroom was packed; many of the great and near-great of Hollywood were there. I danced with some of the most beautiful, famous women in the world. (Jane Powell and her incredibly beautiful blue eyes are my best memory.) It was also a huge financial success, bringing in a great deal of money that always went directly to the kids who needed it.

During the time that I was involved in IOI, in the early, formative years, I had enlisted the aid of Yvonne and Sarah in my quest for a daughter. It turned out that with all that they had done for the country and its people it was to no avail in my search. Firstly I came to find out that before ANY adoptive child would be allowed into the Country you must be approved by the State of California Bureau of Intercountry Adoptions, an appropriately long name with an emphasis on the BUREAU.

Once I realized that I would inevitably have to go through this process I gave in and began what turned into about 18 months of laborious detail. We might never have concluded the work had it not been for a clear-thinking young man named Charles Lingenfelter. Charles worked for the SCBIA. Fortunately, unlike so many others in his profession, he cared very much about uniting good, solid, well-qualified families with orphans who desperately needed safe homes in which to grow and realize their true potential.

I continued my association with IOI throughout this entire period, and was with them, as it turned out, through some very hard times.

During the last few months we began to hear very disturbing stories coming out of Vietnam. I remember a conversation at one of the meetings with the President of World Airlines out of Oakland, California. He was a dedicated member of IOI, and was making frequent trips in and out of Vietnam with his airline.

He told us that he was hearing rumors that as the Viet Cong and North Vietnam regulars were making their way south that when they came to orphanages or Schools, that they were killing any children that appeared to be of "mixed blood:" the children of Vietnamese women and American soldiers.

We decided to get as many of our "kids" as we could out of harm's way. Here is where the efforts and connections of those two great women paid off.

They called in all of their contacts, advisors, and supporters across the country. Somehow, they were granted special dispensation to bring in as many children from IOI orphanages as they could without all the usual endless paper work and approvals.

With the invaluable help of World Airlines, without whom it couldn't have happened, we made arrangements to begin as soon as possible. World would make as many flights out of Saigon with as many of the kids as they could carry. IOI had to take care of the logistics at this end when they arrived.

It was set up like this, by the powers that be in our Government: if we could get the kids onto planes and fly them into the country, we would have to follow these rules.

No child could leave the airplane by itself. They had to be walked off personally by an adult American citizen, preferably a member of IOI. They then must be taken immediately to a sheltered area, provided for in advance, with food, water, cots, blankets, a change of clothes and bathing and delousing facilities. I'm sure that well-intentioned people in the Government whose thoughts were for the welfare of the children and the prevention of what could become a chaotic mess had set up these rules. However, they didn't apply to the situation in all cases.

We were on alert for the arrival of the planeloads of children at all times. I had at the time, as well as my home in Encino, a second home in Big Bear Lake California. Because of that I had purchased a full size station wagon. It came in very handy for when we brought the kids into the United States. I volunteered both my services and the use of my wagon as well for the arrivals.

When the first planeload was coming in, I received a call from Yvonne at about 2:00 AM, waking me from a sound sleep. I had a slate of people that I was to pick up in my seven-passenger wagon and bring to a hanger at the south end of LAX. I leaped out of bed, threw on some clothes, and departed, first calling every one of the other IOI volunteers on my list to tell them I was on the way to pick them up and take them to the airport. I don't remember the times exactly, but everyone was picked up and delivered to the hanger by about 4:00 AM. Then we waited, drinking coffee, anxious about the arrival of what we guessed would be at least 200 kids from one of the orphanages.

Other IOI volunteers had set the hanger up earlier that day. They had done their work well. The cots, blankets, food and water were all prepared.

Another requirement that a change to fresh, clean clothes be provided had been taken care of as well.

Most of the clothing had been donated to either IOI directly or had been collected from a number of different other charitable organizations. All of it was clean, though used.

Then there was the requirement that all of the children, immediately upon leaving the plane, be given water, and then bathed and deloused before they could eat, don their clean clothes and sleep.

Somehow the bathing job became mine. What a strange and bizarre memory I have of that task.

The plane landed before dawn; it was chilly and foggy.

After it had come to a full stop on the tarmac, the engines shut off and the doors opened. This was not the passenger terminal; it was on the far south side of the field, away from the passenger area. Therefore steps had to be brought to the doors of the planes for access and departure.

There were probably a total of about 50 adult IOI members on hand. After a few minutes of discussion and planning, we formed a line at the front door of the aircraft. We then started up single file into the plane. I think it was either Yvonne or Sarah who was first. As each adult walked into the interior of the cabin, they would take the first child they came to by the hand and walk them through the length of the cabin, out the back door of the plane, down onto the tarmac and into the hanger facility.

I was about number 10 or so in the line.

I will never forget the sight of a plane FULL of only small children, probably more than 300. It struck you immediately. Every seat, except those 10 or so who had been taken out ahead of me, was occupied with children between perhaps 3 and 12 years of age. For someone who flew on commercial jets 4 to 6 times every week as I did it was a strange and peculiar experience.

Considering the circumstances it was very quiet inside. The first child I reached was a boy of about 8 or 9. I smiled at him, reached out, took his hand and gently conducted him through the length of the aisle, out and down the back door. We then crossed the tarmac and entered the building. The boy was quiet and cooperative. He didn't seem frightened. More precisely he seemed numb. God only knows what he had been through and seen.

We began to hear stories then from the crew and flight attendants as we passed through the aircraft several times, walking the children out "one on one" as required.

They had flown out of Saigon airport 13 or 14 hours before. It was utter chaos! The Northern troops and Viet Cong had overrun the city. Murder and butchery was out of control. People were being executed in the streets by the thousands.

The United States Embassy was being evacuated by helicopter as our last remaining diplomats and military people were fleeing Saigon. Thousands of Saigon citizens, knowing what their fate was to be at the hands of the enemy had come to the Embassy hoping some how that they would be taken out by our people. Our people were barely saving themselves.

The sounds of small weapons and explosions filled the air, a pall of smoke covered the city as fires burned everywhere. You could hear the sound of human screams constantly over the noise of the gunfire.

Imagine now, these children being taken for a wild bus ride through these streets, not knowing, for hours, if they would reach the airport or perhaps be stopped, taken from the bus and murdered. Being shot at, in constant fear for their lives, they were defenseless. They could only rely on the handful of courageous adults whose task it was to get them to the plane. Those adults who knew, that many of they themselves were not going on the planes. Who knew their own fate was sealed by their actions. Yet they persevered and reached the airport with their cargo.

According to the World airlines employees and a couple of men (who I suspected could be military or CIA) who had accompanied them. The scene at the airport could only be described as hellish.

There was total confusion, panic reigned! Thousands of doomed citizens had come to the airport in a last ditch effort to find space for themselves or at least their children on any plane going anywhere out of Vietnam.

Our plane was being defended by a handful of armed, determined people bent on holding it for the orphans. People were driven back, in some cases shot, to keep them from swarming into the plane.

This is the sight that greeted the children as they reached the airport, drove out onto the airfield and pulled up next to the plane.

Somehow they breached the crowds and began boarding. We were told this was the worst part. Word had spread throughout that section of the airport that a plane was loading now and preparing to take off. Many more hundreds of panicked Saigonese ran towards our plane. It was touch and go for a while. There was a moment when the mob almost ran over and through the defenders, but they were shot and beaten back.

At last all of the kids and a few of the adults who had accompanied them were on the plane.

The majority of the adults, who in my mind earned a special place in whatever you consider the hereafter to be, remained outside the plane as the doors were closed. Facing probably certain death at the hands either of the mob or the approaching North Vietnamese, they continued to protect the plane and its human cargo as the engines started and it began to taxi towards take off. Panicked people were still, in acts of total futility, running after the departing aircraft hoping somehow they could still reach safety.

After a lifetime of seeing their parents killed, living in an orphanage, fearing that at any time they would be overrun and murdered, this was the final horror for them to go through before the flight to Los Angeles and a new world.

It is no wonder that the kids seemed numb.

A few of the kids on board were not identifiable to us at IOI, somehow their parents or someone, had gotten them into the crowd of children, probably at the last minute, and they had just moved into the plane with our kids. What bravery and sacrifice on the part of those parents!

At our end finally all of the children were disembarked and led into the building and that began one of the more memorable experiences of my life.

As I said earlier, I had volunteered (or perhaps Yvonne had "volunteered me") to take charge of the showering and delousing.

The hangar contained two large shower rooms, designated male and female. I of course set up shop in the male shower area. Special soap and shampoos had been selected to provide both cleanliness and an additive to act as a delousing agent. The procedure was that each child had to be showered first with the delousing soaps and then again with regular soap and shampoo.

I had not exactly planned on doing this job. I was unwilling to either undertake it clothed or naked. I decided therefore to strip down to my black jockey shorts. (At least they had the appearance of a swim suit) to accomplish my task.

I began the job of bringing all 150 or so of the little boys, two at a time, into the showers. I would wash their hair, first with the 'special" shampoo, supervise their shower (or in the case of the really little ones, wash them). Then shampoo their hair again, supervise or give them a second shower and send them out of the shower area. Another man at the open doorway who saw to the toweling procedure then met them and made sure they were dry.

This went on for hours! I don't remember ever feeling so soaked and clean. I felt afterwards that I could qualify as a "bather" anywhere. I didn't see a single "louse" and the kids, almost without exception, had already been quite clean.

When I was finally finished I went out for the first time into the hangar and was able to view the entire scene. Most of the children, by then, were redressed, had eaten and were sleeping, or trying to, on their cots.

One of the odd facts of the episode was that in many cases, the clothing that the children had been wearing on the flight was much better and fit better than the clothes that we had provided for them. As I said, I never once saw a sign of a flea or lice, or even dirt on one of those boys.

When they were all fed and sleeping safely, dreaming of God knows what horror. It was about 11:00 AM. I took my leave, closing one of the more memorable experiences of my very "colorful" life.

As it turned out a great many more things were to happen before the successful adoption of my daughter.

CHINA

TOWARDS THE EARLY part of 1974, one of my big CCC clients was Continental Airlines. We were carpeting, on an ongoing basis, all of their facilities, in airports, corporate offices, etc.

The way my trip to China came about was interesting.

At that time my offices occupied most of the top, 9th, floor of a building located at 8899 Beverly Blvd, at the corner of Robertson, in Los Angeles. My personal office was a great corner suite that faced north towards the Santa Monica mountains. Each corner suite had a private balcony. I loved to go to the office very early in the morning and work and wander on and off of the balcony enjoying the spectacular view.

One Monday morning my secretary, Mary Jane, came into my office and said, "You have a call here I know you are going to want to take."

I said "I'm so busy right now figuring sales commissions, why?" She said, "It's Audrey Meadows."

One of the biggest and most popular TV shows of all time, and one of my great personal favorites, was *The Honeymooners*. It starred Jackie Gleason, Audrey Meadows, and Art Carney. It was still showing in reruns for years after it ended live. I was a great fan of Meadows.

It is worth mentioning here that three of the floors below me were occupied by Creative Management Associates, or CMA, owned by Freddie Fields. CMA was, at the time, one of the top companies in the world for managing the business affairs of actors and show business people. They had many of the top stars in Hollywood on their client list. It was a regular occurrence that I would run into big movie celebrities in the elevator when I was going to or from my office or "Mr. D's," the restaurant on the bottom floor. I had met Robert Wagner, Natalie Wood, Stephanie Powers, Cass Elliot and dozens more. So I was well past the stage of being awed by the "stars."

Nevertheless, I was impressed by Audrey Meadows. So naturally I stopped whatever else I was doing and took her call.

After introducing ourselves on the telephone, she asked if she could come by some time that day and spend a little time with me discussing a "project." My first thought was that it might have something to with IOI. We made an appointment for 11:00 AM.

She arrived on time, wearing a strange looking outfit which included, what looked like a toreador's hat, vest and pants that stopped just below the knee, all in red and black.

In that distinctive voice of hers, she explained her reason for coming.

She had been, for years, the wife of Robert "Bob" Six, the founder, owner and CEO of Continental Airlines. He had delegated most of the interior design and selection of interior products for the offices and airport waiting areas to her. She was quite good at it, and took it very seriously.

As mentioned earlier, CCC was, at that time, the premier manufacturer of commercial carpeting in the country. She had become aware of our products after seeing them installed throughout Disneyland. She and Bob had met and spoken to some Disney Executives at a party and heard great things about our products. She was interested in using them at Continental.

For some reason we really hit it off. We became good friends and stayed in frequent touch until her death on February 3rd ,1996.

On the day we met she was a vibrant, funny, lady, in her late 40s. She told me how impressed she and her husband had been with our unusual carpet products. What she wanted was our materials, done in custom patterns, colors and designs exclusively for Continental. That was right up our alley. We ended up going to lunch downstairs, coming back up and spending most of the day creating what she wanted. Continental had a distinctive logo that we incorporated into a pattern on a background of their colors of red, black and gold. The result of those morning's efforts was a business relationship that lasted for many years. We ended up in supplying the company with many thousands of yards of carpet over that time.

I continued to see Audrey and her husband from time to time over the ensuing years. Once we traveled to New York together, just the three of us in the first class section of one of his commercial jets.

One day Audrey called and asked if I had time for lunch, she wanted me to meet someone. I said yes of course. The "someone" was her sister, Jayne Meadows.

The two sisters had led fascinating lives. Jayne was a very well known film actress in her own right. She was married to the legendary Steve Allen. Steve was a true renaissance man: comedian, songwriter, author and the host for many years of the hit "Tonight Show."

The sisters were two of four daughters, born to Episcopal missionary parents in Wuchang, China. Jayne was born first in 1920, Audrey later in 1926. Raised in China, they both set their sights on a career in show business in the U.S. Although they were both excellent operatic singers they seemed, for some reason to gravitate towards comedic acting and made names for themselves in films.

Perhaps because of the good relationship that I enjoyed with Audrey, Jayne and I liked each other as well.

This is the background for what became one of the great adventures of my life.

One day, late in 1974, maybe October, I received a telephone call from Jayne Meadows. She said ' Steve and I would like to discuss something with you, can we meet at out house?" We set a date and met.

Their home was in Sherman Oaks, not far from where I lived in Encino. It was a big, rambling place behind heavy growth. Steve Allen met us, my first wife Louise and I, at the door. He was a very tall, shy, friendly man. I don't know what I expected. As the author, at the time, of well over 20 books, and the writer of songs that everyone in the world was familiar with, and I am told, one of the wealthiest men in Southern California, I guess I expected something else.

After introductions and refreshments Steve and Jayne came to the reason for our meeting.

Richard Nixon was President at the time. Bob Six had been a big contributor to the Nixon campaign and he and Audrey knew the president well. Because of that, and Steve's wealth and fame, Steve and Jayne also had developed a personal relationship with him and saw him from time to time. The President had spent a great deal of effort in trying to establish normal relations with mainland China. Recently he had succeeded, and had been invited to Beijing: the first sitting American president to visit China. The door in the bamboo curtain was opened for the first time since the end of World War Two, just a crack.

While in his meetings with the Chinese Prime Minister, Chou En Lai, and the other Chinese leaders, it was expressed that perhaps the beginning steps in moving towards "normalized" relations would be to first open a United States Liaison Office in Beijing and then look for ways to start normal business dealings between the two countries. One of the expressed interests from the Chinese was that they would like to reopen their rug factories and begin to produce again for export. The President agreed to work towards that.

At some time after returning home, President Nixon had, I believe, seen or somehow spoken to the Allens, knowing that Jayne and Audrey were born in China, and coincidentally that Jayne and her Chinese friend, Lily Wen, owned an interest in a small, high-end custom rug store in Beverly Hills called East West Carpet Co. He mentioned the rug issue to them. Jayne said, "My sister and I have a friend who is the Vice President of a huge Carpet manufacturing Company; perhaps he would help." The President told them to go ahead and contact me about it. To the best of my knowledge, that's how it happened.

We discussed the matter at great length that evening. The plan that emerged was that we would put together a small group. I would be the figurehead because of my position in the carpet industry. Steve and Jayne would go, of course. A few other people would be selected from the custom rug industry. We would plan to all depart and spend three weeks in China in February of 1975.

They were such nice, friendly people; I looked forward to working and traveling with them.

To say that I was excited at the prospect of going to China would be a gross understatement. But not only for the possibility of opening a new business, and helping in the urgent task of normalizing relations with this emerging super power: the other intriguing facet of the matter was the possibility of being the first American martial artist to enter mainland China, at least since the end of the War in 1946.

Since the late Thirties, with a pause of several years to fight the invading Japanese armies, a bloody civil war had been raging throughout China. Mao Tse Tung, and his fellow Communist henchmen, financed and encouraged by the Russian Communist leadership, was fighting to defeat the Nationalist Chinese, led by Chiang Kai Shek. That conflict resumed at the end of WWII in 1946 and ended with Chiang Kai Shek and his loyal followers retreating to the island of Formosa in 1949, where they created what is presently the Country of Taiwan.

At that time the "Bamboo Curtain" fell across the borders of China and no Westerners were allowed to enter. This lasted from 1949 till 1974.

There have been some fictional accounts of "death tournaments" and other nonsense that were supposedly held in China during that time but they are just that, fiction! Probably the best known is an imaginative account about something called "the Kumite", interestingly enough, a Japanese word. It never happened, at least certainly not in mainland China.

Jayne also owned a part interest in a travel agency; she was very entrepreneurial and industrious. It became her job to make all of the terribly complicated travel arrangements. Because we had no "official" relationship with China at that time, everything – visas, entry documents, all the approvals and paper work – had to be handled directly at a very high level of both governments.

The group started to come together. A few were friends of the Allens, whom they wanted to take along. Of course they all claimed some level of involvement in the "rug" business, real or not.

Our final group was assembled. It consisted of Steve and Jayne Allen, Lily Wen (who, born in China and bilingual in English and Mandarin, became totally indispensable); a mother daughter team of Interior designers, Marge and Victoria Levy, from Beverly Hills; a friend of Lily's and journalist from Santa Barbara named Beverly Jackson; Helene Pollack, owner of a rug business and wife of a prominent Beverly Hills surgeon; finally, a man who became a very close personal friend of mine, Herbert Rykoff Cole. Herb was intelligent, funny and the heir to the huge Rykoff wholesale food companies. My wife at the time, Louise and I made up the balance of our entourage. Ten in all

An odd group indeed. All of us were traveling under the auspices of being in the carpet business. In truth, I was the only one who was "for real," and my truer intent was to pursue my love and interest in the martial arts. I became what Woody Allen calls "the Beard." Whenever and wherever we met to discuss the carpet and rug business I was really the only person who could hold a discussion. This fact led to some odd situations. "Wait, Jerry Fisher has to hear this," became a well-used phrase.

After considerable preparation, passports, visas, tickets, etc., our group began to draw together. We had a couple of meetings at the Allens' home to go over all of the logistics and details before departing.

This was 1975. It wasn't like it is today at all. Going to mainland China at that point in time was like going to Mars. We were told that we couldn't buy common everyday items there the way we were used to. We carried all our medications that might become necessary. Extra prescription glasses. Lots of warm clothes. (The weather in The Beijing area in February is about the same as Chicago) I brought a couple of dozen red felt-tipped pens, which turned out to be a very good idea.

Tipping was absolutely forbidden in Communist China, so a "gift" of a red (Red China) pen made an ideal "tip." We also brought plenty of cash, at that time you couldn't use credit cards or traveler's checks.

A few people even brought toilet paper and tissues. Another great idea. Tissues were unknown and the toilet paper was very much like what we called wax paper.

Finally, after what seemed like months, the day of our departure arrived. Jayne and Lily had gone ahead a day early to prepare hotels, ground transportation and other details. We were all to meet in what was then British Hong Kong.

Louise and I left on Saturday, February 22nd, 1975. The adventure had begun!

In case you may be wondering by now how this all relates back to adopting my daughter and subsequently to the martial arts, please read on.

At this time there were NO direct flights to anywhere in mainland China. The route we had to travel was long and circuitous. We left LAX on Pan Am; we had to make a stop in San Francisco, where we waited on board while a few passengers were added. Then we flew directly to Tokyo. We had a little time in Tokyo.

When we went to the airport to make the trip to Hong Kong, an interesting thing happened. Jayne had booked all the flights (except hers and Steve's I suspect) on Coach.

Before boarding for Hong Kong at the Tokyo airport we had to show passports. They asked us for our "final destination." When we said Peking (that's before it became spelled Beijing), eyebrows flew! At that time no one had seen Americans traveling to that destination.

We were passed through, but when they called our flight and we went to the gate to board, we were told we had been bumped to First Class.

I have always been certain that we were being given VIP treatment because of our unusual destination.

The five-hour trip was uneventful but a little more enjoyable due to our upgraded accommodations.

We arrived in Hong Kong about 10:00 PM local time. Just a word about time. When you make a 20-hour flight and cross a myriad of time zones AND the International Date Line, it tends to totally confuse your time senses. It did so with everyone on the trip.

When you fly into Hong Kong at night it is reminiscent of flying into San Francisco because of the lights, hills and water, but also of San Diego because, on your approach, you are actually flying lower than the tops of many of the taller skyscrapers. On many of the top floors there are restaurants, you can see into them and make out the diners at their meals.

The deplaning went smoothly and we were soon on our way to our hotel to meet the others. After check in, we found, Jayne, Lily, Herb and Helene. We were all very excited. However we were to wait a second night in Hong Kong while the rest of our party caught up with us. That is except for Steve, who, due to an unbreakable engagement elsewhere would follow us in 3 or 4 days.

As it turned out I believe we all benefited from the extra day in Hong Kong. We relaxed and did a little shopping, sightseeing, eating and we rested from the long, grueling trip.

When we were all together, except for Steve, we started the final trip that would take us into the mainland of China. This leg of the trip was to be by train. We boarded the coach of a vintage, steam-powered train at the Hong Kong station and began our trip North through what was called the "New Territories," which were still, like Hong Kong at the time, controlled under the remainder of a 99-year lease to the British Empire. We traveled for about 3 hours this way; the countryside began to change. It almost seemed that we were traveling backwards in time as well as distance. Within an hour or so we saw no more motor driven vehicles. Only people, dressed as you have seen in hundred-year-old photographs, walking along dirt roads next to vast fields of rice. Occasionally we saw a field with what appeared to be a different crop, and plows being pulled by oxen.

Finally we stopped and were told to vacate the train. We were at the border. This train was forbidden to go any farther. It was a confusing few minutes, as we hadn't been forewarned of the change and we were each carrying 3 weeks of luggage.

When we, and all of our paraphernalia were off, the train immediately began to back up and leave us standing there. There was no building or any signs.

We did see two armed guards in military uniforms standing on our side of a somehow familiar looking railroad bridge about 200 feet long. Lily said, "This is Lo Wu." We then knew where we were and why the bridge was familiar. It had been depicted for years in photographs and stories. The modest, totally unprepossessing entrance to China!

We realized that we were supposed to walk across the bridge to enter China, so gathering up our tons of luggage, we struggled across the railroad ties. Lily's luggage was by far the majority of the load. As we approached the Peoples Republic of China side we were met by more armed guards. Different uniforms, although the uniforms weren't necessary to see that we were entering another world. The hard eyed stares and the Russian machine guns leveled directly at us were enough. A few very tense moments ensued while Lily, our only Mandarin speaking member, spoke with the guards and showed them our thick papers and entry documents. After what seemed like hours but was probably 20 minutes they allowed us to cross to the other side of the bridge and into what appeared to be a small, very old, freshly painted and clean railroad station. Once inside we were met by a Chinese woman who offered us tea from a large decorated Thermos bottle.

Our luggage was opened and inspected in great detail. Our very first of many problems occurred right then. Lily had family living in the PRC (the People's Republic of China). She had brought many gifts, mostly items that they could not obtain in this impoverished country. Not only was her luggage full of these items but also she had apparently asked each of us if we would mind carrying a "few" things in for her. The accumulation was huge! The inspectors were visibly confused and upset by all the items we were bringing into the country. They were very obviously not for our personal use.

A long dialogue ensued in Mandarin, several hours elapsed, and finally we were allowed to proceed. We knew that Lily had almost ended our trip right there.

We were then escorted to another train. Even smaller and older. We spent about 5 hours traveling across much of the same countryside until we reached the city of Canton.

After we detrained in Canton, one of the many inexplicable mysteries that would continue to happen on a daily basis unfolded. We were rushed, practically pushed, from the train into automobiles and driven through the narrow, cluttered streets of this ancient city at speeds of 50 or 60 miles per hour. There were so few automobiles in China at that time that we were the only ones we saw during this wild ride of over an hour in duration. The very few cars you did see in China in 1975 were all pre-WWII, 1939 and 1940 Chevrolets, Plymouths,

Fords etc. They had been restored perfectly and looked like they had just rolled off the showroom floor. Almost all travel was by bicycle, foot, oxcart or train.

At the end of the wild ride we pulled onto the tarmac at a small airport. There was only one plane, a 4-engine jet, sitting on the ground. We were hustled on to it, luggage and all, the doors closed and we took off at once.

Other than us there were about 100 Chinese passengers. Most appeared to be military personnel. So few people traveled by plane then that I'm quite sure they were all high-ranking communist party members.

There were "stewardesses," a few women who traveled up and down the aisles. We were given, by them, orange juice and hard-boiled eggs.

I have to take a moment here to explain the clothing that we saw in China in 1975.

Keep in mind that it was mid winter and things change when the weather warms up,

There was really only one suit, made with varying tailoring skills; both men and women wore it. It is what was called a "Chairman Mao" suit. You would recognize it if you saw it. A matching pants and jacket, the Jacket has about 10 large buttons that go all the way up to the high "mandarin" style collar, with four big pockets, two on each side. The suit comes in five colors; the colors can designate your rank and or position. The colors are, light or dark gray, and dark blue, (basically civilian colors) black, (the color of important officials) and khaki, which seemed to be mostly for the military. In a "classless" communist society it is important for everyone to appear to be "equal." However, in the words of George Orwell, in his book *Animal Farm*, a parody on communism, "some are MORE Equal than others."

If you wished to add a dash of personal, tonsorial flair, you can make a "Chairman Mao" cap a part of *le tout ensemble*, here you have it. When added to the ever-present black bicycle, you somehow had the feeling you had been reduced in size and were living in an anthill.

Since there was no visible means of telling the thousands of bikes apart we speculated that perhaps everyone just used the first one they came upon and left it where it was when they were through with it.

The plane ride was long; from Canton to Beijing was about a 4 or 5-hour flight. Passenger comfort was not a consideration; if the pilot chose, for example, to change course, he would do so very abruptly. We quickly learned to keep the seat belts tightened down.

BEIJING 1975

OUR LANDING AND deplaning at the Beijing Airport was one of the eeriest and strangest experiences of my life.

First of all, this was THE Beijing airport, servicing a city of over 20 million people. Not some small outer airport.

We landed on an unusually dark and very bumpy runway about 9:00 PM. Our plane was the only one in sight anywhere at the entire Airport. We disembarked onto the tarmac about 100 yards from the terminal building. It was bitter cold, perhaps 20 degrees, and there was a stiff 30 or so mile an hour wind whipping through our clothing. As we followed a crewmember towards the terminal we saw that it was, although a very large building, only lighted in the one small part that was where we were heading.

As we entered the terminal, we could see that only an area about 50 feet wide, at our entry point, was lighted, the rest of the terminal was completely dark and deserted. A heavy silence, punctuated by an occasional echo, pervaded the atmosphere. Gloomy, oppressing, and eerie fail to describe it adequately. The other, Chinese, passengers disappeared into the darkness, seeming to know where they were going. Our party was told to wait where we were. Soon our luggage (happily all of it) was brought to us.

When we were all reunited with our belongings we followed a young man through the darkened terminal, out through the doors to curbside where we boarded a pre-WWII bus. We settled in, just a driver and us.

We then undertook about a one-hour ride down wide, but very poorly lighted streets. The thing that struck you during this bus ride was, the fact that there was only a dim street lamp every 2 or 3 blocks. You were aware of many trees and some buildings, each with only an occasional dim light seeping through a window

By now it was past 11:00 PM Beijing time, it was impossible to tell what our biological time might be. I don't think any of us ever got "right" from the extreme time disturbances during the entire three-week stay.

The Airport and the ride in had put us all in an apprehensive state. Was this the way it was going to be? So little news and information had reached the outside world for the last 25 years that we began to speculate about what really awaited us in China. A little late, we started to think seriously about what our living conditions might be like there.

Finally we turned onto an even wider avenue, huge even by American standards. A little better lit, with street lamps on each intersection. After a few minutes we approached a very large building on our right. It was set back from the street and had small balconies spread across the side facing the Avenue. Still it was mostly darkened with only a few dim lights issuing from the windows behind the balconies, we pulled into a long curved drive way and stopped by wide glass Doors.

The driver said something in Chinese, Lily, who was sitting in front, turned and announced, "Peking Hotel, we are here."

A surprising sense of relief flooded through as we entered the lobby of the hotel.

It was quite beautiful! The lobby of the new wing, where we were to be, was expansive, with a vast marble floor, red carpets, very nice furnishings and four gigantic gold trimmed, marble pillars. Who ever had designed the interior had done their job well. It was very reminiscent of the Fairmont Hotel in San Francisco, with poorer lighting.

The rooms were small by our standards, nicely furnished and with poor plumbing. Our room faced out onto the wide Avenue in front of the Hotel and when daylight arrived provided us with an interesting view.

Except for the 5 or 6 days we spent later, in the city of Tientsin (now Tianjin), this was our home and base of operations while in China.

Morning of the first day dawned; I believe everyone's spirits were lifted with the sun. As always, every morning we found a large thermos full of hot tea waiting outside each of our doors.

Looking out from our small balcony we could see what was our view of Beijing. As one looked out and down, you were struck again by how wide the avenue was. Also you were hit by the fact that automobile traffic of any kind was almost non-existent. Thousands of people were traversing the avenue in both directions on bicycles. Occasionally there would be a horse-drawn cart included. If we leaned far out and looked to the right there was a vast square visible. It was the famous Tian An Men Square, across from the ancient palace of "The Forbidden City."

There was a great dining room, wonderful food. All the food was only Chinese. Actually one of our group who couldn't adapt to the 100% diet of only Chinese food, lost weight and became ill from it during the trip. At this time there was not a morsel of non-Chinese food to be bought at any price in the country, not even coffee. I usually had a large dish of rice with eggs and little green onions scrambled in it, each morning, with tea of course. I very much missed my coffee.

Our trip dates had been scheduled to wrap around the "Chinese Rug Fair" to be held in the city of Tientsin about 150 miles to the southeast. I believe that the Rug Fair was a hastily assembled event that had been created to present the newly revived industry to the handful of Americans and Europeans who had come to China that month for the purpose of trade.

Since the Fair didn't open for a couple of days yet we were to have a little "free" time in Beijing.

We quickly found out that our "free" time was anything but free. That first morning as we each arose at our own time and went down to breakfast we were greeted by Mr. Sung.

Mr. Sung was a serious man of about 40 years of age. I don't remember ever seeing him wear any thing but black, well-tailored "Mao" suits, identifying him as an important man and Communist party member. He became our constant companion through out our stay. He was involved in every detail of our trip and knew everything that we did at all times.

He spoke English, even better, I think, than he let on.

Lily Wen was our spokesperson. But Mr. Sung actually guided us throughout our stay. I believe he was accountable to his superiors in the government for all of our actions.

Along with Mr. Sung was a party of 8 or 9 young people of twenty or so. They were introduced as our "helpers" and English language students. They also acted as additional eyes and ears for Mr. Sung. We were never without them for the rest of our stay. Actually one young man, Wong Chin, became particularly attached to my wife and I. He was the same age and reminded us somehow, very much, of our oldest son Scott. We became very fond of him and had a tearful farewell when we parted at the end of the trip.

With a couple of days of unscheduled, un-carpet related time in Beijing my thoughts naturally turned to martial arts. I began to ask questions of all the locals with whom I could communicate, about the existence and location of any martial arts schools or teachers. My initial reaction was one of major disappointment. I was either met with blank stares, or worse yet, a kind of furtive, fearful reaction followed by an immediate and hurried disappearance.

The overall impression was that it wasn't a subject for discussion.

Finally I asked Mr. Sung, pinned him down, so to speak, and insisted on an answer. This is what I was told, along with other inquiries that I made. I believe the following explanation to be largely true.

During the time of the "Red Guards" in China, a particularly bloody period of "purges" sanctioned by Mao, one of the many targets of the Guard were the "Elitists." (One of the many, self-destructive stupidities of communism.) Millions of people were taken out and summarily murdered by the roving bands of youths called "Red Guards." Many old scores were settled and anyone who had ever or was even suspected as having ever been "special" at something was eliminated. Most business owners, many artisans, teachers, and community leaders were killed.

Among them were a majority of the leaders of the martial arts community. The basic tenet of Chinese communism is that no one is better than anyone else at anything, therefore martial arts "experts" fell into that category. Most of them were identified, found and murdered. Entire martial arts systems had disappeared or been driven very deeply "underground."

I was extremely disappointed, to say the least. I had been driven to make this trip largely because I was going to one of the cradles of the martial arts. However, I decided, fortunately, to continue my search.

The rest of the first day we all wished to "look around," on our own. We heard then, for the first time, the expression that would become the familiar party line for the rest of the trip, whenever we wanted to do anything on our own: "Sorry, that is not convenient at this time."

Everything we did and everywhere we went was under the watchful eye of Mr. Sung. Naturally, Herb and I began to look for ways to "ditch" him. We must have made the poor man crazy by the end of the trip!

At this point, I would like to recommend that if the reader is interested in knowing more details of this trip, read a wonderful book written the following year by Steve Allen. It is titled *Explaining China* (Crown Publishing, 1980). In it, Steve relates his "take" on the trip with lots of photographs, most of them taken by me. He refers to me as "the leader of our group, a martial arts expert who looks like Steve McQueen." We were good friends and we mostly perceived events the same although it is worth reading his book to see the slightly different points of view we had on a few subjects.

When any of us wanted to do a little shopping we were taken, under escort, to a large building, about the size of a modern supermarket, called the "Friendship Store." Here we were allowed to buy gifts, some art objects, and the like. I bought some of the large, decorated thermoses like the ones we found outside our hotel room each morning. Everything there seemed carefully selected for us.

By the second day we had figured out that we were being fully controlled and herded at all times. Being Americans, we balked at the supervision and began to look for ways to get on our own.

One part of our China lives that we became used to quickly was our ability to draw a very large crowd anywhere, anytime. The people of China had been completely cut off from the outside world for 25 years.

Except for Russians, they had really seen no one except other Chinese. The Russians came to China in 1949 as "Comrades," fellow Communists and brothers. In actuality they treated the Chinese Communists as backwards second cousins. The Russians were, rude, swaggering bullies who looked for ways to exploit China. They sold them inferior products and then charged them a fortune to teach them how to use them, all the time looking arrogantly down their noses at the Chinese people. Over time the people of China began, with very good reason, to hate the Russians.

After a couple of "outings" to the Friendship store we were ready for something different, so Mr. Sung pulled some strings and we had an afternoon where, under close supervision, we were allowed to spend time in a part of the city where we could shop and make purchases elsewhere. One of my great treasures was acquired that day. In an antique shop, never before visited by Americans, I found an early Ching dynasty vase that I loved. I bought it for less than $100. It is still today one of most prized possessions.

I continued to hound everyone I could speak with in English, or in Mandarin, if Lily was present, about martial arts in China. I finally began to make a little progress.

A young man from our very recently established United States Government Liaison Office showed up at the Hotel one day. He was quite apologetic; communication being what it was, they didn't know that we had arrived until an hour before. He was conveying a message.

Our presidentially appointed Liaison Officer to the Government of China was in Shanghai attending to some official business and would catch up with us in a few days when we returned from the city of Tientsin and the Rug Fair.

At that time our two countries had not recognized one another as yet so for the time being, our Liaison Officer was basically an "acting Ambassador" to China. The U.S. Government had been allowed to set up a compound of one square block, behind high concrete and stone walls. They were busy creating work areas and living quarters there for the few dozen Americans and their families who were assigned to duty in China.

About the walls: Everywhere throughout the several cities I visited at that time in China, the people's homes were set behind walls. It was generally impossible to see the houses from the street. That was the way residential areas were laid out. If you visited some one in their home, you entered through a door in the outer wall with no view of the actual house itself until you were inside the wall. Once inside, there were courtyards that varied in scope, style, and could be quite unique. The homes themselves were unalike, ranging from very modest to very sumptuous. The overlying idea is that you really "can't judge a book by its cover."

Our visitor from our Liaison Office was very eager to help us in any way he could. Most of our group had personal questions and goals. He spent time with each of us, made lots of notes and tried valiantly to answer all of our questions that he could.

Steve was trying to find an expatriate American journalist, named Rury Ali, for the purpose of including him in the book Steve was writing about this trip. Steve was actually writing two books at once. He always carried two pocket tape recorders and was constantly dictating notes into one or the other of them.

Herb was always looking for the best restaurants. Once he did find one he wanted to try, it was usually, "Sorry, it is not convenient at this time."

Jayne was on a quest for the best Russian caviar, which led to an interesting story for later.

I, of course was seeking any thing I could find relating to the martial arts.

Our new friend from the Liaison office gave me the first information I had been able to glean on the subject.

Here is the story as he related it to me that cold February morning, as we sat drinking hot tea, in the lobby of the Peking Hotel.

After Mao succeeded in winning the civil war in China, he drove the Nationalists and Chiang Kai Shek off the Mainland and onto Formosa. Once Mao had absolute control over the country, the purges began. Most historians seem to agree that, with the exception of Joseph Stalin's purges in Russia, it was one of the bloodiest periods in human history.

Mao began the total and ruthless extermination of millions of Chinese people. As mentioned before, all trace of "Class" was to be eliminated from the new Chinese Communist Society. That could include, for example a piano teacher, a poet, any businessman or a martial Arts Master. Any one perceived to be anti-Communist or "Elitist" was summarily executed.

As victims or potential victims of the mass murders, martial arts masters were either killed or went into hiding. The few remaining had to learn to practice their art and pass it on to others in secrecy for over the next twenty years.

At the beginning of the 70s, for some reason, known only to the communist party leaders, a change occurred. It was decided that the country would have an "official" martial arts program. They decided it would be known under the name of "Wu Shu," which in English literally translates to "War Art." This had to be a culturally approved art, "classless" of course, and could not revere or acknowledge any one master or style. It had to be open to all equally without any recognizable antecedents. This might not sound so bad at first glance. However, the problem was this: who made the decisions as to what to include and what to omit? What kick or block or strike would be included in Wu Shu and what would be discarded?

All of these decisions were made, not by a panel of high-ranking Kung Fu masters, but by political panels of high-ranking Communist party cadres. The decisions were influenced primarily by the investigation of what master of what style is given credit for the development of each technique. If that master was known to be an anti-Communist, even though now dead at the hands of the

Mao administration, still his techniques were deemed as "reactionary" and could not be included in the new, Communist, martial art of Wu Shu.

Now for the good news! I of course asked if I could possibly be allowed any where near where the Wu Shu training was done. My young friend said, "Let's go up to your room." I knew they weren't going to be training in my room, but decided to humor him. When we entered my room, he motioned for me to come out on my balcony. He pointed, directly across the Avenue to a large, open area of perhaps a quarter of a square block. "There it is." From my balcony you could see down and over the ever-present wall and I could watch people working out, performing recognizable martial arts techniques

I was very pleased and excited and could hardly contain my desire to cross the avenue and see if I could somehow gain entry to the Wu Shu school.

However, as we walked back down to the Lobby he imparted one more piece of information that, not seeming as vital at the time, actually turned out to be much more important.

He said, "For what its worth, I have been told, that some of the old Masters still work out in the tree filled parks around Tian An Men Square before dawn." I decided to check that out as soon as possible, but was more enthused at the moment over the unbelievable proximity of the Wu Shu school.

A couple of problems presented themselves immediately. It was a little risky for me to intrude myself into the Wu Shu training area without an invitation. Furthermore, we were leaving for Tientsin and the rug fair the next morning, and other plans had been made for us by our hosts.

That evening, before I could attempt to gain entrance, we had another pressing invitation that had to be honored. Our Group, along with a few European guests of the Hotel had been invited as "Guests of the People" to a "Chinese Opera."

We were assembled and ready in the lobby at about 6:00 PM. Mr. Sung, Wong Chin and a few of the other students escorted us onto a bus to transport us to the Opera house. The ride was perhaps a half an hour through the dimly lit streets.

As an aside, we had discovered that the reason everything was so poorly lighted at night in Beijing was that the city suffered from a shortage of gas and electric power. It also helped to explain why there was constantly a gray/brown haze in the sky over the city. Homes were primarily heated by coal furnaces and lit by kerosene and oil lamps.

Before the "opera" we were taken to a large Banquet hall where we found that, to our surprise, we were to partake in a lavish 22-course meal. This was the first of many banquets in China and I, for one, learned two very important lessons.

First of all, no matter how good any one dish was, or how much you wanted to eat more of it, don't! Because if you eat too much of, let's say, course number 10, you still have 12 more to come! That way lies acute indigestion.

The second lesson I learned that night was DON'T make the toast at the end of each course with a harmless looking Liquor called "Mao Tai." We were given a small shot glass, no bigger than a wine cork, after each course. It contained an ounce or so of that incredibly strong clear liquid. After the first dozen or so courses and following toasts, I vaguely remember making a speech about "hands across the Ocean" or some other ridiculously trite subject and ending with a dissertation of how they could solve all of their Electric and gas shortage problems with a few gallons of "Mao Tai." I'm sure I made a fool of myself.

When the banquet was concluded we reentered the bus and rode for another ten minutes or so to the theater.

Another surprise awaited us. We, the Americans and Europeans, perhaps 20 of us in all, were the Honored Guests for the evening. Everyone else had already been seated, perhaps 800 or so Chinese. I'm sure they had been selected by some official criteria to attend the show with us. I sat next to a very handsome man and a beautiful woman who appeared not to speak English but were very cordial. The thought came to me that perhaps they were Chinese movie stars. The exact number of seats for us had been left vacant. They were intentionally spread out through the theater so that we wouldn't all be clustered together. Each of us sat between and next to Chinese people. It was quite friendly and nice.

As soon as we were seated the show began. It was essentially like an old time vaudeville show, about 15 acts, of jugglers, dancers, acrobats, wire walkers, unicyclists, trained bears, and much more.

Stuffed as I was with a 22-course meal and 22 shots of the most potent liquor on earth, I struggled for two hours to try to remain conscious and appear appreciative. I remember it, through a "Mao Tai" haze as one of the longest nights of my life

The next morning, I awoke, a little the worse for the Mao Tai, to a very busy day. We were leaving by train for Tientsin and the Rug Fair. I still hadn't been able to make it across the street to the Wu Shu school. After packing and gathering all of our papers and the vital "green card" that was necessary for anyone traveling anywhere in China, I was ready for Tientsin with only a short time to spare.

TIENTSIN

SEVERAL OFFICIAL CARS came for us at the Hotel. We had decided that it would be better and safer to take all of our luggage with us to Tientsin. At first it seemed like a good idea to take only what we needed for the four nights there and leave the rest in Beijing at the Hotel. After giving the matter more thought, we decided that it might be better to keep everything with us. It would mean handling all of those suitcases a couple of extra times but there were just too many unpredictable facets on this trip for us to be separated from our belongings.

Therefore we struggled to get our entire luggage into the cars and made the 45-minute trip to the train station. The cars, as always, were pre WWII-vintage American cars in perfect condition.

The Train Station in Beijing was memorable, to say the least. Since the populace of China had no personal automobiles, and air travel was limited to only important Party dignitaries and military leaders, train travel was THE mode of transportation if any real distance was involved.

The station was huge, about the size of Grand Central Station. It was packed with travelers. Many of them were military. Many thousands of civilians were traveling as well. You were struck by the simple, primitive means of transporting luggage. Cardboard boxes, small wooden crates and even items wrapped in paper and tied with string. Ours were practically the only suitcases in view.

We spent an interesting hour at the station watching the people and waiting for our train. As usual we attracted crowds of staring people and were happy when Mr. Sung finally called us to board.

The trains traversing China in 1975, like so many things, transported us again for another trip back in time. They were powered by STEAM engines—something that had disappeared by then in all of the developed countries of the world.

As we entered our passenger car I was astonished by the accommodations. We, the Americans, nine of us at the time as Steve was to meet us in a day or two later in Tientsin, and about a half a dozen Europeans, had two entire cars all to ourselves.

The first, passenger, car had large, old style, comfortable seats. They were covered in a dark burgundy fabric with the ever-present lace doilies on the headrests. The seats were configured so that each two faced two others in half the car. The other half of the car was made up of private compartments. It was all open for our use, as we would see fit. Some of the group napped in the compartments or sat gazing at the passing countryside while others of us talked.

Jayne entertained us with stories of her childhood memories of China in the 20s and 30s. There was an attendant who would see to any of our needs. It made for a very pleasant trip.

Our second car was a beautifully appointed dining car. There was a gentleman working in that car as well who could bring us snacks and tea if we wished.

The entire environment made it seem that we were somehow the cast of an old movie set in the thirties, traveling across China on the "Orient Express." It was High Drama.

I spent most of the trip in the dining car sitting at a table, drinking tea and talking with Jayne, Herb, and Helene Pollock.

We all became friendly with one of the Europeans whom we had first met at the Peking Hotel and who was now accompanying us to the rug fair. His name was Peter Liebentrow, he was a rug dealer from Holland and well known in the industry, having written several books about rugs.

A revealing yet comical note about Peter: We had noticed that he always wore a small red pin in the left lapel of his suit jacket. Because of where we were and a growing, realization that we were under constant study and scrutiny, we assumed that he was a member of the communist party. We were careful never to say anything to Peter that we didn't want to get back to our hosts. This sense of caution superimposed itself over all of our conversations. One night a week or so later, after we had spent a great deal more time with Peter, someone in our group, I think it was Herb, made a comment about the ever-present red pin. "Oh, that," Peter said. " I am an executive with the Red Cross Blood Bank in my country."

How wrong we had been. How easily your surroundings can color your thoughts.

Tientsin, at the time, was a city of about 5 million people, as far as I know, all Chinese. It was an industrial city with a seaport. A great deal of import and export for the country passed though Tientsin. The air over the city, like Beijing, appeared to be constantly overcast, due to the same causes of burning coal, wood and fuel oil.

As our train pulled into the station, we gathered our luggage and when the train had made a full stop, stepped out onto a platform.

One of the weirdest of our many strange experiences on the trip occurred then.

Apparently there had not been an American in Tientsin since 1946. Most of the population, being under thirty years of age, had grown up being immersed in Government propaganda about the "Evil Capitalistic Dogs" of America. Now, because of a pragmatic change of attitude only a few months earlier by their Government leaders, they had reversed their position, made a 180-degree turn and the people had been told that we were OK after all.

As we looked out from the train platform, which was raised about 5 feet off the ground we were stunned and more than just a little fearful to see in front of us, a gigantic throng of people. We later estimated that at least 25,000 people, perhaps far more, had come to the Railroad station to "see the Americans."

As usual the throng was totally silent. Except for an occasional cough or the sound of a baby, not another sound was heard. To say it was unnerving doesn't even come close to describing the impact of this sight.

We must have stood there staring for two or three minutes, not knowing whether to run back onto the train or try to make our way into the station. Then Mr. Sung took command; he spoke to, what we believed were a few Communist party cadres on the platform. . They turned to the crowd, and walking towards them, with a wave of their hands and snapping of their fingers at the assemblage, the crowd just as silently dispersed and left the area.

After that experience I really can't recall much about the ride into the city. It took us all a while to come down from that.

We arrived at what had been christened the "Tientsin Hotel #1." More strange experiences awaited us.

At the turn of the last century, the major cities of China had essentially been "occupied" by the major foreign powers. Economic "interests" such as the British opium trade had made China extremely valuable.

By 1902 the major powers of, Britain, the United States, Germany, Italy, Japan, France and Russia all had holdings and interests in this vast, rich land.

In the major cities, Peking, Shanghai, Tientsin, and a few others, the Foreign Powers settled in. The cities were divided into sections, like slices of a pie, each one called a "Legation" area.

The Tientsin Hotel #1 had been a British "Legation House" built by the Astor family. Since there were actually no commercial hotels in Tientsin in 1975, it had been pressed into service on short notice to be used by the foreigners attending the Rug Fair.

The lobby was very small; it had originally been just the entry area for the Legation House. The floors throughout the entire building were made of hardwood; the halls were dark and narrow. All in all it was a real firetrap. There was what must have been the original elevator, which no one was brave enough to make use of. The rooms were small, sparsely and cheaply furnished, very poorly lit and we only THOUGHT the Peking Hotel had bad plumbing!

When we were shown to our room it was so bad that it was funny. The room was large enough, with very high ceilings and recently painted dark gray paint, which extended down the walls as well. There was no window but instead a glass paneled door that opened out to a small balcony.

The furniture was a sight to behold; there were two narrow, metal, twin beds that sagged badly in the middle like hammocks. Other than that, a large, battered old wooden chest of drawers, one night stand between the beds, with a small lamp. One old, worn upholstered chair comprised the rest of the décor.

There was no closet so we arranged our luggage on the floor for accessibility.

Then we checked out the bathroom. A tub with a showerhead, with a very light stream of water, and no shower curtain made up the bathing facilities. Showers were to be a very unpleasant procedure, with very little water pressure and an unreliable consistency of water temperature.

The *coup de grace* awaited us. I had decided to be good-natured and make the best of it; "it's only four nights." I kicked off my shoes, chose which bed would be mine, and threw myself down on it. As I fell back onto the pillow I thought Benny Urquidez had kicked me in the back of the head. The pillows were filled with RICE!

After doing what we could with our clothes and other items from our luggage, we made our way downstairs and found the dining room. At least it had been painted a cheerful bright yellow and was large with several windows, a welcome change from the dreariness of the rooms.

We met Jayne, Herb, Lily and the Levys at the dining room entrance. We all sat together around a large round table. We were starving so we ordered, Chinese food of course, and tea.

Then came one of the biggest surprises of the trip!

The food, when it arrived, was beautiful to behold, each of us eagerly attacked it. I wish I had a photograph of what must have been the stunned, incredulous expressions on our faces as we each took our first mouth full.

The Chinese government, concerned about the welfare and safety of the foreign guests in Tientsin for the Rug Fair, had taken many precautions. The drinking water in Tientsin was similar to that in Mexico. Even the Chinese traveling to Tientsin were wary of the water. The authorities had decided, to be safe, that they would chlorinate the city water supply. They had never done it before. They grossly overestimated the amount of chlorine required. Everything the water touched reeked and was overpoweringly tainted by the taste of chlorine!

Food, tea, laundry, bathwater, all overpowered by chlorine. It was incredible!

For weeks after leaving Tientsin, we were haunted by the smell and taste of chlorine.

After dinner we tried to take a little walk around the hotel. As usual, before we could walk a half a block we had gathered a crowd of about 50 silent spectators. Although we didn't feel threatened, nevertheless it became uncomfortable so we returned to the Hotel. I found a large, sparsely furnished, salon at the end of the hall from my room. No one else seemed to know about it so I could be alone. There for the first time since leaving Los Angeles I was able to give myself a good, strenuous workout for an hour or so. When I decided to stop, it was still fairly early in China, I have no idea what time my biological clock was set at, but I certainly wasn't ready for bed and that awful pillow. I returned to my room, showered, and redressed. Smelling of chlorine, I decided to go downstairs again to see who else was awake

We had discovered that because of the chlorine situation, the only thing to drink in Tientsin was either beer or a very pleasant locally bottled orange soda.

As I entered the dining room looking forward to my bottle of soda, I practically bumped into Steve Allen. He had just arrived, he missed us by a few hours in Beijing and had just arrived and gotten settled in his Tientsin #1 Hotel room. He was hungry and asked me to join him while he ate a late dinner.

Steve was already aware of the chlorine situation. It was impossible not to be, so he joined me in an orange soda and ordered dinner. Since our waiter spoke almost no English, and my Mandarin is poor, we managed to order Steve's food by using sign language. It would have been a strange sight in Beverly Hills to watch Steve and I making fish faces and gesticulations of fish swimming in a stream to order dinner. It seemed to work. We then turned our attention back to playing "catch up" to bring Steve up to speed on what had been going on the last few days before he arrived.

After hearing of our adventures he had his own story to tell. He had actually arrived the night before but had somehow been taken to a different hotel! The Hsin Ciao Hotel. In spite of all of his attempts to explain that his wife and the rest of his Party were at the Peking Hotel, he was told politely but firmly that he was staying at the Hsin Ciao for the night. "You will see them in Tientsin," is what he was told. He made one final protest that was met with their final answer. "Maybe so Mr. Allen, but you arrived late!" That was the end of that. When I told the others, being familiar with our hosts, all couldn't help but laugh at that.

Then his dinner arrived; it was a whole fish, staring up at us from a large plate, swimming in a heavy sauce. For some reason that struck us as very funny and we laughed and made jokes about his fish while he ate. Steve said it would have been delicious were it not for the overpowering taste of chlorine.

The next day was the first day of the Rug Fair. It was being held in a very large Hall about a 10-minute ride from the Hotel.

It was quite productive, we all managed to find items of interest to us. I was able to choose some products that I thought would sell in the United States; the prices were low and the workmanship excellent. I made arrangements to purchase some samples and set up appointments to visit the factories outside Beijing where the rugs are produced.

All in all we spent about two days at the Rug Fair. They spoke a little English, and when a conversation became too difficult, Lily and Mr. Sung were always there to help.

When we weren't in the building housing the Fair, we were allowed to, with supervision provided by Mr. Sung, see a little of the city.

Although there were many fascinating places to see and go in Tientsin, I will just mention two more.

On one of our excursions, we drove throughout the city in a small bus. After visiting the famous Water Park, a one-time play ground for the long-gone Imperial Chinese family, we came to a large square. It was larger than any square I have ever seen anywhere, Perhaps, as Steve remarked, "the size of several football fields." On one side was a long row of stone monoliths 50 or 60 feet high. They were painted with what we were told were Communist political slogans. Every so often one would instead be painted with a likeness of the great leaders of the Party: Lenin, Marx, Engels, Stalin, and of course, Mao. Opposite these monoliths, across the square, perhaps half a mile away was a huge stone government building with a 100 foot or so high statue of Mao, hand raised in salute towards the other side of the square. We came to refer to this vast area simply as "Tientsin Square."

The other story involves our dinner the last night in Tientsin.

One of the European guests at the Rug Fair had told me about a great restaurant he had been to the night before called "The Little Dumpling." After our last day at the Fair we decided, eight of us, to go there for dinner.

We secured rides, thanks to our hosts, and arrived after dark. As is common in China the restaurant was situated in what had, no doubt, been a private residence at one time. We entered through a door in a wall, into a dark courtyard, through about a 12-foot long alley and into the restaurant.

It was comfortably furnished, not elegant by any means. We were shown into a good-sized room. The walls were lined with about a dozen, upholstered "easy chairs." In the center of the room was a round dining table that could seat 12 or so people. We had, probably the best meal we had enjoyed in Tiensin, if not all of China. After several courses of fish, chicken, noodles and so on we ended with each of us being served 10 of the best meat and sauce filled dumplings I have ever tasted. Somehow the cooks had found a way to eliminate the chlorine. We speculated that maybe they had a separate water source. We were also served all of the excellent Chinese beer we wanted.

After eating we were told it would be about a half hour before the cars would be able to pick us up. Steve and Lily decided to take a walk around the block in front of the restaurant. Herb and I stood in the street in front looking for the cars. After about 15 minutes we saw Steve and Lily returning. Behind them was the usual crowd of as many as 500 people. Once again, as when later, Steve and I wore the "Russian" hats, this crowd seemed hostile. It didn't look good. As they drew near to where we were standing we could hear what sounded like a growling mutter coming from the mob.

Just then a lone man, dressed in the khaki color that usually signified military came walking towards the crowd from the other end of the street. He walked briskly towards them and without seeming to speak, he snapped his fingers several times and pointed back in the direction they were coming from. Silently the crowd melted away and disappeared.

Steve and Lily joined us; even Lily had no explanation as to what had just occurred. I wanted to find out so I went out in the street and approached the man. I was surprised to find that he spoke good English. In a brief conversation he told me something that went a long way towards explaining many of the events on our trip.

It appears that a large element in the Chinese communist society did NOT want détente with the U.S. There was still a large part of the younger population that believed we were their dedicated enemies. They would have loved to see an "incident," perhaps the death of an American or two. That incident could disrupt the government's attempt at normalizing relations with our country. Politically, the part of the city we were in was a hotbed of these people. We had just met some of them. The man who had dispersed them was one of our invisible bodyguards that the ruling members of the party had assigned to protect and watch over us.

Shortly after, our cars pulled up and we were hustled back to the hotel.

As we made U-turns in the street in front of the restaurant, Herb and I saw two open bed trucks full of soldiers, bayonets fixed, parked just around the corner. We knew then why the lone man was able to disperse the crowd so quickly. He had considerable backup!

The following day we packed and returned to the Tientsin train station for our trip back to the Peking Hotel.

Our return trip was totally different from the trip down.

We left just after dark. We boarded a car that was occupied with armed soldiers. About thirty of them were spread about throughout the car. They were cleaning their weapons, sleeping, and talking in low voices. There was a great deal of staring at us as well. We were, to say the least, nervous about this development. I'm sure the thought crossed most of our minds that we might stop somewhere out in the middle of Chinese nowhere and be shot and left in a ditch.

Only later when we were safely back in our rooms at the Peking hotel did it occur to me that these were probably the same soldiers who were watching over us in Tientsin. Our "escorts."

The balance of our time in China, about 14 more days, was, other than a few visits to the rug factories, mostly free time. I was looking forward to resuming my quest for martial arts and artists and doing a little sight seeing.

We arrived back at the Peking Hotel. It must have been about 9:00 PM.

Early the next morning, the first thing I did, with Herb as my companion, was to cross the Avenue and go up to the door of the Wushu academy training headquarters.

To my surprise the door was unlocked, so we entered.

There were a few, obviously shocked men sitting in a small office just inside the entrance. The sight of two Caucasians strolling into the school had them totally perplexed.

Acting as if we had every right to be there and guessing where we were headed we kept going and walked into the gymnasium area. The action was outside so we walked out and sat down in the first row of the bleachers closest to the field. The instructor noticed us but otherwise continued working with his students.

There were about 20 young people, probably between the ages of 10 and 20 years old. They were dressed in either red or blue warm up suits.

They were quite impressive; mostly it was their acrobatic and gymnastic ability. The martial arts had, in my opinion, been added later. This was the National Wushu School. These young people were the best that this land of close to a billion people had to offer. Because of the politically inspired, 25 year hiatus of Martial Arts in China, it is my belief that when the Government decided to create the Wushu program they sought out the best gymnasts and acrobats in the country and brought them to Beijing to learn the fighting arts.

We watched for over an hour. They practiced many of the moves that were familiar to me from the Kung Fu styles I had seen in the U.S. Two of my close

friends were then and still are, Eric Lee and Doug Wong. I have worked out
with them and seen them illustrate their art on many occasions. I thought that
the techniques I saw performed that night were flawlessly done. However, I
could feel a lack of fighting attitude and spirit in the moves. It was more dance-
like than fighting.

At the end of the work out the instructor came over to us, when he realized that
we didn't speak Mandarin and didn't seem to have any reason to be there, he
proceeded, in a calm and friendly enough manner to escort us to the door. I was
never able to re-enter again. On the few attempts I made the door was always
locked. I was, however able to take some good photographs from my balcony
with my telephoto lens.

If the reader is interested in a more detailed description of the Wushu school
in Beijing and this experience, I wrote a long, front-page article about it that
appeared in the September 1975 issue of *Black Belt* Magazine, complete with
photographs.

For the rest of our stay on this trip to China we were able to indulge our
curiosity and enjoy the sights and life of this huge and mysterious land.

TIAN AN MEN SQUARE

I HAD NOT forgotten the information received from the young Assistant to our American Liaison Officer. He had told me that he had heard that many of the older Martial Artists still trained in the parks surrounding Tian An Men square.

We had been scheduled for a trip that next morning after Tientsin through the "Forbidden City," the ancient Imperial Palace of China. It was only about 4 long city blocks from the hotel. The grounds cover many square miles, about the size of Disneyland. The Main Gate in the walls faces directly on to Tian An Men Square.

We were provided with transportation to the palace. It was pointed out, when we entered, that Chairman Mao resided part of every year in one of the structures next to the entrance.

We spent the better part of a day wandering through the grounds and structures. I have traveled over almost all of Europe and large parts of Asia but have never seen anything like the "Forbidden City." I was able to take hundreds of photographs that I still treasure today.

There were still a great many ancient art objects on view to see but it is my understanding that the bulk of the Imperial artifacts were taken by the nationalists when they fled to Formosa (Taiwan).

After my return to the U.S., I made dozens of presentations to groups about this trip and the "Forbidden City" pictures were always a huge hit. To describe it in detail would almost be a separate book. Along with the Great Wall, the Summer Palace, the "Ming Tombs, the Temple of Heaven, and other fantastic sites.

As we were leaving the palace, one of the drivers who was picking us up to go back to the Hotel began speaking excitedly and pointing at the residence next to the main gate. Lily, obviously with great respect and awe pointed and said to us. "Look, there is Chairman Mao." The 82-year-old Communist dictator was standing outside his home getting a little afternoon sunshine and stretching his arms.

I decided not to ride back and instead took a leisurely walk back, making my way around the huge square through all of the tree filled parks that lined the area. It was probably about an hour later that I returned to the hotel.

I now had a feeling for the area where, I was told, the martial arts masters could still be found early in the mornings. I planned to go there before dawn the next day.

Upon returning to the Hotel I ran into Steve in the lobby on his way out somewhere. It was late afternoon. "Where are you headed?" I asked. "I just thought maybe I would see if I can do a little exploring on my own," he replied. "Want company?" I said, and we both headed for the door. It seemed like a good time to sneak out on our own.

Mr. Sung was dealing with one of the ever-present, daily situations with Lily, while Jayne was mesmerizing our young Chinese "companions." She was holding court in her room, teaching them American slang expressions. We had begun to hear contemporary (now quite dated of course) idiom such as, "cool," "I'm hip," "far out," and "heavy" slipping into their conversations.

Steve and I seized the moment to slip out of the hotel. There were always a half a dozen armed soldiers, complete with bayonets, posted at the front entrance, but for some reason they failed to take notice as we walked out the front door on to Tian An Men Avenue, turned left and left again at the next intersection.

Within a few blocks we entered a different world. Real Beijing: a world of Chinese stores, and Chinese people conducting their own daily business. Not a façade that had been created just for our consumption.

We found that if we kept walking we collected only stares.

However, if we stopped anywhere, a crowd would quickly form around us, and if we didn't move on it would continue to grow. This was repeated everywhere we went in the country for our entire stay. It was not at all unusual for us to collect hundreds of people in a matter of a few minutes. They were normally quiet and calm, looking at us the way they might look at handful of 6-foot tall penguins that had suddenly appeared before them.

Steve and I decided to keep moving. We traveled maybe two more blocks and came to a large department store, which we entered. It was somewhat like an American department store, with, of course much different looking merchandise. We had some "Renminbi," Chinese money and wanted to make a purchase. We settled on two large, black, fur hats. We managed to pay an incredulous clerk and proudly wearing our new hats, decided to head back towards the hotel and lunch.

As we turned right to go the 4 or 5 blocks back to the hotel things started to change. Even though we were moving this time, the crowd started to form and FOLLOW us! We knew right away that something wasn't right.

I had made a valiant effort to try to learn mandarin before we left on our trip. My son Scott, a born linguist among many other things, speaks several languages, one of the foremost being Mandarin Chinese. Between Scott, tapes, books and several close friends in the martial arts I had acquired a very rudimentary vocabulary of Mandarin.

When the Communists assumed power throughout all of China there were hundreds of different dialects being spoken across the land. One of the things they did was to make Mandarin, the most prevalent dialect, into the official language of the nation. They call it "Pu Tung Hua" which translates as "the common language."

As we walked, the crowd grew. For one of the only two times during the entire trip we sensed hostility. I could make out a few words, such as *bu hao* (" bad" or "no good"). We didn't know how but we had obviously, somehow, done something offensive. By the time we were a block from the hotel the crowd had reached several hundred people and the sounds were growing and becoming more menacing. Less than a block from the Hotel, Just as we had almost decided to run for our lives, we saw Jayne approaching us from the direction we were heading.

"Where have you two been?" she called out. "And where did you get those stupid hats? You look like Russians"

Steve and I looked at each other and the realization hit us both at the same time. Russians!

I gathered my meager linguistic talents, turned back to face the crowd, removed the hat and said in my best, and loudest, Tournament Announcer's voice: "Wo

De Mei Guo Ren!" "We are Americans!" Several times. The crowd relaxed, several actually smiled and quickly dispersed. In retrospect I believe we had a close call that day. It could have turned really ugly in a few more minutes.

The Russians, with their arrogant attitude and their shameless exploitation of the people, have left a great deal of bad feelings with the rank and file Chinese. They hate them, with good reason. We looked too much like Russians with the hats. I still have mine and get it out once in a while. It always brings back that day in Beijing in 1975. I wish now that I would have purchased more things that day.

Jayne's timely arrival may have prevented an international incident!

Having had enough adventure for that day, and having worked up an appetite, I decided to eat lunch, I went into the lobby and after having some food in the dining room I went back to my room to write a couple of letters and catch up on some badly needed sleep.

On the subject of letters and cards: Soon after arriving, we all realized that all of our correspondence was being read by Mr. Sung, and probably others as well. Too many times he slipped up and made a reference to something that he only could have known by snooping through our mail. One of our party, I believe it was Herb Cole, actually saw him in a corner of the lobby reading one of our outgoing letters. After that we tried to be cautious in our writings.

At the time I was in China, I had, at home, two Great Danes, Garm and Gretta. I have always adored dogs and usually have two at a time. Garm and Gretta were like two more children to me. They had the run of the house and both slept with (on) us at night. They did however have a doghouse in the back for them to use in the case of being shut out on a hot or rainy day. I had made it myself out of 4 by 8 sheets of plywood. It had carpet on the floor, and was located around the house where it was not in view from any of the windows. It was very serviceable but certainly unattractive and very utilitarian.

In one of my letters home to Scott and Kirk, knowing that my mail would be perused, I told the boys, "Our accommodations in Tientsin, reminded me very much of Garm and Gretta's house." Garm and Gretta were our two Great Danes. I used coded phrases and references like this knowing my sons would "get it."

CHINA MARTIAL ARTS 1975

THE NEXT MORNING I awoke early, about 4:00 AM. I showered and dressed in my black Tokaido gi, worn over a t-shirt and sweatshirt; it was very cold. I had a quick bite in the 24-hour dining room to fortify me. Then with my heavy black coat with a fur-lined collar (no Russian hat), I strode out the front door of the hotel.

The guards were there; they saw me, looked puzzled but said nothing. I turned right and walked the few blocks to the Square. Having scouted out the area the day before, I headed directly to the place I thought I would go if I were going to train.

By then it was, perhaps 4:45 AM: still black outside, another hour-plus before dawn. As soon as I reached my destination I perceived at once a small group of Chinese men, fewer than ten, moving about in a clearing in the park. I approached slowly, but kept my distance. They were practicing what I would call crescent kicks.

I decided not to come too close; just the sight of a lone Caucasian in the park at this time of the morning could be enough to set off some kind of undesirable reaction.

I chose a spot about 30 or 40 yards away from them, divested myself of my heavy coat and began a couple of minutes of stretching. Watching them surreptitiously from the corner of my vision I then started to perform a *kata* (form). I chose the most Chinese-looking one I knew, "Chinto" from my Isshinryu studies.

As I finished the *kata*, I then started a good, long, kicking workout. I did several hundred kicks of different kinds. As I continued to watch them peripherally I could see they had stopped and were staring at me.

Taking a break I turned to approach the group, several disappeared immediately. As I drew near to the remaining few, I tried to appear as friendly as possible, attempting in my weak Mandarin to reassure them. I said as best I could "Hello, I am an American."

Their reaction was startled, they looked all around, beyond and behind me, as if they thought I was some kind of bait in a trap, and moved away onto the shadows and were gone. I knew this wasn't going anywhere that day so I returned to the hotel, still before daylight. Disappointed but undaunted, I sat in the dining room drinking tea and planning on how to handle it differently the next morning.

Earlier I mentioned Jayne and caviar. Jayne Meadows Allen has a taste, no, a passion, for good caviar. We had discovered that the best Beluga caviar could be purchased in Beijing for a tiny fraction of what it cost in the U.S. or Europe. We didn't see her all that day, when inquiries were made we found that she had gone caviar shopping and taking her purchases to her room she had consumed a vast quantity of fish eggs and was feeling "under the weather" so to speak.

THE RUG FACTORY

THERE WAS STILL a lot to do that day, so I roused myself from my thoughts and my concerns about Jayne and prepared for a day at one of the rug factories. Most of the group was going. We boarded a bus in front of the Hotel and after an interesting drive through parts of the city that we had never seen before we arrived at the factory about 9:45 AM.

The factory was housed in a very large, old, brick building. Looking like many of the carpet factories still in use in the southern U.S. only older. I would estimate that it had been built in the early 1800s. It was cold and poorly lit. The ceilings were quite low and the floors made of a dark wood. The overall effect was dark and dismal.

We were greeted and ushered into a good-sized meeting room. Fortunately there were large windows in one wall that provided adequate lighting for our needs. Electricity was in such short supply in China at that time that all lighting was kept to the barest minimum.

There were about ten Chinese and six of us. Some of our party had contracted a very bad cold that eventually made us all very sick. This virus devastated everyone in our party. It appeared to be something new to westerners that we had little resistance against. Several of us had to seek Chinese medical help; that is another story for later.

Lily Wen was part of our group that day. Between her and one of the Chinese interpreters who spoke adequate English, we were able to have a decent meeting.

Our concern was to purchase samples and enough room size rugs to test the market in the U.S. (Carpet is machine manufactured in 12-foot-wide, long rolls, as opposed to room-size rugs which are hand made in sizes such as 6x9 or 9x12, etc.) We had already determined that their carpet was not competitive or good enough to stand up against the carpet manufactured in the U.S.

The rugs at this factory were all hand made. We asked for and were given a tour of the manufacturing area. It consisted of huge, ugly rooms, poorly lit, with low ceilings. The weavers were about 80%women, sitting, bent over looms pulling yarn and cutting it with electric scissors. The working conditions were deplorable by American standards. It sickened me to see it.

After the tour we returned to our meeting room. The Chinese all lit up their cigarettes and we resumed our discussions.

Everywhere we went in China, it seemed that the entire population of adults were chain smokers. They were constantly smoking and offering cigarettes. It was a hell for non-smokers, especially those of us, like me, who were ex-smokers.

In this meeting, as in every formal business meeting that I attended in Communist China there is a protocol that was observed. After the cigarettes were offered and lit, the senior member of the Chinese contingent would ask, very seriously, if we would please offer them some criticism of themselves, their facility or their products. This always led to a great deal of embarrassment and discomfort on our part. It was more of a Communist thing than a Chinese thing.

That day I came up with an answer that served me well in all of the meetings from then on.

The inevitable question was asked.

I leaned forward; there was total silence in the room.

I said, "Yes I can." You could have heard a pin drop. The Chinese also leaned forward straining to hear. My fellow Americans, I suspect, must have experienced a moment of panic, thinking,"He is going to get us thrown out of the country."

After pausing a moment for dramatic effect, I said.

"I think you all smoke too much!"

It took a few moments to be translated, and then to my utter relief, the Chinese broke into a prolonged and honest laughter. I continued to use that icebreaker in the rest of my meetings in the country.

My friend and mentor Jim Marcus, whom I spoke of earlier, related some stories to me before I left for China regarding the rug factories. I heard the same thing while in Beijing from Steve Allen's friend who had been living in China since the late 20s, so they were corroborated.

Before the Communist takeover, in the twenties and thirties, life in China was cheap. In one instance in a famine in the late '20s, eight million people died in one province alone. At the time it wasn't even reported in the Peking and Shanghai press. Life had no value.

An 8 or 9-year-old girl could be purchased for a week's supply of food and used for any purpose. The pretty ones were usually used as prostitutes until they died of abuse and sickness by the time they were 13 or 14.

Many went to the factories. At the rug factories, something Jim Marcus witnessed first hand, the girls were purchased and worked in the factory for three years or until they died, whichever came first. They worked 16 hours a day, 7 days a week, 52 weeks a year. They ate rice soup. They didn't have electric scissors. Those who survived had hands that were crippled for life. A high percentage died. There is a large river directly behind the factory; Jim personally witnessed on his trips to the factory to buy rugs, many times, girls' bodies being thrown into the river.

I couldn't help but wonder if any of the men sitting in that room had been at the factory in the old days.

We concluded our business and prepared to return to the Hotel

What happened next was a pleasant surprise.

THE LIAISON OFFICER

AFTER SAYING ZAIJIAN (goodbye in Mandarin), we exited the factory. Sitting in the parking lot in front of the building, we were surprised to see a new, black Cadillac limousine with two American flags planted on the front fenders. Standing next to it was a tall, thin, Lincolnesque American in a dark blue suit. Steve, who had met him in the U.S., rushed to greet him. After shaking hands warmly, Steve turned to us and said, "You finally get to meet my friend, the American Liaison Officer to China."

One by one we shook hands and introduced ourselves. I felt an immediate, friendly reaction to the gentleman and knew we were going to get along famously! Partly, I'm sure since the other four were already seated in the Chinese car; he asked if Steve and I would like to ride back to the hotel with him, Of course we quickly accepted the offer.

As I suspected, I took a great liking to the man and by the time we were back at the hotel the feeling seemed mutual. During the course of the trip back we discussed many things: the future of our trade relations with China, the prospects of détente with them, the residual antagonism by some Chinese people towards America. This, we told him, we had experienced first hand in Tientsin.

At the conclusion of the trip he asked if there was anything we needed or anything he could do for us. I responded with, "Some American food and drink is what I miss the most." He said, "Listen, we have this great big compound over there that the few of us just rattle around in. Why don't you come over for dinner tonight? I'll ask my wife, Barbara, to make us a good Texas home-cooked meal with American coffee and we can drink some bourbon and branch water."

We were very excited at the prospect and rushed to ready ourselves for the evening. At the appointed time the Allens, Herb Cole, Helene Pollock and we arrived at the gate in the wall surrounding the one-block square compound.

The first two things that I saw literally gave me a chill, after about one and a half weeks that seemed like six months in this totally foreign country. We saw two U.S. Marines on guard at the gate and, just past them in the very center of the compound, an American flag fluttering in the night sky, lit up by a pair of spotlights.

The Liaison officer came out of the main house to greet us, ushered us in and made the introductions to his wife Barbara and their Springer spaniel named Fred. I realized that he was the first dog I had seen in China. That little fact gave us something to think about every time we ordered a meat dish during the rest of the trip.

Barbara had made fresh coffee, the single thing I had missed most on the trip. After coffee, some popcorn, and some great conversation in a large comfortable room, we adjourned to the dining room for a wonderful homemade dinner. After dinner it was, as promised, bourbon and branch water, and some quality time with Fred. The evening and subsequent evenings were lifesavers for me. I felt so at home and comfortable.

I became hooked and spent many more nights at the Liaison headquarters and availed myself of that great, Texas hospitality in the middle of China. The Liaison officer himself and I became friends.

After I returned home, I felt so sorry for him, stuck in the center of nowhere that I used to send him funny cards and letters from home to cheer him up. He would respond with cards full of funny and cogent comments about China.

When he finally finished his tour of duty, a grateful President appointed him as Head of the Central Intelligence Agency. He subsequently went on to become the Vice President of the United States under Ronald Reagan and then the 41st President of the United States.

To me he was always my friend George Bush, the good-natured, friendly, Texan who was so hospitable and saved my ass in China.

BACK TO THE SQUARE

THE NEXT MORNING I was up very early to try again to approach the martial artists in the park at Tien An Men Square.

This time, however I was better prepared. I had a thought the night before on the way back from the Bush compound. I had a little good luck and saw Lily in the lobby upon my return.

I asked Lily to write a statement for me on some typewriter paper in large Chinese characters. Basically what it said was;

"Hello, I am an American martial arts Instructor. I am here for a short time staying at the Peking Hotel. I would like only to spend some time training with you, in the spirit of martial arts friendship and brotherhood, while I am visiting your Country."

So armed, once again I left the Hotel and walked the short distance to where I had seen them the previous morning. When I first arrived, it was quite dark and for a few minutes I couldn't find them. I was very disappointed but decided to stay anyway; I still needed a work out.

After 5 or 10 minutes of stretching and doing a couple of simple forms, I saw them watching me from a corner of the clearing, under some trees. Leaving my coat, wearing my same black uniform, I carried my note and a small flashlight and slowly walked towards the group. Of course I couldn't recognize any individuals, but my instinct told me it was the same men that I had seen the previous morning.

As I approached, their body language suggested that they were in a "fight or flight" mode. As reached them I held out my letter and flashlight to the man in front. He was, perhaps 60 years old, maybe more, about my height, 5 ft 10, and solidly built.

After a few seconds hesitation he took the paper and light and began to read. I had a few seconds of doubt. Lily was such a scatterbrain, what if she didn't write what I said? She could have written anything! "I hereby challenge you to combat to prove my Art is superior to yours." Oh no!

Apparently that was not the case. He seemed to read it carefully then passed it to another man, a little shorter, about the same age. I guessed this was the leader. He also read it carefully then gave me along appraising look. I sensed this was the man and the time so I smiled and thrust my hand forward, he reached out, we shook hands and everything seemed to be OK. He turned and spoke for a minute to the others; I could see that they were relaxing.

I walked back a few paces and launched into a hard Isshinryu form, "Wansu". This seemed to be the final test. They all watched carefully, as I concluded the kata, I stopped and motioned in invitation indicating that one of them do the same. The man that I had assumed to be the Master then stepped forward and began to do a medium length form of his own.

It was what I would classify as a "hard style" Chinese form. Reminding me of Hsing-I or Shaolin temple boxing. He performed it with great fluidity and power.

I decided to next do a harder style Japanese form choosing Pinan V. They seemed intrigued buy the longer stances and the emphasis on direct, straight punches.

We went on this way for the better part of a half an hour. First one of them would execute a form then I would respond. I was acutely tuned in to the situation and could see that as time passed they appeared to grow a little more nervous, two or three of them were always looking the other direction. I believe they were "lookouts". After about 30 minutes, the "Master" concluded a form and put his hand out, spoke for a bit in Mandarin, smiled and they all turned and disappeared into the darkness under the trees. That was it! It was over. I would have given a lot to know what he said.

I felt that I had a good morning and decided to go back to the hotel for my rice and eggs. This time however, I saw a few more clusters of people in different parts of the park and made a mental note of the locations for the following morning.

Back at the hotel, I found that my wife had finally contracted the virus and was becoming quite ill. Her jaw was swollen badly. After a quick shower I decided to see if we could find Medical aid.

We went downstairs to the lobby and approached the three Chinese men standing behind the long counter. Knowing that they spoke no English and in the absence of Lily I had practiced what I would say in Mandarin.

As we approached they all three came to stare at us and see if they could determine what we wanted.

In my best Mandarin I said something like this: "Wo de Tai Tai bing, yi shing she me de fong?" The meaning of the Chinese language is dependent upon the intonation of each word. You can say the exact same word, but its meaning changes totally depending on the inflection. If your word rises at the end it means one thing, if the same word falls at the end it means something entirely different.

In my mind I was saying, "My wife is sick, where is a doctor?"

The three of them began to laugh. I was totally frustrated and becoming angry. I repeated my request in a louder voice, they laughed all the harder. Because of the seriousness of Louise's condition I was becoming furious. One of them particularly incensed me to the point where I was about to pull him over the counter and do something that would probably have caused my immediate expulsion from the country. It was a very volatile moment.

Just then I felt a hand on my arm, I turned and saw Lily, she was laughing as well.

The last straw! "What are you laughing at?" I practically shouted.

She said, " Sorry, I think I know what you are trying to say, but what you ARE saying is "My wife is a panda, where can I find a soldier?"

As I stood, chagrined, Lily spoke quickly to the three. They became all seriousness and in a moment Lily said they would contact a doctor for us at once.

I learned yet another valuable lesson and made a vow to myself to be more aware of my limitations.

When the doctor arrived, about 45 minutes later, we met him in the lobby. I was glad to see he was a man in his 50s.

While we were in Tientsin we had a conversation with Wong Chin and a few of the other students, wherein they were explaining the way the Communist system worked in regard to "Elitism."

In order for anyone to join and then to rise to a position of leadership in any field, whether it was Architecture, Law or Pipefitting, they first had to be selected and approved by a Communist party committee.

There were no exceptions. In order to make any career plans, you must first be passed on as a good Communist party member.

I was debating the point with them good-naturedly and asked questions. I was trying to make a point and decided to use doctors as an example.

"Suppose," I said, "that a good Communist party member from a small village wants to be a medical doctor, but they aren't qualified intellectually?"

"That doesn't matter," they said. "If the local Party leadership wants to send them to medical school, then they can go. Everyone is equal so any one who is approved as a good party member and endorsed by their local party leaders can become what they want."

In an effort to make my point I used as an illustration, a person who doesn't have the academic ability to earn what is necessary to become a doctor. What then?

They explained to me that if that person were designated to be a doctor by the Party then he or she would be a doctor. If the person has difficulty with their studies then it becomes the responsibility of the other students to help them until they can pass, no matter how hard or how long the process may be. No elitism can be allowed in any case.

Later I had a private conversation with Wong Chin alone. He and I had become quite close, he reminded me so much of my son Scott.

I said, "So if you are very sick, how do you know that your doctor is not one of those who had to be carried through medical school?" He lowered his voice and said to me, "What you want is a gray haired doctor." I must have looked confused, he then said, "That way, you know that at least he has had a lot of experience."

Our Doctor was " a man of experience." However, instead of the antibiotics that we had expected, he left a number of herbal and homeopathic medicines. It is my belief that antibiotics were practically non-existent in China at that time. Perhaps that was one of the many factors that had driven the Communists to seek trade and détente with the United States at that time in history. Every member of our group fell very ill with the disease. It was like a super bad chest cold that came close to pneumonia and as far as I know, no one received a badly needed antibiotic until they reached the U.S.

Most of the rest of that day we stayed around the hotel, resting and eating; we had all been driving ourselves very hard for ten days or so. That was probably not helping our resistance to these unfamiliar bacteria.

The next morning I was out of the hotel before 4:00 AM again. With my letter ready I made my way to the park.

First I went to the site of the previous day's success, but there was no sign of yesterday's group. As I continued to walk through the dark I would catch glimpses of people but they didn't seem to be engaged in any martial arts activities, more walking and stretching. After about 20 or 30 minutes, it was freezing cold, I was beginning to feel as though I was out of luck today. Then I saw what looked for all the world like a class being conducted in a good sized, treeless area.

There was one man, facing a group of a dozen or so, leading them in the practice of a combination kicking and punching routine. As usual, everything was done silently, if the leader spoke it was in a barely audible whisper and the followers were noiseless.

After watching for a few minutes, knowing that they had seen me, a total oddity, a Caucasian in the park before dawn, I decided to try again.

Taking off my heavy coat, with my black *gi* and belt in view I began to do a combination similar to but yet different than one they were practicing. I was careful not to look directly at them but to head in a direction at a 90-degree angle from them. I thought it might be bad to look as if I was trying to join the class without an invitation.

It was adequately lit from a street lamp located where the park met the square for us to see each other well enough. I was aware that they had stopped to watch me. I began to expand my workout, adding more high, power kicks and spinning kicks. After a few minutes I stopped and turned to look directly at them; trying to appear friendly, I waved and slowly moved toward the group. I held my letter out towards the teacher. He took it and with the aid of my little flashlight read it. As he was reading other members of the class was reading over his shoulder.

At the end, they looked around at each other then they seemed to relax. I felt a change of attitude from one of suspicion and tension to relief.

This group was different from the first group I had met the previous day. It seemed to be a little younger and more athletic. The teacher was in his early to mid 40's.

He was quite friendly; he motioned for me to watch him as he did a kick combination. I copied it. Then I did a combination and he copied me. We communicated in this way for several minutes.

After a while he turned and spoke to his group. Two of them faced one another and putting their left wrists together back to back they stood for a second. Then on a command from the teacher they moved into a controlled attack. Sparring.

This was what I had been hoping for. I watched the contact level very closely. Since it was bare knuckle, the way I had sparred for years I could see that they were utilizing good control to the head and face. Each "match" was over quickly. As soon as one of them scored a telling point it stopped. One Point sparring.

I couldn't wait to try it but knew I had to be invited. Sure enough, after most of them had taken a turn I was asked, through gestures, if I wanted to participate.

I faced off with, who I thought was, a high ranking student, At the command to begin, I pushed his left hand downwards and away and hit him with a reverse punch on his left floating rib. They all laughed good-naturedly, I think at the expense of my opponent.

This scenario, in one way or another, was repeated several times. I believe that the system that they were practicing was very stylized, and they were not fully prepared for something different. Furthermore, it appeared that their punches were all or mostly circular and the straight punch was faster. In kicking the same held true. They seemed unready for a sidekick or thrust kick. They relied mostly on crescent kicks and a kind of roundhouse kick. I was also able to score with a spinning back thrust kick. This went on for about a half hour. I was having a wonderful time. Finally the teacher and I engaged in a couple of minutes of free sparring. That was very enlightening.

He was a very capable fighter, reminding me of my old friend Willie Williams. We each scored several good points during the match. I had trouble with his crescent kicks, inside or outside; they were extremely fast and accurate. I gained a new respect for that kick which I still have today. On the other hand he was not used to straight linear techniques and I was frequently able to score in that manner. I also found that a left hook was difficult for him to block.

We went on probably too long as the sky began to turn gray. At that point I could see that they were ready to go. We all shook hands warmly. I returned to the hotel, sore in a couple of places but very happy.

THE GREAT WALL

IT WAS TO be another very long day. No sooner had I showered and dressed that it was time to eat something quickly and board another bus.

This time it was to see something that I had looked forward to the greater part of my life: The Great Wall of China.

Our entire group was assembled for this trip; sick or well, no one wanted to miss it.

It was an adventurous 2-hour plus trip. We were soon out of the city and into the rural countryside. That part of the country in February/March is yellow and dry. It is also very rocky. The scenery was drab and featureless except for the rocky crags that appear occasionally. It reminds one of the high desert area between Victorville and Apple Valley, California, in mid-winter.

Every few miles we would pass a small village or isolated farm house, always with a wall around the courtyard entry. We noticed a few walls with what appeared to be broken glass set into the mortar on the top of the wall. Cheaper and more effective than barbed wire.

The high, or low, depending on your point of view, part of the trip to the wall were the "rest stops." I have many photos taken at the toilets.

After a little more than an hour, the bus driver pulled up next to a small stone structure situated at a point where two narrow roads crossed. There was nothing else in sight. He spoke to Lily who announced, "Potty Break," and exited the bus.

The little structure was perhaps 6 feet wide and 8 feet long at the most. There was a single door in the front. Lily entered first and reappeared in a few minutes. "Next" she called.

One by one the women entered first, only to re-emerge with various cries of disgust or outrage. I was so curious that I could hardly wait my turn. As I entered the first thing that assailed me was one of the worst smells I have ever known. I can still remember it!

Inside the four bare, tan brick walls which were covered with Chinese graffiti, in the middle of the floor, was the "facility."

It was a trench dug in the center of the floor, lined around the sides with ceramic tiles for about 6 inches. The trench was about three feet long and 10 or so inches wide. There was nothing else. No washing facilities, no paper. It was, of course, very dirty around the edges and impossible to tell how deep.

Imagine if you can, Helene Pollack, a cultured, beautiful woman, her perfect blonde hair coiffed by the best that Beverly Hills had to offer, nails perfectly manicured, and wearing a mid calf length dark mink coat, standing and staring at the "toilet" in utter disbelief.

Although we had all, by now, become quite good friends, I for one was not going to ask her if she had used the facility.

We soon reboarded the bus and continued on the way to the Wall. When we arrived, there was a mad dash by the ladies to the "rest rooms" there. They were exactly the same, only cleaner.

As to the Wall itself, it was everything I had ever imagined it would be. I couldn't wait to climb up the stairs onto the twelve to twenty foot wide aisle or walkway between the protective three to four foot high battlements.

The walkway was designed to be wide enough to allow the movement of large groups of soldiers. The battlements were an average of four or so feet high with cutouts every three feet or so to allow archers to launch their shafts.

The original wall was started about 500 BC. It was originally made of packed earth and was about ten feet high. These early walls were built, during the "Warring States" period, to protect the Qin dynasty from northern invaders. It did its job until about 221 BC. At that time, the new Emperor, Qin Shi Huang, destroyed the existing walls and constructed a new one to protect his newly unified China from invaders from the north.

In about 1450 AD, the Ming dynasty decided to rebuild the Wall, pretty much as it is today. This time it was built to a height of 20 feet or more and made from stone and bricks. It was the Mongols who were the invaders at that time. Later, in 1600 or so, the wall was there to stem the tide of the Manchu invasion.

The Wall is 3948 miles long. There is an "Urban legend" that the Wall can be seen from the moon. The fact is that the Astronaut, William Pogue, was able to see it with the aid of binoculars from the moon. However, it is visible from the Space stations with the naked eye.

My favorite picture from this trip to China, of the many hundreds that were taken, is of me standing on the wall. You can see it stretching upwards and behind me for miles.

One incident that occurred that day was, I think, worth the telling.

The part of the wall where we were taken had been repaired for visitors. The repaired area, where we were allowed to go, started at the stairs that we had ascended and then meandered for about a mile, quite steeply upwards and to our right.

We had all pretty much clustered in an area 30 or 40 feet from the spot at the top of the stairs to talk, look and take pictures. I could see off to the right about how far the way was open for us to go. I decided to go to the end. No one else was ready to undertake the trip at the moment, as the climb was obviously quite steep.

As I started off, the only people, other than our party, on the Wall were two young Chinese soldiers. They appeared to be just sight seeing like us. The three of us started up at the same time. I was wearing one of my usual outfits that I wore throughout the trip: a dark blue suit, white dress shirt and red tie, with a little American Flag pin in my lapel. I left no doubt in any ones mind as to where I was from.

As we started the mile or so climb up the Wall's steep grade, in the high altitude, I noticed that the two soldiers, both in their early 20s, had looked at me, spoke something to one another, and started to walk a little faster. At first I thought it was some kind of cultural paranoia on my part, but as I thought more about it, it seemed to me that they had decided that they wanted to get to the top first. They didn't want to be beaten to the top by some "decadent" 39 year old American in a suit.

In order to test my theory, I started waking a little faster. As if to prove my point, they increased their speed as well. The race was on!

What they didn't know was the kind of condition this 39-year-old American was in, and that he was also a warrior! A warrior who usually ran 3 or 4 miles every day.

My added years may have put me at a sight disadvantage to their youth but I had two things going for me: surprise, and a plan,

It turned into quite a race to see who could reach the top first. It was touch and go for a while, but as I suspected, they had made the serious mistake of underestimating me.

The last 50 yards or so we were all practically running. I beat them to the top by ten paces or so. I had been thinking for the last couple of minutes about what would happen at the top. I didn't know how they were going to take it so I was ready for anything.

I turned to face them, with my back against a stone wall just in case.

As they caught up, we were all three breathing heavily, hands on our knees. I thought, "What the hell" and reached out my hand to shake. They stared for a couple of seconds, then started to laugh, I couldn't help but join in. We shook hands all around. Once again, as they spoke to me in Mandarin, I would have loved to know what they were saying.

Earlier I mentioned the red felt tip pens I had brought with me. Tipping was absolutely forbidden in China, so they replaced cash as a "Thank you." There was nothing like them available in the country and the red was certainly appropriate for a gift to anyone in "Red China." They were also perfect for occasions like this. I gave each of the young soldiers a pen and a handshake. After a few minutes they waved goodbye and started back down, I decided to stay, as a few of my party had decided to walk up. I waited for them. They had watched the "race" and we talked about it a bit, and then we all meandered back down, taking more pictures, and slowly went back to the bus. All together we probably spent three hours or so on the wall itself.

The ride back was fun but uneventful and we arrived back at the hotel in time for a dinner at a restaurant with George and Barbara bush.

Dinner that night was at the "Bi Lou' restaurant, famous for its Mongolian barbeque. We all sat around a circular table and cooked our own food in the huge metal pot in the center. It creates a relaxed, fun, atmosphere. George and Barbara are wonderful company and we all had a great time.

On another evening we joined George at a restaurant that was known for its Peking duck, the Beijing Kao Ya Dian restaurant. It was excellent. The most memorable event that evening, for me, was that Steve Allen mistook the sauce for a sweet Plum sauce that he loved and used a great deal of it on his duck.

Only to discover that this was much spicier and had a different, bitter taste. He pretty well ruined his meal.

During the rest of our stay the Bush family, including Fred of course, made our stay much more pleasant. They were warm, friendly people and wonderful hosts. Later George and I exchanged cards and letters until he returned from China a year or so later.

We made many more side trips to historical wonders, such as the Ming tombs, the city of Xian, the Temple of Heaven, it was all unforgettable. There are so many more stories that I don't want to take the time to tell here

Maybe just one more: If you read Steve Allen's book, "Explaining China," you will see that he writes a great deal about the honesty of the Chinese people. As I mentioned earlier, Steve and I had a slightly different view of some things, each from our own perspectives. (Rashomon, if you will.) I agree with Steve that the Chinese people seemed to be very honest. Nothing ever went missing. However my take on it was that as well as honesty there was a great deal of fear of reprisal from the Government involved as well.

Case in point, while in Tientsin, my wife suffered a "run" in a pair of panty hose. She tossed them into, or maybe next to, a trash can in our room.

When we were back in Beijing a few days later, we returned to our room from lunch and discovered a small flat box on the bed. We opened it and there inside were the panty hose, washed, and pressed, run and all. My theory was that someone had found them and, not believing that something so valuable would be thrown out, and not wanting to be suspected of having taken them, had turned them over to a person in a position of authority. That person then decided, to be on the safe side, to have them sent on to us.

I continued to go, almost every morning to the park around Tian An Men Square to work out with and train with the Kung Fu Masters. I felt a great empathy with them and wished so much that we could exchange thoughts as well. I thought about taking Lily with me, but there was no way I was going to get her up at 4:00 AM.

I believe that I was able to acquire some valuable new skills from the time I spent working with and exchanging ideas with these men in Beijing. Although it was probably only 15 or 20 hours in total, I was so focused on learning everything I could it was if I had spent a year with them.

The last day in China was one of mixed emotions. We were ready to go home, see our families and friends, eat American food, drive our cars, play with our dogs, and just generally revel in the freedom and glory of America.

Yet, at the same time, it was hard to leave. I think most of us had developed a lasting attachment to the Chinese people themselves, if not their government.

George Bush came by the hotel to bid us goodbye. I promised to write, and I kept my word, sending him cheerful, humorous cards and letters in an attempt to ease the isolation I knew he must have felt.

We packed, gathered our treasures and left for the airport.

The plane we were departing on had just arrived, late, from India. The passengers deplaned and we were ushered on at once. The smells on the plane gagged us, we flew to Tokyo directly, most of us ill from the incredible stench.

Arriving back in Los Angeles was a great feeling. My sons met us at the airport and we returned to the house and our two Great Danes, Garm and Gretta. One only has to travel abroad to begin to truly appreciate our wonderful country. The things we take for granted, such as personal freedom, cleanliness, easy access to good, safe food and trustworthy medical care are not to be found everywhere else on the planet.

Word had spread about the trip, and I was soon besieged with requests to speak and show the hundreds of slides I had taken to many various groups. I tried to comply with as many as I could, what with the carpet business, the new rug business, the karate school, and the weekly tournament schedule.

I was approached by Black Belt magazine and did write a lengthy article that appeared in the July issue of 1975.

Once back to what was "normal" for me, I returned to my quest for a daughter.

XIAN

I HAD MADE many inquiries while in China, through many sources and was told flatly that it would not be possible for me to adopt a Chinese child! It was a political decision. The Communist government did not want it perceived that they could not care for all in their society, and the last thing they would allow then was for a Chinese child to be raised in a Capitalistic society.

In later years, that policy was changed. I have a Chinese niece who was adopted and brought here in 1999.

So I redoubled my efforts. I was told by the Inter Country Adoption people that my best chance would be to adopt from Korea. We went after the home study and approval with new determination. The final result of all the work was my daughter Xian.

When she arrived in May of 1976, I fell immediately in love with her.

She was about 4 ½ years old and spoke no English. I had tried to learn Korean, but found that the Koreans speak almost a different "baby talk" language to small children, so she didn't understand my Korean much better than she did English.

I turned to all my Korean martial artist friends as translators. I would take her to Chong Lee's School every day with a list of things that I wanted him to ask her. She soon came to know him as "Uncle Lee."

In retrospect I think it is very funny that, when I couldn't find Chong Lee I would call Hee il Cho or Bong Soo Han, and put them on the phone with her. I remember occasions saying "Cho, can you please tell me what she is saying?" and hear the deep voice of the man we called "the Korean Charles Bronson" say, "Baby say she have to go potty," or "Baby afraid of pussycat."

A few side notes on Hee Il Cho. He was, at that time, one of the most common figures seen on the covers of the several karate magazines.

I used to help him direct all of his tournaments, usually at Beverly Hills High School. At one of these events, there was, in attendance, a Tae Kwan Do Black belt known as "Master Suh."

During the Black belt finals, in the last match, one of Suh's students was fighting. All five officials were Tae Kwon Do black belts. The Tae Kwon Do fighter was, however, being devastated by one of the best American tournament fighters I have ever known, Barry Gordon from the BKF.

Barry ultimately became a very good friend of mine. At this time, however, he was known as a great fighter with a really bad attitude. Every time he would score a point on the Korean opponent, he would laugh and deride him. It was infuriating Suh!

When the final point was scored and Barry proceeded to perform a "Victory Dance" around his opponent to further humiliate him, Suh totally lost it.

He tried to attack Barry, when the officials tried to stop him he turned his anger towards them. Punches and kicks were flying. Suh's shirt was ripped off; he picked up a chair, broke it into pieces and started throwing the pieces at the officials and into the audience in the stands.

Soon he had cleared the floor, everyone was standing far enough away to hopefully be out of range of the flying wood. The audience had vacated the first seven or eight rows nearest the gym floor.

I was in the announcer's booth, about 10 tiers above the floor, using the microphone to do my best to maintain order and prevent a panic or riot.

Someone had called the police. Three of LA's finest entered the auditorium, crossed the floor, drew their batons and approached Suh. There was complete silence in the building as they circled the maddened Tae Kwon Do Master; he was bare to the waist and holding a large wooden chair leg in each hand. I could sense an impending disaster so using the Microphone, I spoke into the silence.

"Officers, if you hit him with those sticks, you are just going to make him angry!"

It had the desired affect, the crowd laughed, the tension eased, and with perfect timing two of Cho's biggest students tackled Suh and pinned his arms and legs, holding him while the officers managed to handcuff him. He was removed from the auditorium and soon sent back to Korea in disgrace.

Another of my favorite Hee Il Cho stories is of the famous lawsuit.

My friend Johnny Vaneck was present first-hand for all of this.

One day, Johnny had gone to train with Cho in one of his advanced classes at the Santa Monica school. During the class a stranger entered and strode out on the mat and challenged Cho in front of his class.

Cho was not a man to let this pass so they prepared to fight. Apparently the challenger came at Cho with a barrage of kicks and punches.

Master Hee Il Cho was very famous even then. He had appeared on the cover of many Martial Arts magazines. He was best known for, first of all, his incredible jumping, spinning back thrust kick. He once appeared on the cover of Black Belt in a famous photo that showed the bag tearing in half as his kick struck.

The other thing was his breaking ability. Cho held many breaking records. I have personally seen him doing demonstrations at his Beverly Hills Tournaments where he would drop a 2-inch thick, 12x12, pine board from his left hand and break it in mid-air with a right punch. His right hand was quite misshapen from all of the years of breaking and almost had the appearance of a hoof.

What happened that day was this: Cho threw his famous kick, and missed! It only angered him more and spurred him on and with a single; follow up punch, caved in the side of the other man's face, breaking several facial bones.

All of the proper calls were made, ambulance, police, etc.

A short time later the intruder filed a lawsuit against Cho for medical expenses and damages.

The matter, in time, went to court and Johnny Vaneck was called as a witness for Cho's defense. The opposition made their case, making heavy use of the fact that Cho was a "trained killer" and providing all of the publications and written material that had appeared over the years about him as evidence. Their case was based on their position that Cho had, "over-reacted."

Cho's defense attorneys called Johnny and the other witnesses to testify that the other man had challenged and made the first aggressive move. Still, it was touch and go on the issue of "overreacting."

In summation the Plaintiff's lawyers finished by stating that "Why Mister Cho, you could have killed him!"

Then Cho took the stand, his attorneys had barely begun to elicit his testimony when the Judge interrupted. "Mister Cho, I have a question for you. COULD you have killed the Plaintiff?"

Hee Il Cho drew himself up, looked the Judge straight in the eye and in his best, deep, voice replied

"CERTAINLY"!

The judge believed him, and the case against him was dismissed.

This was the same man who listened to my daughter and relayed messages to me concerning her potty training and her uncertainties about "pussycats."

When my daughter arrived, on her papers, her name was spelled Seon Soon Kim. We found the first name very difficult for people to pronounce, so it came out " See-on". By the time her adoption was final we were used to calling her that, but we changed the spelling to XIAN , pronounced basically the same, but also the name old the old Capital City of China.

Her legal name finally became, Xian Sunsoon Fisher. It remained that until June of 2006 when she married a nice young Man named Adam Chapman, who is the editor of the widely acclaimed Animal Planet series "Whale Wars." They now live on the Big Island of Hawaii, with frequent trips to Los Angeles.

Xian grew up in the karate school and at tournaments. My sons Scott and Kirk were, respectively, 11 and 16 years older, so as Xian started school they were pretty much out of the house and on their own, having finished school, Scott from UCLA and Kirk eventually from Cal State Northridge. They both still taught martial arts and worked out. I had sold the Tarzana school again and opened a new school in Encino, California, where they both taught on a regular basis.

When Xian started the 1st grade, her English was still poor. As luck would have it there was only one other Asian child in the 1st grade at Wilbur Avenue Elementary School in Tarzana. She was Japanese-American, her name was Ali Morita. She and Xian became life long friends. Ali's father was Pat Morita, at that time he was starring in the TV series "Happy Days."

Ali decided to take Xian under her wing. Ali somehow, although she spoke neither Korean nor Japanese, could seem to understand Xian's broken English better than anyone except our family. At school, Ali would translate for her. Sometimes she would even do it for us. She would say to me something like " Xian wants a peach and an apple." I would say "Thank you Ali. But I get it."

It was very funny how attached they became. This lasted through most of grammar school. I believe they are still in touch occasionally today.

Xian's other best friend was Pilar DeMan. She was a beautiful, calm little girl, a good counterpart to Xian's excitability. Pilar would spend the night frequently. They were very good friends. Pilars father, Freddie DeMan, was an agent and business manager in the music business. At that time he had just taken on a young performer who was trying to break out on his own: Michael Jackson. Freddie handled him for years and when that ended Freddie took on a young singer named Madonna. Freddie and his wife Candy were great people, and we were close friends for a few years.

All we knew about Xian's background was that she had been found wandering the streets in Seoul, Korea. It was common then, if a family had too many girls and couldn't afford to feed them, they would drop off the one they wanted the least in a section of the city where they might be found and cared for. If they were lucky!

Xian had been such a foundling, taken in by a Christian organization. When they found her she was suffering from pneumonia, malnutrition and covered with rat bites. She had been in the care of the organization for a few months when our paths crossed.

The way it worked was like this.

Once we had been approved for inter country adoption, our file was sent to one of the agencies in Korea. They would read about us and send us ONE file of a child. If we, for ANY reason, did not want to go forward with that child, we would return the file, no explanation required, and we would be sent another, and so on until we decided on the one we wanted.

Xian's was the first one we received. It told us briefly of how she had been found, her condition, now healthy, and a little bit about her personality. They said she was, "smart, happy, good natured, liked to do chores, liked to sing a song, and was somewhat negative with her friends." The picture they enclosed in the file was atrocious! It was in black and white, her clothes were too big for her, she had what looked like a large bruise or maybe a skin condition on her face and her hair had been chopped off. Furthermore you could see the little spots all over her, which we later learned, were scars from rat bites. At the time we saw the picture we had no idea what they were.

The picture was enough to put us off. At first we considered returning the file, the more I read about her the more I thought, "What a sweet, nice, little girl." Then I was struck with the thought: "If we don't take her, no one will."

After a great deal of soul searching, we decided to take her as our own. The file was returned and in a few months she was our daughter.

The scars went away, the bruise healed, her hair grew out. Today she is a very beautiful woman, married and living in Hawaii, with a nice career. She, who could just as easily have grown up in a Korean orphanage.

She became my constant companion. We were inseparable; I still traveled about 2 or 3 nights a week. However when I was not out of town, Xian was with me. She went to the karate school when I went, excelling at it. She went to the tournaments with me. We were "joined at the hip".

When she was eight years old, I bought a new, bright yellow, Porsche. The first week I had it she wanted to know how fast it would go. I strapped her in tight, opened the top, and took her for a ride up on Mullholland Drive. We were going through some turns (safely) at about 70 mph when I got trapped by a policeman's radar. It was a 30 mph zone. The only reason I got away with just a ticket was because Xian was with me and obviously having the time of her life.

Already I had made many friends in the Korean martial arts community, but as they began to see me with my daughter I was even more accepted.

At this time there was still some division in the tournaments caused by race and origins of styles. Everyone knew me as being "color blind." I think I was able to help prevent and to heal many of the racial problems of the times.

I was frequently sought as a center referee when there were different races fighting for important divisions. Everyone knew I would always be fair and impartial.

If the BKF (Black Karate Federation) had a fighter in a division that perhaps also included a Korean, a Japanese and a Caucasian fighter, I would usually be asked to leave my usual spot on the microphone to referee.

I made many great friends in the BKF. I was invited to train with them and did so when the opportunity presented itself. Steve Muhammed, who first became famous after winning the Internationals as Steve Sanders, is, in my opinion, one of the greatest fighters of all time. He was one of the original founders of the BKF. He taught at night in a portable classroom at a public school in South Central LA.

The first time I went there to spar, it was about 1974 or 75. It was 9 years after the Watts Riots, yet there was still some real concern about the safety of a blonde haired Caucasian in a white Corvette driving around alone in that part of Los Angeles.

They made arrangements to meet and escort me to the workouts. We chose a gasoline station in Inglewood to meet. When I arrived there would be two cars waiting. We waved and I followed one of them about 10 feet behind it while the other one followed about ten feet behind me. "Close quarter escort."

We would spar then for a couple of hours and then they would escort me out the same way. I made friends for life during these workouts: Ray Wizard, Dexter Brooks, Sam Pace, Billy Washington. Conrad Simms, Hot Dog Harvey, Robert Temple, Alvin and Cynthia Prouder, Big John Robertson, Ron Chapel, Nate Moore, Donnie Williams, Lenny Ferguson, Eddy Newman, Kraigar Dupree. And many, many more.

Many of us met again recently, in 2006, in Pasadena, at the funeral of another of my dearest friends, Howard Jackson, the ex-middleweight champion of the world kick boxer and Chuck Norris' long time friend and training partner.

Leslie and I attended along with about a thousand of the old time, real martial artists who were there. Donnie Williams, now a Bishop in a large Christian Church denomination, delivered a fine eulogy. Then, one by one, about ten of us including Chuck Norris, Benny Urquidez and I, each spoke and shared memories of Howard with the assemblage.

I shared two stories.

The first was that I had been the center referee in the Black Belt division at a Tournament produced by Gordon Doversola, a hapkido master, at Valley College in Sherman Oaks California. It must have been about 1972; there was a shy, respectful, young Marine from the east, who swept the division. I spent a long time talking with him afterwards and we became friends for life. That was Howard Jackson.

My second story occurred about 15 or so years later. Howard had gained international fame. He was the champion of the world kick boxer, had enjoyed an incredible history in tournament competition, was the bodyguard for the Temptations, and was starting to work with Chuck as his regular training partner.

I had produced one of my many tournaments at the Culver City Auditorium. That night we were holding the black belt finals up on the stage. I was the center Referee and had asked some of the famous martial artist's friends in attendance to be the four corner judges; as I recall, they were, Eric Lee, Steve

Fisher and Ron Chapel. In the corner closest to the front left side of the stage was Howard.

This was during a period when it was fashionable for men to wear an Afro hair do, if they could, and high heeled boots.

There was a clash for points; all of the judges threw their flags to call a point. Howard was so carried away with the moment that in addition to throwing his flag, he also stepped back to illustrate the high hook kick that he was calling, and fell off the stage!

Chuck told a wonderfully funny story. He and Howard were extremely close, if not best, friends. They were on a movie shoot together in Africa. Chuck's wife told him that the local villagers had arranged a celebration in their honor. Chuck and his wife and several others from the movie cast and crew attended.

There were several dancers around a huge fire. Chuck had brought his personal camera and was filming the dances.

The village elder, who spoke some English, announced that the witch doctor was going to perform a special dance just for Chuck. He came out in full regalia: painted face, feathers, bones, a short skirt like garment tied around his waist, and began to dance in front of Chuck while he filmed it. Looking through his lens and totally absorbed in his filming Chuck saw after a few minutes, to his amazement that the witch doctor had the rim of a pair of Jockey shorts appearing at the top of his skirt.

He looked again carefully and with sudden realization said, "Howard??" It was Howard, made up as the Witch Doctor; he had arranged the whole thing as a joke on Chuck.

A very funny, typical Howard Jackson story.

Of the well over a thousand people at Howard's funeral I would guess that 98% of them were martial artists. I only wish Howard could have been there to see it. He would have loved it. (Who knows, maybe he was.)

Xian grew up in the Martial Arts, a few years later she was joined by her stepbrother John.

In 1979/80. I was divorced from my first wife. It was a difficult, time for Xian.

I met, fell in love with and married a beautiful young woman. Leslie Sexton, my second (and last) wife. We met when I was 43 years old and she was 26. She had a 5-year-old son, I ultimately adopted him and his name became John Sexton Fisher.

John is 3 years younger than Xian. They shared a life together for the next 10 years or so as brother and sister. Both of them were "dojo rats," studying and growing up in the Martial Arts environment.

They went to most of the Tournaments that I attended, so that means almost every weekend. Both of them had hundreds of tournament matches and won loads of trophies. On the rare occasions that they had to defend themselves in real life neither ever had a problem doing so.

Both became fine Black Belts with plenty of tournament experience. I have always been secure in the knowledge that all of my kids can take care of themselves.

The Tournament circuit continued to occupy all of my time outside of the carpet business. Leslie, 17 years my junior, who had been a dancer and dance instructor, was quickly brought into the martial arts, and now, 27 years later, holds the rank of 7th degree black in my PUMA system. Until January of 2008, she taught 5 days a week at our Big Bear headquarters. We try to stay at a Maximum of 100 students, going to a waiting list when we hit the Max. Leslie loved teaching the 5 and 6 year olds and is also an excellent fighter and our bo staff and kali stick instructor.

Leslie, Xian and John were with me practically every weekend at a tournament somewhere. Leslie learned every aspect of tournament production. The kids competed every weekend. I remember that time with fondness. (Prior to that time, pre-Leslie, Xian and John, it was Scott and Kirk who were my constant tournament companions.)

This was during the TPA, and Internationals, period. Leslie was an integral part of the annual Internationals project and was also a good friend of all of the martial artists I mention.

In 1983, Leslie was getting close to her 30th birthday. As I think it is for most people, it was looking like it was going to be a hard one. She was feeling that special stress that goes with leaving your 20s behind you forever. I wanted to do something to make her feel better and still celebrate her birthday. I decided to have a surprise party for her at the house on Gable Drive. It was a great party house. We had a private, gated, driveway with a parking lot in back that held more than 20 cars. Perfect for a surprise party. The first 20 cars could kind of sneak in. As I started making the guest list I had an idea.

The night of the party arrived. As expected, she had mentioned several times that day, how old she felt and what a sobering experience it was to turn 30.

About 7:00 PM the first of the Guests arrived, we pretended that they had just "dropped by." Then two more, then more, it wasn't too long before Leslie realized what was going on. By 8:00 PM a total of 40 plus people had "dropped by" and her birthday party was in full swing.

As the evening wore on and she bemoaned her birthday and the tragedy of turning 30. She received no sympathy. Every person she spoke to said something like "Oh, you're just a baby," or "I would give anything to be 30 again." The result was that she started feeling better. It was a great party, and a successful remedy for turning 30.

I hadn't invited anyone under 40!

During that time from 1980 until 1984, a great many things happened. Some of the great tournament stories, at the Internationals, and the TPA occurred then. CCC ceased to exist and although I continued in the carpet business, as Western Area VP of Patcraft and later Hartford carpet mills, then President of Westweave carpet Mills, what little commitment I had was pretty much gone. More and more martial Arts became my primary *raison d'etre* with the carpet business being only a necessity for supporting my lifestyle.

THE KARATE KID MOVIE

THEN IN AUGUST of 1983 another interesting event in my life and martial arts career began to unfold.

I was still living in that great house on Gable Drive, in the Encino Hills. It had somehow survived my painful and expensive divorce. Leslie and I were sitting in the dining room after dinner, as usual, enjoying the "one of a kind" view when the phone rang. It was my friend Pat Johnson.

Pat Johnson was, even then, a well-known personage in the film industry as well as the martial arts. He had done fight choreography for many major films and was probably the most sought after fight consultant in the industry, with the possible exception of Gene Labell.

He asked me, "Would you be interested in working with me on a picture I am doing for Columbia?" I, of course said yes, I was excited by the prospect of working with Pat. My first thought was that he wanted me to do a fight scene with him in front of the camera.

We made an appointment to have lunch at the studio in Burbank the following day. When I arrived there was a pass and a message waiting for me at the guard station at the entrance to the studio. The message instructed me to park and go to the commissary and meet Pat, which I did.

He was standing outside when I got there, we shook hands and he said, "Come on in, there are some people inside who want to meet you for a lunch meeting."

We entered and were shown to a large table in the corner at which 3 men were already seated. Introductions followed. The three were:

Jerry Weintraub. At the time I think he was best known as a very huge and successful producer of music concerts, for people like Elvis Presley and Frank Sinatra. He was the producer of the film in question.

John Avildsen, Best known for having been the director of *Rocky*, with Sylvester Stallone.

And, R.J. Louis, the Executive Producer of the film.

After we had met and lunch had been ordered, Jerry began to explain what this was all about.

He was producing a film, written by Mark Kamen, to be directed by Avildsen. It was going to be called *The Karate Kid*, starring a relatively unknown young actor named Ralph Macchio and a veteran named Pat Morita. I explained to them that Morita, Ali's father, was my daughters "Uncle Pat." This certainly broke the ice a little bit. Jerry Weintraub took most of the lunch to explain the film to me. He told me the plot. He explained to me that the last third or so of the movie was the all-important climax and that it took place at a karate tournament. He explained that Pat Johnson was doing the martial arts training and fight choreography for the actors.

Weintraub had asked Pat, "Who is the top Tournament expert in the country?" Pat was kind enough to recommend me. Their offer to me was that I assume the responsibility of tournament consultant. I would actually have a large budget and basically a free hand in creating the actual tournament for the film. To say it was flattering and exciting is an understatement. We finished lunch, they gave me a copy of the script to study and we made an appointment for me to meet with R.J., John and Pat the next day.

I spent the intervening hours reading and studying the script, especially the tournament scenes. The script might simply say:

"Mid morning, inside a large auditorium, Tournament in full progress"

From that it would be my job to bring it all to the screen. I loved it!

By the time we met in their trailer at Burbank studios the next afternoon, I had the beginning of a strategy.

We met in R.J.'s office. Before we got into the ideas for the tournament scenes, they had a couple more people for me to meet. the location manager and the set director. These two had some definite ideas that would affect the tournament scenes.

The location man had just about tied up a deal with my son Kirk's school, Cal State University Northridge (CSUN).

The real impact, however, was from the set director. He had a full "mock up" about 3 ft by 4 ft of the way the set would look. I was surprised. Having never been to a karate tournament and letting his imagination go after speaking with Pat Johnson, he had come up with the idea of a circular layout.

My initial reaction was rather doubtful. I decided, however, to remain silent and hear the man out and keep an open mind. I'm glad I did. The more I thought about it, I could see the dramatic affect, and the unusual aspect of the circular ring layout.

The more I looked at it, the more I thought, "What a great idea, *if* you could afford it." The cost of setting up a configuration like this would be totally out of reach for a tournament promoter. The promoter set his rings up in a rectangular formation with the cost of some tape and a few chairs borrowed from the venue. The cost of setting up a configuration like the one planned for the movie was way into the six figures. Still you couldn't help but love it and, after all, this was a movie!

What they were after was something as close as they could get to a *real* tournament, with all of the spontaneity and excitement! They weren't concerned about the cost. The problem for them was they hadn't come up with a way to do it. It was going to take at least 5, maybe 6 days to film the tournament scenes. They had to have, basically, a real tournament going on for that entire length of time. The solution had evaded them. That's why I was there.

After the set and location people left, R.J., Pat And Avildsen turned their attention toward me and R.J. said, "You understand our dilemma. I know it's only been 24 hours, but do you have any ideas yet?"

"The only way to make it look real, is to really do it," I said, "Here is how I think it could work.

"It is now August; you want to shoot the Tournament scenes by the end of this year. Here is my suggestion. Starting in September, we will promote an actual tournament for September, October and November. Each one will be held at CSUN, where the filming will occur in December. They will be the same as the script, an Under Eighteen Tournament. We will advertise them as The Karate Kid Tournaments, with the top 4 competitors in each of the many divisions, from each of the three tournaments, moving forward to compete for prizes and to appear in the movie. We need to be able to make use, in our pre-tournament advertising, of the film and Columbia Pictures.

"The final tournament, where the filming will occur, will be held at CSUN, in the circular ring configuration, during Christmas vacation. The kids who won the earlier Elimination Tournaments will compete then for prizes and will be seen in the background shots of the Movie.

"I believe this will capture the excitement you are looking for. The competitors will be fighting their very best, for bicycles, TVs, etc. and to look good for the camera.

"The spectators will be made up of the parents, instructors, relatives and friends of the kids competing in the rings.

"I will provide the necessary Black Belts to officiate, the scorekeepers, time keepers and other helpers to run a good, smooth event."

All three of them agreed that this was a good idea for achieving our goal and signed off on it enthusiastically. I had prepared a written proposal and approximate budget to accompany the presentation. R.J. felt the budget was more than reasonable and said there would be more money available if needed.

Over the next few months I had many financial dealings with R.J.Louis. He held the purse strings, accountable only to Jerry Weintraub, whom the rest of them saw infrequently.

R.J. was a completely honest and honorable man; we sometimes made financial decisions over the phone or in person with nothing in writing. Never once did we have a misunderstanding or a problem. We eventually became friends and spent many enjoyable evenings together with Leslie and Joanie, his wife.

Work started on the tournaments immediately. We had to secure the site, create and print flyers, contact all the TPA members, purchase the equipment, and start the "buzz."

The thing that made these Karate Kid events so special was, obviously, the tie in with the release of a big movie from a major studio. People were very interested. I received great support from my fellow TPA members especially. Soon things were moving at full speed. I met with R.J. almost daily at Burbank Studios, in order for me to feel more involved in the picture, he wanted me to be "in the loop." To do so I attended a great deal of the actual filming and was present during all the important scenes.

Word of the project spread quickly. By the time we held the first event there was great interest. We had labeled them as "The Karate Kid Elimination Tournaments." The advertisements said"

"Top three Winners in each division will advance to the Karate Kid Finals, December 28th and appear in the motion picture "The Karate Kid" to be released by Columbia Pictures in the summer of 1984."

Once we knew the date for the filming, to begin on December 28th, things fell into place and a few modifications were made. Instead of the original plan of three elimination tournaments, I decided to have two, to be held on Nov 27th and Dec 11th, with two Semi Final Tournaments on Dec 23rd and Dec 27th. This would keep the excitement and enthusiasm at a high pitch. It worked, as can be seen in the film.

The elimination tournaments were large and successful. We achieved our goal, with 42 divisions, of having 3 winners move forward from each division. By the end of the second Elimination we had 252 kids going into the Semi Finals.

From there we took the top 4 contestants from each division and moved them into the Finals to start on Dec 28th. At this point we were down to the best of the best! We announced to them that not only were they going to appear in the background of the film, but they would also be competing for some fantastic prizes: a free 24-inch color TV for first place in each division, with bicycles and video games for runner ups!

We had a lot of fun doing the pre-movie tournaments. The kids were happy and excited. For those who didn't make it into the finals, there were still nice trophies and the fun of being able to tell your friends that you competed for the "Karate Kid."

During the filming of the non-tournament scenes of the film, R.J. was, as always, a man of his word. He kept me advised and invited me to come to all of the filming. I was a regular on the sets.

It was always hilarious to watch Pat Morita work. Born in Isleton, California, he started his career in show business as a stand-up comic. He was so funny!

There is no way of knowing how much Pat must have cost the production; he was always doing something to crack up the cast and crew. Most of his antics were visual so they are hard to describe. For example, in the well known scene where Miyagi has taken too much to drink on the anniversary of the death of his wife and newborn son in Manzanar. In the first take of this highly dramatic scene, Pat is supposed to act as an inebriated Miyagi, suffering from the sad memories of the tragic event. He decided, for fun, to go way over the top, portraying instead, for laughs, a silly, sloppy, fall down drunk. It was hilarious, but of course had to be reshot.

We never knew what to expect next.

My favorite took place in one of the final scenes. Daniel has been kicked savagely in his injured knee, Miyagi runs to the mat, kneels down and takes Daniel-*san* in his arms, his back to the camera so that you can witness the pain on Daniel's face.

In this dramatic moment, the audience is supposed to register shock, fear and dismay. Instead the "audience" made up by now of film extras, starts to laugh uproariously.

"Cut!" called John Avildsen, not seeing or knowing what has happened to ruin the moment.

Unbeknownst to John, or the film crew behind Pat, when he scooped Daniel san into his arms, with his right hand he had extended his middle finger towards the "Audience" while making one of his incredibly funny faces. I was on that side, portraying one of the instructors of one of the fighters, and I too was unable to stop from laughing. It took several minutes to restore order and retake the scene properly.

In my opinion, Pat Morita was actually a very fine actor. Like most Asians, his roles were limited and he was frequently type cast. For example, he was the Captain of one of the Japanese ships attacking Pearl Harbor in *Tora Tora Tora*. He also played a recurring Korean character on the TV show MASH. He was unassuming, and funny, yet he could rise to the occasion and do a fine, professional job on even the most dramatic scene. He was nominated for both an Academy Award and a Golden Globe for his work as Miyagi.

Pat and his family were actually detained in an internment camp in Gila River, Arizona, for the duration of World War II—an experience that he could draw on for the "Manzanar" scene in *The Karate Kid*.

We remained friends for years. One time we took our girls to Disneyland and while Xian and Ali did the rides, Pat and I took turns carrying his sleeping 3-year-old daughter, Tia, all over the park.

After the release of the movie, which, as almost every one knows, was Hugely successful. It was the number-one box office money maker of 1984.

Pat would still come to my martial arts school (by then I had moved to Woodland Hills, California), and play with the kids and sign autographs, usually wearing his "Miyagi" clothes.

Pat passed away in November of 2005 and is mourned and missed by so many.

Many people thought that Pat did his own martial arts for the movie, but that was not true. A very fine martial artist and Shotokan master, Fumio Demura, did all the fight scenes. He and Pat were the same height and general build, although Fumio was more muscular. With the same clothes, a little aging makeup and a "Bald wig" on Fumio, they looked very much alike. Fumio was a pleasure to work with. I was there to watch the fight scene where the "bad kids" are beating Daniel up by the cyclone fence. Fumio was flawless in every take.

Speaking of the "bad kids," several of them had a little martial arts training. Chad McQueen, Steve's son, had as I recall trained with Pat Johnson. Billy Zabka , who played the "bad" kid, was a green belt in a style I can't recall. Billy's brother, Guy, trained with me for a while.

It all came together under the tutelage of Pat Johnson, not only is he a great karate Master in his own right, but he has such a "feel" for the camera. Pat always felt the camera angles and had everyone trained and positioned perfectly for every shot.

Under John Avildsen's direction, the film progressed inevitably towards the "finals." There was a certain amount of pressure, always the fear that something could go wrong. As we concluded the semi-finals on December 27th, we had the required number of contestants; I was, however, a little worried about the "audience." Many of the parents had lost interest after doing two or three Tournaments to get to the finals and also it was the week between Christmas and New Years. The martial arts schools slow down during that time. We still, at the time of this writing in 2007, close our schools that week. I did whatever I could on the 27th to assure attendance the following day.

The ring configuration, seating, red carpet (which I provided), all of the trophies, etc. had to be completed the night before. The set crews worked all night to have them ready by 10 AM the morning of the 28th.

On the day of the 28th of December, we started early doing sign-ups for the "Finals" and the filming. Pat Johnson had done his usual superb job of preparing the actors for their scenes.

The participants and their families began to arrive and Leslie and her father George checked them in. Leslie had to have help because she was also working in front of the cameras portraying one of the scorekeepers. Once George and a helper, my old friend Bob Esmay, had a handle on it, she was free to go inside where I was making last-minute touches to the rings and holding a meeting with the officials.

The officials during the eliminations, the semi-finals, and the filming were hand picked by me, and in a couple of instances by Pat Johnson. We wanted the best!

Those who know, as you watch the film will recognize, Steve Muhammad, Bob White, Clarence Magee, Kirk Fisher, Barbara Goldstone, and Johanna Williams, to name a few.

The filming of the scenes that portrayed the eliminations went off without a hitch. In spite of some occasional moderate body contact, no time was lost. I believe that much of the flavor of the background tournament scenes was created by the fact that the kids fighting in the other rings had forgotten that they were "in a movie." They were real martial arts students fighting for their honor, their studio, their pride, and a color TV set!

My daughter Xian, who was 12 at the time, and son John who was 9, were both competing during the filming. If you know where and when to look, you can see them kicking and punching in the background.

I had a small part, and can be seen during the "finals" wearing a white *gi* top and black bottoms, standing at ringside between the fighters, portraying the instructor of the semi-finalist who was the last one to fight Billy Zabka before Daniel-*san*.

The night scenes filmed at the "finals" presented a problem. As I had feared the day before, we lost a lot of our audience. They were needed to fill the stands. What happened was that as their kids were eliminated or won their prizes, the parents wanted to go home and enjoy what remained of their Christmas vacation.

Jerry Weintraub was rightfully concerned and sent out a call for 100 or so extras to come in and fill the empty seats in the stands. That worked!

Filming was completed over the next couple of days except for some second unit work.

I would like to mention one more person. This was the first starring role for Elizabeth Shue, playing opposite Ralph Macchio. She went on to be a fine,

Academy Award-nominated actress. Many of us had a feeling that she was destined for stardom and she was.

During the filming, Leslie played a scorekeeper wearing a black "official" T-shirt. My son Kirk can be seen frequently in the rings, judging, wearing a red T-shirt.

Kirk and his stepmother shared a good friendship, full of lots of kidding around.

For the Finals scenes, they were sitting ringside together. Kirk still had his red and white flags from calling points earlier in the day. Every time the camera would point towards the two of them, Kirk would position his flag in front of Leslies face.

My son Scott was working in the computer business nearby, and came by one day at lunchtime to watch the filming of some of the final scenes. Members of the "audience" were cautioned that if they had to leave between takes to always return to their exact positions upon their return.

I invited Scott to stand next to me in a point in the center of the camera view. He watched for a while and then had to go.

In the background of the scene he seems to just disappear!

The filming was wrapped up in a few days and the set was taken down.

However, my Karate Kid story was just beginning!

Refereeing Grand Champion fight at the "Internationals"
Barry Gordon vs. Leonard Creer about 1993

With He-Il-Cho at one of his Beverly Hills High School Tournaments in the late '70s.

with my friend Ed Parker at the Internationals, about 1992

With Chuck Norris about 1992

My last tournament fight. Culver City, California 1977. Grand Champion against "Ted", one of the original BKF organizers

1986 with Alvin Prouder

Me

Tarzana, California about 1987 with Dexter Brooks. Johnny Gyro in the background

1984 Northridge, California. Setting up a scene for "The Karate Kid"

Encino, California 1999 with Howard Jackson the night we first heard about his cancer

1973 My tournament at Culver City, California with Steve Muhammed (BKF). Cynthia Prouder, mother of the goddaughter She-ra and Mark Zacharatos, one of my 5th degree black belts.

1988 Woodland Hills. Leslie, me, Carol, Ron Pohnel (now an
8th degree Puma black belt) and Bobby Burbidge

1975 The Great Wall of China. The first American black
belt in China since 1941 or maybe ever.

refereeing at the Internationals, Ray Wizard and "Satch" Williams

Woodland Hills, California, abaout 1988 with Johnny gyro, now
an 8th degree black belt in Puma, and Bobby Burbidge

1972 Encino, California. Sparring with my son Kirk Fisher

1972 Encino, California.

My beautiful daughter Xian, a 3rd degree black belt

My son Scott about 1973, now an 8th degree black belt

John Fisher 1999

My son, Kirk Fisher about 1975

Simon Rhee at the Internationals 1986

THE KARATE KID TOURNAMENTS

ON DECEMBER 23RD, just prior to the filming of the Finals, I was having lunch in Burbank, with R.J. Louis and John Avildsen.

A very attractive woman joined us there. Her name was Judy Schwam; she was the head of Promotion and Publicity for Columbia pictures.

I had not met her before so introductions were made. R.J. explained to Judy that I was the "Tournament Consultant" and what my role was in the making of the movie. And then lunch was ordered.

While we were eating, Judy told us of her reason for coming.

She said, " I wanted to speak to you," meaning R.J. and John, not me, "about the Publicity campaign for this film."

"The studio Heads seem to think this might just be a big hit," she continued. "They have given me a huge budget for the promotion, I'm looking for some fresh publicity ideas, other than the usual newspaper, TV, etc."

We continued to eat in silence for a while. Then an idea occurred to me.

"What about this?" I said, putting down my utensils. "Since the movie is largely focused around a karate tournament, why not stage tournaments all across the country, call them Karate Kid Tournaments, and use them to advertise the film?"

There was silence for about a minute while everyone gave it some thought. It was such a long minute that I began to think that I might have broken some "advertising rule" and offended Judy.

Then they all put their utensils down. "What a great idea!" Judy exclaimed. The others agreed. "Could you DO that?" she asked.

I said, "Sure, it's very do-able, it will take a lot of organization but it can definitely be done."

Judy said, "Can you put your idea in the form of an official proposal and bring it by my office, complete with a budget and time line?"

"I will have it for you in the morning," I said. She gave me her card; we set a meeting time for the following morning and finished our lunch.

Immediately I went home and started to work.

There is no way that any one could, single handedly, produce a large number of Tournaments across the country. Tournaments rely on reciprocity! In order to give a successful event, you must have the support of other local promoters, and the help of dozens of instructors and their students. It would be impossible for an unknown person, no matter who, to fly into a strange city and produce a large, well-run Tournament.

So my plan relied on one essential ingredient: the involvement of local tournament producers and the use of the word "affiliate."

The plan that evolved relied as much on my experience an executive with Large corporations as it did my tournament experience. It required experience in organizing a national sales force as much as it did in knowing the intricacies of tournament production.

The proposal that Judy Schwam received was this.

My corporation, "Yin and Yang International," proposes to do the following. (This is just the gist of it)

We will undertake to cause that a specific number of karate tournaments be produced in major cities across the country, time and place to be decided and approved by Columbia Pictures. These tournaments will be co sponsored in affiliation with local tournament Producers.

Columbia Pictures will agree to provide certain aids, such as tournament patches, Karate Kid participation certificates, T-shirts, advertising flyers, banners and posters.

Advertising tie-ins will be established at each local level with newspapers, local Columbia reps, TV and magazines. Furthermore, the local Producer will schedule three demonstrations prior to the tournament to further advertise the connection to the film.

A booth will be set up and manned by a Yin and Yang representative at every tournament. From this booth, information will be disseminated to the participants and spectators extolling the movie.

The cost to Columbia for this program will be $******** per tournament. (It was a very significant amount)

In my proposal I had suggested that we undertake a total of 40 events.

Judy read it, choked a little at the total and asked if we could cut the costs. I said, not really but we can reduce the number of local events.

We agreed on 30 rather than 40 and she signed off on it.

That's when the real work began. In order to coordinate this many events within a short period of time I would need a lot of help from the best people in the business.

I already had Leslie, Scott and Kirk so I set my sights on the rest of the essential people.

My plan was to divide the country into regions and assign a regional manager to each. Those were the key people in the plan. They had to be high-ranking, well known black belts in order to command the respect of the local tournament producers, They also had to have a great deal of tournament experience and be mature, honest and self-motivated.

After giving a great deal of thought, not only to the selection of the people, but also to the areas where they would be the most effective, I made the decisions and set up the organization.

I contacted the people I wanted and explained the project to each one of them, first, by telephone. After hearing the explanation of the project, every one wanted "in." So the next thing I did was to set a dinner meeting at Chui's Dumplings restaurant in Los Angeles Chinatown.

We had a great dinner and a very productive meeting. Every one that I had hoped for wanted in on the project.

My plan was to divide the country into 6 regions. A Regional manager would be assigned to each. He would be responsible for 5 "affiliated" Tournaments and one Regional Championship Tournament.

It shaped up like this:

Region #1 The Northwest
    Regional Manager Kirk Fisher

| Seattle | Spokane | Denver |
| Tacoma | Portland | |

Region #2 Central
    Regional Manager Dave Torres

| Chicago | Detroit | Cleveland |
| St.Louis | Indianapolis | |

Region #3 Eastern
    Regional Manager Ron Chapel

| New York City | Philadelphia | Boston |
| Pittsburgh | Washington DC | |

Region #4 Southwest
    Regional Manager Steve Fisher

| Houston | Dallas | Fort Worth |
| Oklahoma City | New Orleans | |

Region #5 South
    Regional Manager Bob White

| Atlanta | Miami | Tampa |
| Memphis | Charlotte | |

Region #6 West
    Regional Manager Ron Pohnel/J.Fisher

| Los Angeles | Orange County | San Diego |
| San Francisco | Sacramento | |

All of these tournaments had to be held during January through April of 1984. I would help and participate in the contacts and scheduling.

Additionally, each regional manager would select the promoter in the city that offered the most in the way of attendance and organization, and schedule a "Karate Kid" regional championship tournament with that promoter for May of 1984.

Yin and Yang Int. would pay all expenses, and then some, to each regional manager. We would provide all of the materials, shipping, etc. The regional managers would take charge, coordinate all of the tournament details, travel to the city and be there for the tournament. At the event they would set up a booth, with a large gold banner, and hand out; literature, T-shirts, patches, and certificates and make a short speech about the forthcoming movie.

As added inducements to the local promoter who ended up working with us on the regional championships, we would provide trophies, prizes such as movie soundtracks (a great one written by Richard Conte), the full support and effort of our regional manager for tournament direction, and additional grand prizes from Columbia. One such grand prize was a private showing for the winner of the tournament at a theater of his choice in his or her hometown. This winner would be selected by a drawing between the winners of each division.

We started immediately. The key to the success of the project was setting up the local tournaments as quickly as possible. This is where the "affiliation" was so important.

I sat down with all of the martial arts magazines I could put my hands on, and looked at the "upcoming events" sections. I called every promoter who had an event scheduled in our time frame. After explaining what we were doing, I don't think a single one of them did not want to join us.

As soon as I had made a deal with the local promoter in the city we wanted I would then turn the rest of the detailed arrangements over to the proper regional manager. It started coming together very quickly.

Some of the arrangements had to be altered as it took shape; we might, for example, not be able to find a tournament in Fort Worth so we held one in Yuma, Arizona instead. We couldn't do one in Philadelphia so we did one in York, Pennsylvania. It all worked out.

We received a great deal of support and publicity in the martial arts magazines. People like my old friend Emil Farkas gave us great coverage in his "Western Wrap Up" feature in *Black Belt* magazine. The local papers were interested in the local tie-ins with a major film release.

All in all it was a great success! Through the tournaments themselves and all of the resulting local media coverage we reached millions of people. I believe our efforts helped make the movie an immediate hit!

It cost Columbia a lot of money but Judy told me that she thought it was worth every penny!

Besides being very well paid for my efforts, all of the proceeds from the Regional Championship and the National Karate Kid Tournament that I held in Cypress College in southern California were the regional managers' and mine. Columbia didn't care about the "gate" from these, so that was all ours.

We had a lot of fun doing them and we felt like an integral part of the success of the film.

Some funny stories came out of the work.

David Torres' first "Karate Kid" Tournament was in Chicago. As David tells it, he is an East LA, southern California product. He left for the Chicago tournament from LAX on a typical February day. It was sunny and 75 degrees.

When they landed at O'Hare airport in Chicago, David was wearing one of his trademark blue TKFT T-shirts.

He picked up his luggage, and looking for a cab, he walked out through the airport doors.

Here it was a typical Chicago February day, overcast, about 9 degrees with a 40 MPH wind knifing through you.

David took about 10 steps, turned around and went back into the airport. There he opened his suitcase and put on every single article of clothing that he had brought with him before venturing out again.

Ron Chapel was responsible for the East. Our principal contact there was Grandmaster Manuel Agrella. I had met Manny and most of the other promoters over the years at the Internationals.

Manny headed up a large system called "Tong Leong Gwo Shuh Goan" with 4 or 5 schools in and around Pennsylvania and Maryland. He had hosted one of the Elimination Tournaments and Ron and I had selected him to partner with us on the "Regional Finals."

The finals were to be held in York, Pennsylvania at a large venue there. All the arrangements were made ahead of time, and Ron, Leslie and I flew into Dulles Airport the day before. There we rented a car and drove a few hours to York.

We had a great drive; we were such good friends, and we made up a game of taking turns naming a TV western shows. I won, but they wouldn't accept "F Troop" as a Western so the game ended inconclusively.

We arrived in York in time to check in to the Sheraton Hotel, where the tournament was being held the next day. A dinner was being held there for the officials and contestants and we were treated as honored guests.

Grandmaster Agrella was a real stickler for respect and protocol. Any of his students who wanted to approach him first bowed then knelt on one knee with the opposite fist on the ground and waited for him to acknowledge them. We saw that repeated many times for the next two days.

Dinner was good and Manny relaxed with us at the head table and we had a lot of laughs.

The next morning, before the Tournament, we had to walk through the Parking Lot to reach the adjacent building where the Tournament was to be held. There were hundreds of people streaming towards the entrance to the building, past all of the parked cars. We became aware of a strange sight. People kept popping up and down all over between the cars. It was strange and unsettling for a minute, then we realized, Manny's students, and parents as well, were under strict orders to bow to us whenever they saw us. That's what we were seeing; it gave the appearance of a bunch of meerkats popping up and back down again.

Once inside, the tournament went smoothly and finished up at about 8:00 PM. There was a short and potentially serious misunderstanding between Manny and me which almost became physical. We were able to locate the source of the problem and fix it. We parted friends the next day after he took us to lunch somewhere in Washington D.C.

My son Kirk, although only 23 years old at the time, did a great job with his assignments in the Northwest. He ended with a very successful regional championship held at the Flag Pavilion in Seattle on June 16th, 1984. He combined all of his Promoters to host this one, a great idea and achievement. Jerry Gould, Morris Mack, Ken Low, Pat McCarthy, Fred King and Steve Armstrong collaborated to make it a huge success. It was a terribly busy six months. Every one of our people performed admirably. The tournaments went as well as we could have ever hoped for; Columbia and Judy Schwam were very pleased by the results.

During all of the time that we were working on our promotional efforts, the movie was moving towards its finalization. Editing was almost completed, and in, I believe, late January 1984, a preview of the film was scheduled to be held at Jerry Weintraub's mansion-like home in Bel Air, California.

Most of the cast and crew were invited. Leslie and I were included. We arrived at about 7:00 P.M. The house was huge and beautiful as you might expect. Weintraub was rumored to be one of the wealthiest men in Hollywood at that time. He ultimately became even more wealthy, a great deal of it from the Karate Kid, and bought large holdings in Las Vegas.

Once inside the mansion we were escorted into a large, beautifully furnished screening room. There were perhaps 100 guests, made up almost exclusively of those who worked on the film. Even then the room was not filled to capacity.

We saw and gravitated towards our friends, the Louis', the Moritas and the Johnsons. Drinks and hors d'ouevres were served.

While we waited for the Weintraubs to make an appearance, we strolled through the beautiful screening room admiring the art.

We came to a very large and beautiful painting that depicted a scene in China that I recognized. It was a very well done Oil that represented, accurately, the huge square in Tientsin, China where I had spent several hours, nine years earlier.

Shortly thereafter Mr. and Mrs. Weintraub entered the room. Slowly they made their way through the throng of guests greeting each in their turn.

When they reached where we were standing by the painting, Jerry and I shook hands and he said," I see you are admiring my China painting."

"I certainly am," I replied. "It's a wonderful depiction of the square in Tientsin" He looked at me in surprise.

"How did you know?" He asked obviously puzzled. "I was just there last year."

I told him briefly about my trip to China in 1975, including my trip to Tientsin.

He asked me, "Then you must know my friend George Bush."

At that point I made an unintentional but bad blunder!

Forgetting that I was in the heart of the entertainment business where "one-upmanship" is a serious and deadly game, I jokingly said, "Yes I do, and Barbara and Fred Bush, too."

Weintraub looked at me and asked "Fred Bush?"

I said, "Their Springer spaniel."

He never spoke to me again, and I didn't work on the next Karate Kid movies!

I believe that without intending to and without realizing it I had really embarrassed him. He thought I was trying to "one up" him. It was a case of my saying something to be funny without thinking it through first. It was much later that I realized what I had done.

It has been over 25 years now and I'm long past caring about it except I do regret having said something that looked as if I was just being a smart ass, to a man I respected.

So if you are out there, Jerry, I'm sorry!

We then watched a showing of the not quite fully edited movie.

The film, although not the finished product—there was more editing to do—was still obviously going to be special! I think everyone connected with it could feel it.

In "the business" they talk about a film having "legs," meaning it keeps on going and going. I don't know of too many movies with the kind of legs that this one has. It is showing everyday somewhere in the world, it is still a very popular rental. The kids in my martial arts schools, who think of any thing from the Nineties as being an "old movie," all know and love it. It will go on for many years yet, probably until they make a bad remake and kill it.

After this experience and in spite of my having incurred the ill will of the producer, we worked very hard on the promotion and publicity. The tournaments went very well!

We had held a "Regional Karate Kid Championships" in each of the regions. They all led up to the "National Karate Kid championships" held at Cypress College in Orange County, California on June 3rd, 1984.

One of my favorite stories from those tournaments concerns my good friend Barry Gordon.

Barry is one of the great enigmas of the martial Arts.

When I first met him, he was THE Bad Boy of the tournament circuit. Everyone hated to see him coming. He was banned from the TPA tournaments for a year. He hated everybody—mostly, it seemed, me. He would continue most of his matches after the fact in the stands or in the lobby. He was loud, insulting and mean. He could think of more insulting ways to call me "white" than I ever thought possible.

That was in 1973 or so.

Then he began to change, I think the fact that he won almost every tournament he competed in, including the Internationals, combined with the fact that he knew he would always be treated fairly by me began to make him different. We slowly became friends.

We also sparred one another almost every Wednesday night at the Sherman Oaks Karate "Fight Night." That tends to make you friends too.

The fact that I was "family" with Cynthia and Alvin Prouder and Robert Temple, three other BKF veterans, probably helped as well. Leslie and I had gone to Church with the Prouders and Cynthia's husband, Robert Temple, and became godparents to their daughter She-ra .

By the time we were doing the Karate Kid Tournaments in 1984, Barry and we had a great friendship.

He was by then a schoolteacher. He taught 3rd grade in the San Fernando Valley. Leslie used to go in and act as his "aide" occasionally and said he was a different person in the classroom.

To digress for a moment, it was during the time of the filming that an interesting situation occurred. I was driving to my office in Beverly Hills from my home in Encino. It was early in the morning and I was in my Corvette, with my top down. As I stopped at a signal nest to the Catholic Church on White Oak blvd at Ventura blvd, I heard shouting. Some men, working on top of a building on the East side of the street were shouting and pointing to the other, west, side of White Oak.

I turned and saw, in front of the church rectory, a catholic priest, in his mid 60s, in a struggle with what appeared to be a homeless man in his mid 30s.

I found out later that the younger man had come into the rectory demanding money, and when told they had none he had punched one of the nuns several times. The priest had managed to force him outside where the younger man was viciously attacking him.

I jumped out of my car and said, " Father do you need help?" To which he replied with a vehement "Yes."

As I approached him, the attacker turned to me and threw a wild right hand. I blocked it and took him down, very hard, with a foot sweep and strike.

As he hit the ground on his back I mounted him and gained control

He began to verbally assault the priest, swearing at him and calling him every vile name imaginable. I said, " Father you don't have to listen to this, go inside." As he complied he turned to me and said, "He says he has a knife."

As soon as the priest was inside I shoved my fingertips into the assailants throat, very hard, and said, "Now that the priest is gone, you keep it up and I will shove my fingers through to your spine."

Soon two police officers arrived. As they approached I warned them, "He says he has a knife." They took a firm grip on him, one by the arms and one by the legs; I jumped off and they picked him up, turned him over facing downward and placed him on the cement walkway none too easily. A search revealed a long butcher knife taped to one leg.

The situation in hand, I said my goodbyes to the priest and nuns, after hearing their story and made my way to work, a little disheveled.

Back to my Barry Gordon story. At the last Karate Kid tournament we had a couple of 1st prize TVs left over so we decided to raffle them off. I called the stub number over the microphone to the crowd of perhaps 800 people. After a few seconds, Barry stood up and started yelling, "I won, I won, I can't believe it! I never win anything!" As he walked towards the announcers table he continued to proclaim, at the top of his voice, "I can't believe it! I won!"

The people in the stands began to applaud and by the time he reached me everyone was on their feet. I shook hands and hugged him warmly, happy that my friend had won. He picked up the huge box with a 24-inch color TV and smiling broadly began to return to his seat.

For some reason it occurred to me to call out to him, "Barry I didn't get your ticket." He started laughing, walked back, put the box back where it had been and returned to his seat.

He never had the ticket! A classic Barry Gordon story!

Later that night, Barry, Leslie, Cynthia, Ray Wizard, Alvin, his wife Lambie and a few others went with us to get something to eat at an "All You Can Eat Buffet" place. Barry had two huge Rottweilers. He asked Leslie to come with him to the buffet table where he proceeded to fill two large take home containers with ground meat to take home for his dogs.

With Leslie acting as an unwilling look out he filled the containers as fast as he could before the management could see him. She was nervous and apprehensive about it but Barry assured he did it all the time and got away with it. Just as they completed filling the containers and turned to go back to our table a manager strolled onto the scene. Acting completely nonchalant, Barry turned to go back to his seat and accidentally dropped both containers full of ground beef at the feet of the manager! Leslie continued without looking back, returned to where we were all sitting. We all turned our backs on Barry and pretended not to know him.

When Barry finally married we were all guests at his wedding. There is a custom where guests can "pay" to dance with the Bride or Groom. Usually its $5 or $10. Barry made it very clear to all the guests that he couldn't and wouldn't SLOW dance, he was bad at it! I paid $10 to dance with his lovely bride. Then after everyone had heard him announce several times that he would not slow dance under any circumstances. I slipped Leslie a $100 bill. She made sure everyone saw what it was as she held it up under Barry's nose. He couldn't refuse and danced an entire slow dance with my wife. Very funny stuff.

On June 22nd of that year, we were invited to and attended the premiere of the film in Hollywood. It was an exciting culmination to nine months of hard work and fun. The premiere was held at a well-known theater in Hollywood and was attended by everyone involved in the making of the film. It was a fun and exciting experience!

During my time in the martial arts in southern California I was to work on some other films, but nothing even close to the caliber of "The Karate Kid."

Another film of a slightly different caliber that might make an interesting story is:

"Chawks Revenge"

In March of 1986, I was contacted by a fellow martial artist and friend, Nate Moore, of the BKF (Black Karate Federation). He wanted to meet with me to discuss a movie project.

We met for lunch and he explained that he was one of the producers of a forthcoming film entitled "Chawks Revenge." It was going to be about a psychotic, cop-killing criminal who, having seen his father shot to death, by a police officer in a case of mistaken identity, vows revenge.

They wanted me to play the title role of Chawk. Nate would be the lead "good guy" detective opposite my villainous lead character. Almost the entire balance of the cast were BKF members.

Some very close old friends were also appearing in the film, such as "Big John" Robertson, Ray Wizard and Cynthia Prouder (wife at the time of Robert Temple and the mother of my goddaughter, She-ra Temple.)

It was a very low budget film, produced and directed by beginners. I saw an opportunity to have some fun, work with some great martial arts friends and gain some interesting experience, so I agreed to do it.

We started shooting in April, since we all had other aspects of our lives to deal with, we usually met three days a week. Some of the initial problems were quite funny. Initially shot on videotape, we had real racially related problems. Not what you might think since we had all been very good friends for years. They were caused instead by the difficulty of getting the lighting and film color right. I am very white, with light skin, blonde hair, and blue eyes. Nate, Ray and Big John are all very black.

When they would get me right, Nate would appear as a dark smudge, when they got him right I would appear as a white blur. It took a lot of work to get so that you could see both of our faces at the same time.

My character was a truly evil sociopath, killing police officers with martial arts techniques (or sometimes with a gun).

The filming took us all over Los Angeles. In a few words, the plot called for Chawk vowing revenge on the entire LAPD, recruiting other bad guys by breaking them out of prison, and terrorizing the City. There were plenty of fight scenes. That was the one thing we did quite well.

In the end, after killing dozens of people, Chawk finally finds the officer who actually shot his father. After killing several more policemen, Chawk is shot dead by Nate's character. A true morality play, Good triumphs over Evil, and it was a wrap.

Lacking the equipment and sophistication to add sound later, all of our dialogue and sound affects were done live at filming. This proved to be our undoing.

When we had our first showing for cast and crew and a few Hollywood people that might be interested in it, the film was bad enough to be embarrassing. Reminiscent of a very bad Hong Kong film of that era.

I stayed in the back in the shadows. Since I was in almost every scene, I was afraid that I might be assaulted by an irate viewer.

After the conclusion, the lights went on, many people just quietly left without a word.

Still lurking in the shadows, hoping not to be recognized, I overheard someone from the business say, "How did you get permission to use all of that great background music?"

Permission?

No one had bothered with that little technicality. If they wanted Ray Charles, Stevie Wonder or Marvin Gaye in the background, they just put on a tape. Consequently the film had no commercial value as it could not be legally released anywhere. I was told that it did play for a while in Southeast Asia.

Still, I had a great time doing it, working with my friends; we had a lot of laughs.

I have, I believe, one of the only copies in existence today. Every other year or so, when I am all alone in the house, I watch it. Even under those circumstances I still try to stay in the shadows of my den so that no one can see me. I have never shown it to anyone.

After the Karate Kid was released we were very busy with the schools. The film had a great effect on the nation's interest in martial arts. Other than a large general increase in enrollment, the other big difference was a huge swing towards more kids. It hasn't changed since. Prior to the Karate Kid, my school enrollment usually consisted of 70% adults, 30% kids. It has been reversed ever since; it still is today.

Another trickle-down effect from the film was that, with the increase in students, there was a resultant increase in interest and attendance at tournaments.

My tournament schedule became even more hectic. Still heavily involved in the TPA, I was at someone's Tournament every weekend, at least 50 per year. I was still involved in the carpet business, but it was just a means to an end. After the collapse of CCC, my heart was never in it again. I managed to do enough to still make very good money at it. I used to think of it as a "trick" I did for a few hours a day to make money.

My passion was and is the martial arts.

During the 70's, I had met and become friends with so many martial artists through the tournaments, especially the Internationals.

One of them was Mike Stone. Mike was already a legend in karate by the early 70's. He had won over 100 tournament fights in succession, devastating his opponents with power and ferocity. To never lose, in those days, was an incredible achievement especially with all the rules conflicts and poor or questionable judging.

I had refereed a couple of Mike's fights and we started hanging out together at the tournaments and became friends.

Mike had started a series of tournaments he called the "Four Seasons," held every three months. They were very popular. I started helping him by first officiating and then announcing.

Mike was, at that time, living with Priscilla Presley. I spent time with them frequently, usually after Mike's "Four Seasons" tournaments. This was about 1973 and 1974. Lisa Marie was about 5 or 6 years old. We would usually all have dinner together after the Tournaments; Lisa Marie, Elvis and Priscilla's daughter, used to like to ride with me in my new white Corvette convertible. She was a cute, sweet little girl.

Some time in 1974, Mike produced a very ambitious event that was intended to be both a tournament and a presentation of a showcase of all the different Martial Arts. Steve Fisher won the karate tournament portion. My son Scott and a couple of his UCLA friends put on a fencing demonstration in complete Three Musketeers costumes, and almost every other art from Judo to Aikido was represented as well.

I remember the moment when Mike and Priscilla showed up at the event, where I was acting as Master of Ceremonies in a tuxedo, of course. Mike was wearing an ankle length fur coat and they were driving a Stutz Bearcat automobile.

Some time after Mike and Priscilla split up, he dropped the Four Seasons; I saw much less of him for a long time. He was doing films and seminars all over the world. I was involved heavily in IOI, China, tournaments and CCC.

Fast forward to 1980.

Mike and I had stayed in touch, randomly speaking every few months, then one day we ran into each other at a karate event and ended up talking for hours, catching up. Mike had married a beautiful Korean singer named "Woni" whom Leslie and I met and became friends with. They were living in Studio City, close to our home in Encino. Out of that long conversation two very interesting ideas emerged.

First of all, Mike was convinced that the whole "ninja" thing was going to be a wave of the future. At that time, in 1980, little was known about the Ninja in this country. Mike was working on a film he wanted to make about a contemporary Ninja. He was trying to sell the idea around Hollywood. He finally did but they put another actor named Franco in the lead role that Mike had planned portraying. The film was moderately successful and did a lot towards interesting the American public in the Ninja mystique.

The other idea was that he and I would revive the "Four Seasons" tournaments. It was agreed that I would put up the money to reactivate it, which I did, and he and I would act as 50/50 partners in the events.

It worked well. We were good together and produced many more Four Seasons throughout 1980 and 1981.

During that time we were playing racquetball a lot, it was very popular in the early eighties. No one could beat Mike. He was the ultimate racquetball hustler. The same as in martial arts, he was also the undefeated champion in racquetball.

We had a good time doing the Four Seasons. They were all successful. Mike's name was a big part of the appeal. One of the reasons that we worked so well together was that we were both always willing to try new, innovative techniques.

One innovation we made was actually paying our officials. We asked them all to attend 2 meetings prior to the event where we went over the rules of judging and of conduct. The day of the tournament they had to wear black corduroys and a white Izod shirt. After the tournament, if they had worked the rings they collected their money.

It wasn't a lot of money, but it made a big difference in the attitude and deportment of the officials—it made them Professionals. Heretofore all tournament judging was on a volunteer basis, you took what was available and crossed your fingers.

Mike and I shared a lot of good experiences during those two years. We haven't seen each other for a while now. When I last saw him, he and his new bride Tyna came for a visit with us about 1990 when we were living at the ocean in Laguna Beach. I have spoken to him a few times on the phone since.

Tyna came from an old Filipino family that had some property in the islands. Mike and Tyna were living on an island, in a converted, old Portuguese lighthouse. It was built of local stone 250 years ago. Mike is still traveling all over the world doing seminars and personal appearances as far as I know.

In my opinion Mike Stone is the fiercest and most focused fighter I have ever known. There are a few who could maybe have beaten him for points in a ring but no one could have ever defeated him in a life or death struggle.

In the early to middle eighties the Mecca of fighting was the Sherman Oaks Karate school on Ventura Blvd. at Van Nuys Blvd.

Chuck Norris and Pat Johnson had opened the school originally; later on it was taken over by Harold Gross, one of their students. That was when I first started going there to spar.

After that a druggist named Bernie Krasno purchased it. He was only a blue belt at the time he bought it, so he hired one of my long time black belt students, Ron Pohnel, to run the school.

Ron started with me at my Tarzana school 38 years ago, in 1971; he is now an 8th degree black belt in my PUMA system.

At the time he was running the Sherman Oaks school, he was a 3rd degree and was, and still is, one of the premier tournament fighters of all time. His team "the Oreos" (so called because there were 4 black fighters with Pohnel, a white man, in the center) was undefeated in tournament team fighting for many years. The original Oreo team included, Pohnel, Dexter Brooks, Billy Washington, Conrad Simms and Alvin Prouder.

Pohnel and the others were very well known on the tournament circuit and it became known far and wide that Wednesday night was "Fight Night" at Sherman Oaks.

Before long, all of the best fighters in Southern California and the rest of the world started showing up there on Wednesday nights.

I almost never missed a Wednesday. On any given night you might see, of course, all of the Oreos, and maybe, Bill Wallace, Johnny Gyro, Ray Wizard, Barry Gordon, Ken Firestone (another of my 8th degree black belts) Bobby Burbidge, Howard Jackson, Mark Zacharatos or many other well known fighters.

Fighters came, literally, from all over the world.

One night the French Silver Glove (the highest rank) Savate champion visited the school with his entourage. Savate is a very effective form of kickboxing that the French have practiced for over 200 years. He chose to fight Alvin Prouder first.

At that time Alvin, who was like a son to me, was one of the best martial arts fighters on the American scene. He was then in his early twenties and had been training in the BKF, under Steve (Sanders) Muhammed, since he was a child.

Alvin had won most of the major western Karate Tournaments, including the Internationals. He was the reigning welterweight champion of the WKA kickboxing League and was 10 and 0 as a professional boxer as well. He was a regular fixture at our Wednesday night workout.

After doing an impressive stretching routine and a warm up designed to illustrate his very fast and effective kicks, the French Champion looked around the room and gestured that he was ready to go with someone, and with a disdainful jerk of his thumb selected Alvin, not knowing, I'm sure, whom he was selecting.

The routine of these Wednesday nights were that we all went at full speed but with very light head contact and light to moderate body contact. It was a gentleman's agreement that everyone, except an occasional visitor, maintained. The occasional visitor who wanted to go hard would usually be warned once, and then ended up having to be carried off the floor.

The Frenchman didn't bow when Alvin did but instead launched an immediate attack with full power kicks. Had it been some of the other of us he might have ended the fight right there.

Savate as practiced by this man, has all targets open including the Groin. As the fight progressed—and it was a fight, not sparring—it was evident that the Frenchman was a great kicker. Alvin was, however a great kicker as well, but showed superior hand techniques. (It has long been and still is my opinion that American boxing is the ultimate hand system.)

The fight lasted maybe 3 or 4 minutes, and is a fight that many people in the world would have paid a lot of money to see.

It became evident about half way through that the arrogant Savate champion realized that he was in trouble. He had underestimated American martial arts, the Wednesday night fights and most of all, Alvin Prouder. He was obviously trying as hard as he could to knock Alvin out.

Finally Alvin set him up, and with a straight front left hand, followed by a hard right cross, he then kicked him in the groin so hard that it lifted him off the ground. He flew about 6 feet back and landed in a fetal position from which he did not uncurl for at least 5 minutes.

When he did revive, after vomiting for a while in the men's room, some of his supporters half carried him out of the dojo. We then resumed our normal Wednesday night work out.

There were so many great stories from those days. I was always the oldest person on the floor, in my late 40's. We all used to get a big kick out of the fact that I was 47 or 48 years old and always wore a yellow, cut off, "Disneyland" sweat shirt to the workout. Frequently a first time visitor would stretch, look around and say "I'll start with him" (the old guy in the Disneyland shirt). It was usually an eye-opening experience for them that we all got a big laugh from.

One night a well known, Chinese 6th degree black belt, who shall remain nameless here, came for the first time. He had made a point of saying to several people at different Tournaments that he would like to come by Sherman Oaks some night and "check us out and maybe show us a thing or two."

There was a back entrance to the school from the parking lot. Many of us came in that way. The dressing room was right next to the back door.

We were just starting to stretch and start the good-natured insults, threats and banter that went on every Wednesday. That part of the evening was usually dominated by Johnny Gyro, another "son" of mine and now an 8th degree in my PUMA system. John was a practical joker "par excellence" and a master of insults. His only equal in that department was Barry Gordon. They would usually start the warm ups with detailed descriptions of their relationships with each other's girl friends and mothers.

Our 6th-degree visitor entered in his street clothes, saw everyone sitting around stretching, talking and laughing, and without a second glance went into change into his *gi*.

By the time he came back out everyone was on the mat sparring. Included were, of course, the 5 Oreos, Gyro, a very muscular Black Belt who had just won the Police Olympics whose name escapes me, Bobby Burbidge, Barry, Ray Wizard, Joey Escobar, a brown belt student of Pohnel's at the time, Ed Anders, now a 6th-degree of mine, Dexter Brooks, a couple of others, and me.

I was sparring with Dexter Brooks when I saw the visitor come out of the dressing room. I put up my hand and indicated to Dex to stop for a second. We observed him for a couple of minutes.

The visitor strode proudly onto the edge of the mat. He was finishing adjusting his decorative 6th degree Belt and began to watch.

He watched intently for several minutes. Then I saw him slowly walk backwards into the dressing room. A few minutes later I was sparring with Gyro, I think, and we saw our guest, back in his street clothes, slipping quietly out the back door. Obviously, he wanted no part of what he saw.

As I look back sometimes across the lifetime I have spent involved in fighting and in the martial arts I think I miss those nights the most! I was always sore somewhere on Thursdays but I wouldn't trade a minute of it.

I am still in touch with many of the great "fight night" survivors. Unfortunately just this last year, 2008, my dear old friend Dexter Brooks chose to kill himself. He will be missed.

Bill Wallace was a frequent participant at Sherman Oaks.

One Wednesday night in 1983 or 84, for some reason that I don't recall, Bill and I were almost the only two fighters that showed up.

We decided to give ourselves a half hour or so sparring workout.

Bill, known to the entire world as "Superfoot," was undefeated as a professional kick boxer. He and my good friend Benny Urquidez can share that claim.

Bill had an uncanny ability that I have never seen before or since. Once he raised the knee of that kicking leg to his chin, there was no way to know what was coming next. From the exact same position, he could execute a blazing fast kick. The amazing thing was that it could be either a roundhouse kick, a sidekick or a hook kick. He could perform any of the three equally fast, hard and well from there. So the odds were always 2 to 1 that you would guess wrong. "The Shell game."

That night as we started, my wife Leslie, a good Black Belt in her own right was there watching.

She said, "Bill, don't you dare break anything on him, we are leaving for two weeks in Hawaii in the morning"

Bill and I smiled and started sparring. About 15 minutes into the workout I tagged him with a pretty good left hook, no doubt harder than I meant to. Champion that he is, he immediately responded with a hook kick that broke my cheekbone.

Leslie and I spent the next two weeks in Hawaii with me looking like I had been in an automobile accident.

I don't want to leave anyone out and if I have its certainly not intentional. Cynthia and Lambie Prouder, Alvin's sister and wife respectively, trained there from time to time, as did Leslie.

One time a 16 or 17 year old, Rick Roufus, who later became a World Champion kick Boxer came from back east to train with us. Johnny Gyro took him under his wing and helped him a lot.

Gyro is one of the greatest jokesters of all time, unfortunately since I want to keep this rated PG, I can't relate many of his tricks and jokes. He now owns and operates a huge school in Agoura, California. As mentioned earlier he is presently ranked as an 8th degree in my PUMA system. He and his beautiful wife Noel and their sons, all great black belts, do all of the teaching there.

There are so many wonderful Gyro stories. He is an incorrigible gagster and all of us have felt his touch at one time or another.

Many years ago, Ron Pohnel, now an 8th degree in the Puma system and a master in his own right, was a victim of Gyro's on a number of occasions.

On one particular occasion, Gyro had met the legendary Bob Burbidge for the first time at the Internationals. Bobby, now deceased, was another of my "brothers."

They both knew each other only by their well-earned reputations. At this first meeting Johnny said to Bobby, "I'm very happy to meet you, you seem like a really nice guy, not at all the asshole that Pohnel made you out to be."

Upon hearing this Pohnel (no doubt fearing for his life) rushed to Johnny and demanded that he explain to Bobby that he was "only kidding."

Typical Gyro!

Two other fighters who would occasionally show up on Wednesday nights were Burnis White and, Mark Zachoratos. Burnis is ranked as a 6th degree and Zack as a 5th degree in PUMA.

Burnis White was the middleweight PKA Kick Boxing Champion of the World right after Bill Wallace retired undefeated. I sat ringside and saw them fight one another at the Hemeter Center in Honolulu, Hawaii. It was November 28th 1977. Bill Wallace won and retained his Championship. It was a split decision that could have gone either way.

Burnis and I trained and worked out together a great deal in the Eighties. As mentioned earlier, he was a member of the LAPD and the senior training officer for the Arrest and Control Division that I spent a great deal of time with working as a consultant.

Mark Zacharatos, "Zack," was a successful full-contact fighter, ranked in the top ten in the world. He has been a well-known instructor in Southern California for many years. He is married, to a beautiful, woman black belt, and has a successful teaching set up in Calabasas, California.

Joey Escobar, who was a student of Pohnel's and therefore in my "down line," now owns a nice school in Malibu, California.

I have a very funny Joey Escobar story that is worth telling here.

One Sunday, in 1985 or 86, I believe it was, I had held one of my frequent Culver City tournaments. Those readers who might remember Culver City and those Tournaments may recall this one.

Usually, by the time the Black Belt Finals are run, much of the audience, those with younger children, and those that have lost already, have left the premises. This has always been a problem; by the time the best fights occur, there are very few people left to witness them.

On this night the finals had come down to the last two fighters: Ray Wizard, of the BKF and Joey Escobar, the student of my long time black belt, Ron Pohnel.

The remaining witnesses to the last match were about 15 BKF black and brown belts and a few other die-hards.

I, as usual, was the center referee with four good corner judges sitting at their appointed posts; Leslie was keeping score and Cynthia Prouder was sitting next to her keeping time. The black belt finals were set to be three two-minute rounds, total accumulated points.

We were in the third and last round, the score was very close. Ray and Joey, who were not friendly to one another to begin with, had let the match become very personal. Both were already bleeding from some very hard contact.

I called a time out and motioned both fighters to come to the center of the ring for a discussion.

"You are both going full contact," I said. "It isn't necessary, we aren't fighting for money here, it's a trophy, you have known each other for years, one or both of you is really going to get hurt, it's not worth it, I will call it right now as a draw and we can all go home in one piece."

Since Joey was Pohnel's student and I had sat on most of his panels when he tested all the way up to black, I thought he would be easier for me to control. Ray was a friend and frequent training partner at both the BKF and Sherman Oaks Wednesday nights but he looked much angrier.

Therefore as they stared holes into each other about two feet apart in the center of the ring, I turned my back to Joey and faced Ray. While I was trying to calm Ray down and reason him out of his anger, suddenly, Joey reached over my right shoulder and punched Ray full in the mouth!

I don't know who present was the most stunned. Then all Hell broke loose! The BKF spectators and Ray Wizard erupted with one desire: "Kill Escobar." Joey, realizing what a stupid thing he had done, ran up onto the stage and leaped up onto the announcer's table.

He had picked up a six-foot staff on the way. The BKF fighters were in a circle around the table trying to take him down while he was swinging the staff in big looping arcs to keep them back. Cynthia, Leslie and I were trying to stand between Joey and the mob and calm things down. We had to keep our eyes on the people circling the table yet also be careful that Joey didn't hit us in the back of the head with the staff.

It was a very tense and potentially dangerous minute or two. The three of us were trying our best to keep the 15 or 20 BKF fighters from undoubtedly seriously harming Joey.

Just when we thought we might have some order reestablished, Joey threw the staff, full force, at the hostiles and made a break for the side door of the auditorium. Joey Escobar used up a lot of his good luck right then because the door was unlocked. He pushed it open and ran outside into the night.

The angry mob followed him, pushing and shoving to get all of them through the door and outside, that slowed them down just enough.

When Leslie, Cynthia and I followed just behind the last BKF fighter out the door, we looked to our left and saw Joey, who was fortunately a very good runner, sprinting west on the wide street heading towards the ocean with the entire pack close on his heels.

We watched until they all disappeared into the darkness and then the three of us returned to the inside of the auditorium.

By the time we had packed up our things and were ready to leave we still hadn't seen or heard from any of the participants in the melee.

Cynthia promised to let us know as soon as she heard what the final outcome was.

True to her word, she called us late that night to tell us that Joey had managed to elude his pursuers.

It was a few days later that I spoke to Escobar again. He had lost them in the dark and had spent the night on the beach.

I think tragedy was only very narrowly averted that night.

Most of the "Wednesday Night Fight Nights" experiences were during and after the "Karate Kid" period. It was a great time that I miss a lot. Some of the best fights I have ever witnessed were just sparring matches at the old Sherman Oaks karate school.

During the mid to late 80s, I was headquartering out of my school on Ventura Blvd in Woodland Hills. We were only a few blocks from Simon Rhees' Tae Kwon Do School.

Simon is a wonderful young man and a fine martial artist.

We became good friends. I have some great Simon Rhee stories.

When we first met and became friends, my daughter, Xian, was probably about 12. Simon was perhaps 20.

I once came into Simon's office, pulled up a chair and with a stern look said to him, very seriously. "Simon, I have met with and spoken to your father and we have decided that it would be very beneficial for both of our families for you to marry my daughter, Xian, as soon as she turns 18."

Being old-school Korean, Simon was quite concerned and believed me for several minutes before I couldn't keep it up any longer and started to laugh.

It became a running gag that went on for years and I would sometimes refer to him, in his presence as "my future son in law." This was always good for a few laughs.

One day we met at a tournament in Woodland Hills. Simon was there with his then fiancé. I was on the microphone, directing the event. I made some comment about him marrying my daughter. He explained to his fiancé that "oh yes we are planning to be married." Then after a while said, laughingly, "She is just a baby."

Just then Xian happened to walk up. Simon hadn't seen her for years. She was no longer 12 but a beautiful 17 year old, with a great figure. The look on Simon's face was priceless. He looked at her and then at his fiancé, then back to me again and said, "This is Xian?" I'm sure he had a lot of explaining to do later.

Another memorable Simon Rhee story that I will never forget concerns a Red Dragon Tournament.

The Red Dragons are the product of Grandmaster Lou Cassamassa. One of the greatest of the Old School instructors and a great friend! Their schools are located throughout San Bernardino County and are generally all big and successful.

For many years in the eighties I came to almost everyone of the Red Dragon tournaments and usually acted as the MC and was the Center Referee for the black belt fighting and finals.

It was at one of the biggest "required" tournaments, where all the Red Dragon students are expected to attend and compete or help. I would estimate that there were way more than 1500 contestants, most of the Red Dragons themselves and hundreds from other schools as well.

The black belt finals had come down to the last 8. There were 7 Red Dragon Black belts and Simon Rhee, contending for first place in the black belt fighting division.

One by one six were eliminated. Only Simon and the number one Red Dragon black belt remained. As usual it was going to be three two-minute rounds, with the total accumulated points deciding the winner.

All day we had allowed, in the black belt divisions, moderate to hard body contact and "kiss" touch to the head and face.

It soon became obvious in the finals that the rules were being "bent" by my four corner Judges, all of whom were Red Dragon black belt instructors. From the start of the first round, the contact escalated and soon it was very hard.

Several times I questioned points that were being given for what was obviously very hard face and head contact from the Red Dragon to Simon. Each time, as I made the rounds to each corner judge and questioned the severity of the contact, I was told, "this is the black belt finals, there isn't too much contact."

We were down to the last few seconds of the third and final round and the score had been tied by a full power punch to Simon's face that almost broke his nose. I called a time out.

I went to the other fighter and said something to him like, "This next point will probably be the last one so make it a good one." Then I crossed over to Simon and said to him so that only he could hear.

"The only way you are going to win this thing is by knocking this guy out." He looked at me and said, "Yes sir!"

I called them back up to the line and with about 10 seconds remaining and shouted, "Go."

What happened next was one of the best things I've ever seen in the martial arts.

Simon came off the line and performed a perfect aerial cartwheel and came down with an ax kick right in the middle of the other fighter's forehead. The man dropped like a shot and was flat on his back as the time ran out. I had motioned Simon back to his line to wait.

I then walked around to the ring to each judge, looked him straight in the eye and said "THAT WAS A POINT!" To their credit not one of them argued the matter. They had been letting the Red Dragon fighter go full-contact during the entire match and could see that fair was fair.

I made sure the other fighter was back on his feet in a few minutes and was not seriously hurt then turned to Simon and announced "Winner." He picked up his trophy and exited the building.

It is not my contention that there was any cheating or even any serious favoritism involved, because when faced with the doing the "right thing" they all did it. I might be able say however, that they were "Hoisted on their own Petard."

Simon has appeared, along with his brother Phillip, in dozens of movies. Frequently he is cast as a "bad guy." Nothing could be farther from the truth!

It was about that time that another of Leslie's birthdays was coming up. It was April of 1985. She needed a new car, her 1980 Mercedes was starting to give us some trouble and the mileage was getting high. I thought that a new car would make a nice birthday present.

One of the hot cars that year was the French Peugeot. It was very sleek and beautiful and had been recently popularized in a James Bond movie.

We went together to the local Peugeot dealer in Woodland Hills California to look.

The dealer had several in stock in different colors. Leslie was smitten with the silver.

They had two brand new silver Peugeots available for sale. One was much less equipped; it had no power options. They looked the same except for the obvious sunroof until you checked for the options.

The second one had everything that you could put on it. Sunroof, all power, special stereos, even seats warmers!

There was, of course a difference of several thousand dollars in the prices. I explained to Leslie that it was a great deal of money for all the extra gadgets and since I was paying cash with our trade in, we would have to settle for the lower priced one. As always she was Ok with that, she was still very happy to have a new Peugeot.

It was about time for the dealership to close for the night when made the deal. Therefore it was arranged that we would pick the car up in the morning to give them time to wash and detail it.

We left the dealership in our two cars; hers would be traded in the next morning. When we arrived home I told Leslie that I had left my calendar at the Peugeot dealership and had to go back for it.

Hurrying right back. It was only about a 10-minute drive. I caught the Sales Manager, as I knew I would. I said that I had changed my mind and wrote him another check for the difference to buy the more expensive "loaded" car.

The next morning we arose early and cleaned out her older Mercedes. We drove the short distance to the dealership. She was naturally very excited about the prospect of picking up her new car. I didn't say a word about the switch.

When we arrived at the dealership (I had cautioned them not to say anything either), Leslie bid farewell to her old car as we waited for them to bring her the new one. At last a lot boy drove it up and handed her the keys.

As she slid in behind the wheel I watched her face. The expressions were priceless. It suddenly dawned on her that this was not the car I had bought for her the previous night. Sunroof, all power, and multi-speaker stereo, SEAT WARMERS! I would not make eye contact with her and feigning interest in something from my brief case I turned away.

A moral dilemma! For several minutes she didn't know what to do. I was no help because I was not looking at her. She believed that they had given her the wrong car by mistake. Her thoughts raced. Should I tell them? No, I should just shut up, after all I didn't do anything wrong! She was frozen in time. I finally could contain myself no longer and started to laugh and told her it was a surprise!

It was a very funny memorable experience that we still laugh about.

HAWAII

THAT SUMMER OF 1985 we made one of our many trips to Hawaii. Over the period from 1967 through 2001, I made over 75 trips to Hawaii. Many of them were while I was in the carpet business. Many more were vacations or martial arts related. At an average of over a week each, I calculated once that I spent over a year and a half of my life in Hawaii. Leslie and I were married there at the old Kuwaiahao Church in Honolulu.

Every year for 11 years, after each Internationals, Ed Parker would treat Leslie and me to the airline tickets for 2-week sojourn in Hawaii.

I had made a number of friends there over the years. One of them was Hubert Ho. We met through a huge carpet project that CCC was providing for the Federal Government in Honolulu. It was over 80,000 square yards of commercial carpeting to be installed in the new federal office building on Nimitz Street. I retained Hubert and his company to do the installation. It was one of the biggest carpet labor contracts ever awarded in Hawaii. Hubert and I worked through the entire project, frequently making adjustments of prices and extras on nothing more than a handshake or a phone call. We learned that we could trust one another implicitly and became close friends. We found that we were born on the same day at the same time on June 19th 1936. He, however was Chinese/American born in Honolulu and I, a Caucasian, born in South Dakota. We found over the years that we seemed to share so many of life's ups and downs at the same time. Enough to make us wonder about the astrological significance.

That summer of '85 we were planning a two-week, vacation trip to the Islands. I called Hubert to see if could find me any hotel "deals" as he frequently could

He told me that there weren't any deals that he knew of available because it was the height of the tourist season and I was calling on short notice. The only thing that he could even suggest was this.

Hubert was a member of the "Carpet Installers of America," a large national organization. He had been appointed Site Selection chairman to choose a location for their forthcoming annual National Convention, the following fall in Hawaii.

Hubert said, "I will make a reservation for you and Leslie at the Sheraton Waikiki Hotel, we will tell them that YOU are the Site Committee Chairman instead of me, that way they may give you a discount." He continued, "I have planned to put the convention there anyway so no harm is done."

Good idea, so we made our airline reservations and flew to Honolulu. The checkin went as planned, and we were given a suite high up on the Diamond Head side of the hotel with an incredible view of the Beach and Diamond Head. A beautiful room and view.

That night after we returned from dinner at the "Tahitian Lanai" (it was our custom for years to always eat dinner there by the pool and beach the first night in town), there was a surprise waiting for us in our room: a huge bouquet of local flowers and two very nice "Sheraton" bathrobes.

The following day was the day of the "Aloha Day Parade." We were early on the street to get a good spot. Leslie was dressed in very small white shorts, a white bikini top, white high heels, a large white straw hat, and dark glasses.

She has always had a phenomenal figure and great legs. This day was one of her best ever. Several times as groups, of servicemen or police or firemen marched past, someone would say "Eyes Right" and they would all stare appreciatively at her as the marched past.

I told her later that "the parade watched you" rather than the other way around.

I had a pedometer that I wore strapped to my ankle to measure how far we walked each day in Hawaii. It was not at all uncommon for us to walk 7 miles in a day. That day, after the parade, was no exception.

When we returned to our room that evening after dinner at The Chart House, one of other favorites, there was yet another surprise. A very large plate of "pupus", Hawaiian hors d'oeuvres, and a bottle of nice wine.

This was repeated every night for 2 weeks. It might be little flashlights or gift certificates for lunch at one of the Hotel restaurants, or tickets to Sea Life Park.

Every night there was a nice gift waiting for the "Site Committee Chairman" and his wife. Thank you Hubert!

Because of the wonderful suite and the many special attentions we received, it was one of the best trips we ever made to Hawaii.

Before we left we were taken to a fine dinner one night on the roof top restaurant of the hotel by Annette Parker, a distant cousin of Ed Parker's, and the convention manager for the Sheraton.

I told her that I was almost positive that the Sheraton would be the site of the big Convention coming up that fall with over 1000 registrants.

That night I called Hubert and ascertained that it was indeed the selection, Hubert positively guaranteed me that it would be. I felt OK then about everything.

The next morning our fabulous trip had to end. We packed, sent our luggage down to our rental car and went to the check out desk. I was expecting a bill for at least $5,000. For 14 nights in one of the best suites plus several nice restaurant charges and lots of poolside food and drinks.

They handed me the bill, it simply said "Complimentary."

I was in a state of shock. I took the bill, turned to Leslie, grabbed her arm and steered her towards the front doors and our rental car. She said, "What's the matter?" I simply said "Just keep walking and don't look back."

We had a very pleasant flight home!

I have so many wonderful memories of Hawaii.

My first trip in 1967 was not long after Hawaii became a State. It felt quite "foreign" then. The Royal Hawaiian (the pink one) and the Moana Hotel at the other end of Waikiki were the biggest hotels in Honolulu. None of the high rises were built yet. The Tahitian Lanai, the old Surfrider and the Halekulani made up most of the rest.

The first time I went to Hanauma Bay, it was very hard to find. I only heard about it from my friend Hubert and he had to draw a map for me to use to locate it. At that time there was a narrow one-lane road that you could take right down to the beach where there was a little parking lot that could accommodate about 10 cars. The first time I went there, I was the only person on the beach. Today, any time you go, there are tourist buses pulling up into the 1000 car parking facility at the top of the bluff and there are literally thousands of people on the beach.

In those early days, the trip from Honolulu to North Shore was like a jungle ride, dark and mysterious!

I had a good friend in Hawaii named Charles Black. In those days, I was a pretty good swimmer. Charles was born and raised in Honolulu and was a great swimmer and surfer. The Blacks, like the Parkers, were an early missionary family and had been in the islands for over 100 years. Charles introduced me to body surfing. We went together a number of times and I thought I was really getting the hang of it.

One day, I believe we were at Makaha or maybe Kuilima Beach; we had been body surfing for an hour or so. There were huge waves that had originated with a big storm out in the Pacific. We had been getting some incredible rides.

I was out over 100 yards and saw a big one coming in, I didn't notice that Charles had chosen to stay away from it; it looked good to me so I started to swim in with it.

I don't know how far I was from the beach, perhaps 40 or 50 yards, I was swimming on the crest of the big wave, when suddenly I looked down to see that all of the water below me had disappeared and had been sucked back into the ocean. I was suspended about 12 feet in the air with nothing below me but a couple of feet of rapidly receding water and a lot of rocks, sand and coral.

I fell straight down. There was just enough sea in the receding tide to somewhat cushion the fall. No sooner had I thanked God for not being killed in the drop when the wave I had been riding landed on me with the force of being struck by a school bus.

It almost knocked me out, and then I felt myself being dragged back out to sea. I thought I was dead for sure. I was tumbling, disoriented under tons of water, I didn't know how long I would be under, my lungs were near bursting when I popped up a little farther out than when I started.

I turned to see Charles swimming toward me; he had seen what happened and later told me he was positive that I was dead. We swam back to shore. I was very scratched and beat up and profoundly affected. I have never really enjoyed swimming in any thing but a pool since that day.

It didn't, however, at all dampen my love for Hawaii. I was the happiest ever when I was there so much in those days.

I miss the way it was then. I miss the smell of pineapple cooking in brown sugar at the old Dole canning factory as you drove past it coming in from the airport in a rented convertible on your way to Waikiki. I miss the way you deplaned down a moveable stairway directly onto the tarmac. I miss the Hawaiian music and the girls in grass skirts welcoming you with a hula and placing a flower lei around your neck as you stepped down from the plane. I miss the lei stands that lined the 2-lane road that was the only way in and out of the airport. I miss the way everyone dressed in aloha clothes. Long muumuus or bikinis for the women and white slacks and aloha shirts for the men. I miss the original "Eggs and Things" restaurant. I miss the way the trade winds smelled before the faint aroma of exhaust fumes tainted them. I miss "Hawaii Time" when 9:00AM meant, "Maybe see you by noon, brudda."

I miss swimming on Waikiki beach with a total of maybe 200 other people on the entire beach. I miss the sounds of 1000 doves cooing in the early morning on the huge Banyan tree at the corner of King and Beretania. I miss the old Pali Lookout when there was only one narrow road and room for only 5 or 6 cars to park at the tiny little "lookout point." I miss the old original "Crouching Lion" restaurant and "DaPie." Mostly I miss the wonderful, genuine, loving attitude of the Hawaiian people towards visitors to their island paradise.

On one of the many trips to Hawaii I was walking down Kalakuaua and ran straight into my old dear friend, and incredible martial artist, Eric Lee. We ended up spending the next few days together. I still see and speak to Eric frequently.

If there is an afterlife and you can choose where you want to spend eternity, for me it would be in the Hawaii of the 1960's and 70's.

Feeling as I do its no surprise that we made a serious attempt at moving there in the Eighties.

On one of our trips, Leslie and I were taking a normal, marathon walk, as was our habit. As we passed in front of the International Market Place the familiar "Cookie Smell" that pervaded the Market Place assailed us. We decided to pick up a dozen and headed towards the aroma.

It was the "Famous Amos" cookie store that had been there for years, and where we frequently assuaged our desire for sweets.

We ordered our cookies and while they were being bagged I struck up a conversation with the manger. It turned out that Amos had decided to divest himself of all 5 of his Hawaii stores.

In talking with the manager over the next half an hour I gained a great deal of information about the store, its sales gross, costs, problems and profits. Interesting.

That night I kept thinking about it. Leslie and I had dinner at the Ilikai Hotel and discussed the matter thoroughly. We thought that it might be a good investment and perhaps provide the base for a life in Hawaii.

Upon returning to the Mainland a few days later I contacted Amos. He was very forthcoming and told me of his good reasons for divesting himself of the Hawaiian operation. It made sense. He opened the books for me; we discussed a fair price and came to a tentative agreement for my purchase of just the International Market Place location, lease and all.

My thoughts were that we could use the profits from the cookie store as a base from which to build a life in Hawaii. It wouldn't stop there; we would also then open a martial arts school as well. The lease on the cookie store was a good one and had a long time to go on it. We thought that we might expand on the operation to include more items in the coming months. It looked good.

We had finally sold the wonderful house on Gable drive to satisfy the terms of my divorce from my first wife. We bought another nice house on Avenue San Luis in Woodland Hills, California. We had been there for about a year and made some profitable improvements and investments in it so that we would come out quite well on a sale. We listed the house for sale with a real estate broker and flew back to Hawaii.

We started looking at houses in Hawaii. We loved the Kahala neighborhood just around Diamond Head from Honolulu. After spending several days we discovered that there were a number of houses that we could afford and that would be more than suitable. They wouldn't be on the beach but very close to it. It was coming together.

My carpet business was in transition and was not something that I had to have or could not do without. We began to see some interest in the sale of our house.

I started seriously looking into the possibilities for a karate school in Honolulu. There were a lot of them already there, but I felt that once we had found the right location we could have a successful operation in the area.

It isn't easy to move 5000 miles away, across an ocean. There were many considerations, family, friends, business etc. We loved Hawaii so much that we continued to move forward.

Then, just before we signed the sales papers on our home in Woodland Hills, I received a call from Amos. Another buyer had made an offer to take all 5 of the Hawaii locations. Our deal was off!

Of course we were quite disappointed, however it could have been much worse if we had been a little farther along in the move.

We pulled back to lick our wounds and regroup.

On April 8th 1986, I had just come home from working on a large carpet project for General Dynamics. It had been a long day of driving to Pomona and back. I arrived home hoping for a quiet evening.

ALVIN

THE PHONE RANG just as I was preparing to eat dinner. It was Cynthia Prouder calling from Cedars of Sinai Hospital in LA. Her brother Alvin had been shot. She was terribly distressed and in a state of near panic. I told her I would be right there. Leaving Leslie at home with Xian and John, I made the 45-minute trip to the hospital.

Cynthia met me outside of intensive care and told me what had happened. Alvin's wife, Lambie, was sitting outside his hospital room door.

Alvin was in his early twenties at this time. His younger cousin, Michael, was about 17. Michael sometimes came to the Wednesday night fights with us and, although a lower belt, red I think, he was showing a great deal of promise.

Apparently, a few hours earlier, Michael had an altercation with some serious gangsters in South Central LA where they all lived. It had turned ugly and a fight ensued. Alvin was close by and came to Michael's aid. At that time Alvin was the World Welter Weight Kick Boxing Champion and had a record of 11 and 1 as a professional Boxer as well.

The only boxing match he had lost was one that came only a week after a Kick Boxing match, and Alvin had lost his concentration and inadvertently thrown a kick at his Boxing opponent. Alvin was so startled at throwing the kick that he had dropped his guard to apologize and been knocked out.

When Alvin jumped into the fight to help Michael, the scales immediately tipped into their favor and they began to beat the hell out of the gangsters. One of the bad guys pulled a gun and fired two shots into Michael, killing him instantly, then fired another shot into Alvin's brain.

Alvin had already been in surgery for an hour or so when I arrived. Cynthia and I sat in the waiting room, holding hands and waited for word.

Finally a doctor came out to speak with us. He was quite grim. He said there was very little chance that Alvin would survive the night. Cynthia and I sat down outside his room to wait it out.

After an hour or two, a second doctor came to speak to us. He said it was looking as though Alvin might live but he would probably be a "vegetable." The damage done by the bullet and the resulting surgery had removed a piece of his brain bigger than a golf ball.

We were allowed to see him briefly. Cynthia and Lambie were first, of course. After spending a few minutes with him at the side of the bed, while I waited by the door, they turned away and went to the window. As I approached Alvin, I stopped at the foot of the bed and rested my hand on his shin. As I did, without any other movement or sign of life, he turned his right hand over and gave me the "thumbs up" sign. I was the only one who saw it.

I knew then that he was going to survive this in spite of what the doctors said. They didn't know they were treating a perfect physical specimen of a young man with the heart of a champion!

As the evening turned into early the next morning, other friends and relatives began to show at the Hospital. The doctors' reports went from "He can't live" to "He might live but will be a vegetable" to "He may live but will never walk or speak again" to "He looks like he may survive, but he will never be normal again."

Each time they would give us some dire prognostication, Alvin would prove them wrong. The Heart of a Champion!

I spent all of that first night there at Cedars. Finally after dawn I went home and slept for a little while, then returned to the hospital early the next afternoon. Alvin had made further progress and people around the Hospital were starting to use the word "miracle" in reference to him.

It was just getting dark, it was raining very hard, and Alvin was continuing to utterly amaze the Medical Staff at Cedars. They were bringing many other doctors in to see the "miracle."

I heard my name paged over the intercom. When I picked up the phone it was Leslie, very upset: her Father, George, had just been rushed to the VA Hospital with what appeared to be a stroke. I was a good two hours away on rainy freeways. I made arrangements to meet her there as soon as I could get there. I called one of her "best friends" who lived nearby us and asked her if she could meet Leslie at the hospital and stay with her until I arrived. Her answer was, "I can't, I'm fixing dinner." So much for "best friends".

When I did arrive it looked very bad. George died 6 days later, never regaining consciousness. It was a horrible time for Leslie and all of us. George was a very funny and beloved man.

Alvin continued to improve and was released from the Hospital, sitting up in a wheel chair. His recovery was one for the medical books. His conditioning, personality, support system and heart drove him to come back. In months he was training again. Although his professional fighting career was over, he went on to compete in tournaments again and became a great teacher himself.

A few months after the incident I held an "Alvin Prouder Benefit Tournament" to raise money for his medical bills. It was well attended and, I believe, helped to improve their financial situation.

When Cynthia married Robert Temple, a top BKF fighter, I was very happy for them. I had known Robert for several years and have always been very fond of him and respected his ability as a great fighter.

Cynthia is like another daughter to me. She and Robert soon produced a daughter of their own, whom they named "She-Ra," which means "the princess of power."

When they asked Leslie and I to come to their Church and become She-Ra's godparents we were very honored. Xian and John attended the ceremony with us.

When we lived in Woodland Hills and later in Monarch Beach, She-Ra used to come to stay with us quite often. I still remember, in Woodland hills, when she was only a couple of months old, her sleeping in bed between Leslie and me at night.

One time when she was about four years old, Robert and Cynthia had to take a trip somewhere and they brought She-Ra down to where we were living at the time in Orange County. Our home was right across the street from the Ritz Carlton Hotel and on the Monarch Beach Golf course. It was at Christmas time. Leslie took She-Ra into Laguna Beach and bought her pretty new dress .We were taking her, that evening, over to the Christmas festivities at the Hotel.

When she arrived, Cynthia had tied She-Ra's hair up into about 30 little pigtails, each with a small brightly colored toy at the end. It was very cute but didn't fit the new dress that Leslie had bought for her. Leslie decided to give her a bath, and wash her hair out to make a simpler look.

It was Leslie's first experience with doing a black person's hair. As I watched, she removed the toys and pigtails, stuck She-Ra in the tub, leaned her back and began to shampoo her hair. As she did, it started to grow! It got bigger and bigger. It was out of control!

By the time she had finished shampooing and towel drying, the hair was now, literally, bigger than the kid!

We didn't know what to do.

After several experiments, it was time to leave for the Ritz. Finally, out of desperation, Leslie pulled it up into a knot on top and tied a ribbon around it.

We had a terrific time and She-Ra spent a few days with us, hair and all.

ALWAYS TOURNAMENTS

DURING THE YEARS of '86, '87 and '88, while we were living in Woodland Hills, I had a school there. My son Kirk was doing a lot of the teaching with me. I traveled a great deal in my business so he was there when I was not. We continued with the tournaments of course.

We turned out a few good black belts at that school during that time.

The tournaments continued unabated. I averaged at least 45 per year. I almost never turned anyone down who asked for my help.

One of the reasons that I can write a journal like this, besides being blessed with a very good memory, is that I have a calendar system.

Since 1967 I have kept the exact same kind of "day runner" calendar. I make notes daily of where I was and what I did. It's almost a diary. I have every one of them still. I have a note of every tournament I worked on or produced, or directed or MC'd or acted as Head Official. When I look through the calendars the notes bring back vivid memories of the events. I'm so glad now that I started and kept these records.

David Torres and I worked on the majority of the tournaments together. We both finally, David, I think a little sooner than me, burned out!

David and I have remained very good friends; we speak on the phone from time to time. Neither of us is active in the tournaments any more. I was giving inter-school tournaments with Johnny Gyro once or twice a year up until we moved to Big Bear Lake and opened our school here in 2002.

The only tournaments I have attended since then have been the big Stan and Tina Witz Tournaments in Las Vegas, or Mohamed Jahan Vash's tournaments in Ontario. Only then because I have students here who really wanted to try the experience and I love and respect those two men very much. When we go we always do quite well.

In 2005, I was inducted into the Black Belt Hall of Fame at the U.S. International Championships in Las Vegas. Along with the honor, another unforgettable experience occurred there for me. I was acting as the Tournament Director, running the 17 rings for Stan Witz; it was a very good-sized tournament, probably close to 3000 competitors. It was June 19th 2005. My 69th birthday. I was so busy with the Tournament that I had completely forgotten about it. An announcement came over the loudspeaker, "Mr. Fisher please go to ring 17 at once!" I extricated myself from the problem I was dealing with and made my way to 17, that was the main ring, on stage, in the center of the huge room. As I arrived there, I could look down at the other 16 rings and into the crowded venue. I didn't see a problem. Then another voice came over the microphone, it was Stan Witz!

"Stop all the matches!" when it was quiet throughout the huge Vegas room, he continued. "Today is Grandmaster Fisher's birthday, please join me in singing Happy Birthday"!

What a feeling as I stood there feeling incredibly humble, lucky and embarrassed while about 6000 Martial Artists and supporters sang. It's something that I will never forget!

That Tournament also gave me an opportunity to see many of my old Martial Arts friends and students. Among them were Ron Pohnel and Ken Firestone.

Ron Pohnel, whom I have mentioned earlier, first joined me about 1970. At that time, I had my first school that I had purchased from Bob Ozman. Pohnel was a brash, swaggering 15 year old with hair down to his belt and a bad attitude.

His first serious attitude adjustment came at the hands of my son Scott.

I was sitting in the office, there wasn't a view of the mat unless you stood and looked out the little window provided for that purpose. I was speaking to John Atkinson who was seated across from me. Scott was working with Pohnel, who was then a yellow belt, on sparring techniques. Obviously Ron must have given Scott some "attitude" because suddenly John and I heard the sounds of several hard punches and kicks, followed by a loud crash on the wooden floor.

Standing up, we peered out the window and saw Pohnel on a heap on the floor. With a shrug we sat back down and continued our conversation. It was lessons like that which made Ron Pohnel the fine man that he is today.

After a few more of those, he began to come around. I have some great photos of the early Pohnel. One was taken at his very first Tournament when he was a yellow belt, being coached by my son Kirk who was, at 12 the youngest Black belt Ozman had ever promoted. Another vintage photo is of a sparring night at my Tarzana school. Bobby Burbidge and I used to take turns bringing our students to each other's school for sparring. In this photo is an orange belt Pohnel and a young, yellow belt, Roger Lacombe, one of Bobby's beginners. Lacombe has since owned successful schools in the 1000 oaks area of California and is, I believe presently ranked as an 8th degree Black Belt under Pat Johnson as Pohnel is in my system. Lots of history there.

Pohnel went on to be one of the top Tournament fighters in history. At the time of this writing in 2007, at the age of 51, he is still competing and taking first place in the open Black Belt competition at major Tournaments! He had a school in Honolulu for many years but in 2006 moved back to Southern California with his wife Charlanne. She is a lovely Hawaiian woman who is a fine black Belt competitor in her own right. She has many Grand Championships to her credit in fighting and weapons.

Ken Firestone was at the same event in Las Vegas. It was at this Tournament that I called both Pohnel and Firestone up on stage and promoted them to 8th Degree Black Belt.

Ken Firestone was about 13 years old at the time that he and his father walked into my Tarzana school one day in 1971 or 72. They were looking for a school for Ken to start studying karate.

They entered while I was in the middle of a "situation."

I had competed in a Tournament the week before. These were in the bare knuckle days; I had suffered a broken rib. Although I was teaching a sparring class I had advised the class of my injury and was not so much participating as coaching the sparring.

A student of mine, a 20-year-old green belt named Mike Johnson was in the class. Johnson was known for his weird behavior, which was why he was still a green belt after more than two years of study.

As Ken and his father entered the school they stood just inside by the front door to observe.

They hadn't been there for more than a few minutes when I was saying something to Johnson and for absolutely no reason he punched me, hard, on my broken rib! I rarely lose my temper but this time I did.

There was a low divider, about 2 feet high and 1 foot wide, between the hardwood Dojo floor and the little lobby where the Firestones were standing.

I hit Johnson 3 or 4 times then kicked him over the divider where he landed at Ken's feet.

Then, still angry at Johnson and now also at myself for losing my composure, I crossed the room to where an old canvas heavy weight bag was hanging by a chain in the corner.

I executed a hard step across sidekick, and the bag, having seen a lot of use, tore in half! The bottom part spun around and flew through the air across the Dojo while the top remained attached to the chain.

As Ken tells the story, he then took his father by the arm and said, "Let's go back to Mr. Ichikawa's school down the street."

His father said "NO, this is where you are going to learn to fight."

He stayed with me for many years. Firestone and another student of mine, Ed Anders, who is now a 6th degree in my system, became partners with my son Kirk in a school in Studio City California throughout the early eighties.

They ran the school successfully for several years, actually expanding to a second school in Woodland Hills, California. It was that Woodland hills school that I ultimately ended up owning.

Firestone also went on to be a famous tournament fighter. He has owned several schools and has presently owned and operated a successful school on the island of Kauai in Hawaii for many years. He is recognized, along with Ron Pohnel as being the one of the top fighters in Hawaii. Between them they have won the large, prestigious "Tournament of the Kings" every year. My old friend Ted Tabura is the owner and Producer of that Tournament.

BOBBY BURBIDGE

AT THIS POINT I have to devote some time to some wonderful stories about one of my closest martial arts friends of all, Bobby Burbidge.

I first met Bobby when I bought the Tarzana School from Bob Ozman in 1970. My partner John Atkinson and Bobby were close friends. They had competed with one another for years, neither one holding an edge.

At that time Bobby was 20 years old. He was already a well-known Tournament competitor. He had received his Black Belt from Chuck Norris and Pat Johnson. You can't get any better than that!

Early in his tournament career he had gone to Oakland, California to compete in a big event. This is one of the only stories in this book that I did not actually witness myself. However I have it on the authority of several impeccable people who were there, including Benny Urquidez and Bobby himself, that this is the literal truth!

At that time, Bobby did not like to wear a Jock Strap. He would just take his protective cup and stick it down the front of his Jockey Shorts when competing.

He was fighting in the middle of a huge arena in Oakland, there was a clash with his opponent in the center of the ring, and the bystanders heard a loud crack and Bobby fell to the floor writhing in pain. First the referee knelt next to him then his teammates from southern California surrounded him. He was finally able to make them understand that he had suffered some kind of groin injury.

It was up to one of his teammates to make an inspection. They all surrounded him in such a way as to make a wall to prevent the fans from seeing what was at stake.

When they pulled his *gi* bottoms out to look at the injury what they saw was hard to believe.

The opponent had kicked Bobby so hard that it had split his cup in half lengthwise. Bobby's manhood had come through the cup, which had then closed back up on him pinching his member in a vise like grip.

Working out of sheer desperation, his friends, one in particular whose name I wont mention, managed somehow to pry the broken cup open and somehow push his Johnson back through the opening thereby saving it from the possible threat of amputation.

After that Bob Burbidge never wore a cup again. Throughout the next 30 plus years of competition and training he never wore one. He told me once that he had taught himself a yoga technique to protect himself without the aid of an external protective device.

About that time Bobby celebrated his 21st birthday. It was on one of the nights when he had brought his students to my school in Tarzana for a "fight night," something we did every other week.

After the conclusion of the sparring, we all wanted to celebrate Bobby's 21st, so we sent the little kids home and bought a few cases of beer.

My partner, John Atkinson, was no stranger to the brew. In a short time the 20 or so of us who had remained for the celebration were "feeling no pain." I believe that Brett Gold and Van Moomjian were present along with Greg Zem, my sons, some other students and Ron Pohnel.

Bobby and John had gotten way ahead of us in the beer count and were participating in some good-natured rivalry. They were arguing about who had the fastest back knuckle, who had beaten who more times in Tournament competition, who was the best fighter they had ever fought. (John said Skipper Mullins and Bobby said Pat Johnson.) The argument went on.

I have to remind the reader again that this was in "bare knuckle" days. Points were decided by how close you could come with a full power technique without making contact. Speed and "control" were the deciding factors. Much different than today.

They reached an impasse when it came to a disagreement about who had the fastest yet best-controlled roundhouse kicks.

They decided to have a contest. They selected Ron Pohnel as their unwilling assistant in the competition.

Ron was taken onto the middle of the dojo floor. Here he stood, back straight, eyes alertly focused ahead, hands behind his back. All of the rest of us sat in a circle around him, beers in hand, as Bobby and John took their places on either side of Pohnel. I was to be the judge so I took up a position about 2 feet in front and to the side of Pohnel's nose.

Then the contest began. John first threw a fast round house kick at Pohnel's, nose missing by about 2 inches. Then it was Bobby's turn, at least an inch and a half. John took careful aim and launched his second effort, amazingly fast and less than an inch from the target.

By then Ron had started to sweat profusely.

Bobby tried again; from my vantage point it was about half an inch away. Then John, with at least 6 beers in him by now, came within a quarter of an inch with a kick that could have caved Ron's face in easily.

By now a single drop of sweat had formed on the end of Pohnel's nose. Bobby leaned forward and looked carefully at it. He drained his 7th or 8th beer. Then with lightning speed he kicked the drop of sweat off the end of Ron's nose.

Finally they decided to throw kicks at the same time, John to the back of Pohnel's head and Bobby to his nose. John's kick just tapped the back of the head, pushing it forward a fraction of an inch. Just far enough to make Burbidge's kick connect with the end of Ron's nose.

A great argument ensued and it was decided by all present that Bobby won by default since it was John's kick that caused Bobby to strike Pohnel's nose.

We all leaped to our feet, congratulating Burbidge while Pohnel collapsed in a heap on the dojo floor!

Another great story of Bobby and John is the "Dairy Queen" story. One hot summer night, they had just finished working out at my school in Tarzana, California. They decided to buy an ice cream cone at the local Dairy Queen drive in. Some rowdy young men, three of them, jostled John, making him drop his ice cream. Words followed and John started to fight all three of them.

Bobby sat on the hood of his car watching. After a minute John said, "How about some help?" Bobby said, "I don't have anywhere to set my ice cream, wait till I'm finished." He calmly finished his ice cream cone and stood up.

By that time John had finished off the last of his assailants. He demanded of Bobby, "Why didn't you help me?" Bobby replied, "I hadn't finished my ice cream and besides you didn't look like you needed any help!"

Bobby had several schools over the years. My favorite was in Woodland Hills, California. He was there for several years. My oldest son Scott had a falling out with John Atkinson and consequently trained with Burbidge in Tang Soo Do for about a year at that school. When Scott returned, he had acquired some new skills from Bobby. They were assimilated and incorporated into the PUMA system.

Burbidge was the best foot sweeper I have ever seen. He had decided, about the time he opened that Woodland Hills School, that he was going to be the best. He focused on foot sweeping for a year or more. Never mind if he got hit or kicked he worked on his foot sweeping. With a single-mindedness that was one of his great characteristics he worked until, I believe, he was the best in the world. He could sweep anybody off his or her feet.

One time, when he and I were sparring at the Woodland hills school, it was a fight night and I had taken 15 or so students there to work out. Bobby and I had waited till last to fight. For one of those weird, unexplainable reasons, we started to take the contact up. It was bare knuckle of course. At first we were just having fun letting go and then for no reason it turned bad. We started going very hard. The contact was furious. My hands had a slight edge and I hit him with a two-punch combination that resulted in a cut lip and a black eye the next day. He led me into another onslaught and then caught me with a jumping, spinning back kick that broke two of my ribs and cracked one of them loose from my spine. We continued for a minute after that, then, by mutual agreement, we stopped, gave each other a hug and turned it off. I don't remember either of us ever mentioning it again. I think I definitely got the worst of it. That place on my spine still hurts often, to this day, 35 years later.

Bobby lost his lease on that school sometime later. For a while I let him use my Tarzana school to teach his best students privately. John Atkinson and his girl friend Robin were living at the school at the time, sleeping in a dressing room at night.

Between our 100 or so students, John and Robin living there, and Bobby giving private lessons whenever we didn't have a class going, it was a hectic time at the Tarzana school. I was traveling 2 or 3 nights a week, which at least gave me a little break. That situation lasted for about 6 months until Bobby could find another location for his next school.

I was away when Bobby found his new location. I returned from a trip and he announced that he had signed a lease on a big space in a shopping center at the corner of Ventura Blvd. and Topanga Ave. in Woodland Hills. I was surprised that he had found such a space at a very reasonable price in one of the most desirable locations in the Valley.

I think that even though I loved him like a son/brother that I was so happy to see an end to the overcrowded conditions at my school that I didn't pay enough attention to the details of the space when he described them. I had a lot going on in my life at that time; it was during the IOI Orphan ordeal, which, along with my business was occupying most of my thoughts.

He told me that he was taking all of his bags and workout paraphernalia out of the back of my school and my garage and would have his new school open very soon. I was happy for him.

Time flew by I was very busy that next week, and before I knew it he told me that everything was in place and he was having his students in that week for an "Open House and Workout." I couldn't come; I had an urgent meeting in New York City and had to fly out suddenly. I still hadn't actually seen the new school.

I returned two days later; Scott told me that something had apparently gone wrong at the opening of Bobby's new school. I drove the 3 or 4 miles from my school to Bobby's new location.

What I found was dumbfounding!

I knew that Bobby was no businessman. I had helped him over the years many times in that area. This, however, transcended that!

He had leased a space on the second floor. A long flight of stairs led to the door to the school, I've only seen a couple of martial arts schools before or since on a second floor, and they didn't work out so well either!

That was only a small part of the problem. The school was right over a large, successful, lighting fixture store that had been there for years.

The ceiling of the huge lighting retailer beneath Bobby's school was packed with lighting fixtures. Crystal chandeliers abounded, hung from golden chains: hundreds of them. Every time anyone in Burbidge's classes executed a jumping kick, a foot sweep or even when the class was performing basic kicking drills, all of the hundreds of ceiling hung lamps would swing and sway. A few of those less securely fastened crashed to the floor.

It was an unmitigated disaster!

Needless to say the lighting people were furious and had a lawyer on the case at once!

Bobby had to close and move out within days. The fault had to be shared by the leasing agent so I don't think it cost Bobby much money. There was, however, a considerable cost in time and pride.

He returned to teaching at my Tarzana school for a while longer. Then he found a good location and opened a dojo in Thousand Oaks where he remained for a couple of years at least.

Bobby loved dogs, as I do. He always had 3 or 4. On more than one occasion when I had been invited to one of his barbeques, he would disappear. I would find him outside, cutting up the left over steaks and giving them to his dogs.

My favorite Bob Burbidge story is this one.

One day, I'm not sure of the year, I would guess 1976 or 77. Bob and a couple of friends, Brett Gold and Ron Pohnel were there, were having lunch at a Mexican restaurant on Ventura Blvd. in Woodland Hills Calif.

During lunch Bobby excused himself to go to the bathroom. While he was in there a man came in, obviously drunk, and while Bobby was washing his hands the inebriate started to tell him to hurry up and get out of the way. Bobby let it pass until the man grabbed his arm. No one could do that and get away with it. Bobby hit him a few times, knocking him through the wooden divider around the bathroom stall. Leaving him laying there Bobby returned to finish his lunch. As he sat down, in his understated, laconic fashion, he said, matter of factly, " I just got in a fight in the toilet." The others said "Oh," or words to that affect and continued to eat.

Soon the man in question came to their table with two others. One of the others said, "You just hit my brother in the bathroom." Bobby continued to eat, and without looking up simply nodded his head.

The next words from one of the trio were, "We are going to kick your ass."

As Bobby continued to ignore them they became even angrier and attacked him.

From there it turned into a full on brawl. Bobby's friends continued to munch tacos while they watched. Later it was said that it looked exactly like a movie fight scene. Bobby literally mopped up the floor with the three men. At one point he kicked one of them over and through the large salad bar, destroying the bar and its contents totally. He threw one of the others completely through a wall between the restaurant seating area and the bathroom aisleway. It was utter chaos, yet his friends continued to sit and eat and watch, occasionally ducking a body or a flying object. I don't think it ever even occurred to them to help him.

After a few minutes, the other patrons had already run screaming into the street; calm resumed. The three assailants were unconscious or otherwise immobilized and laying in various postures around the restaurant. One of Bobby's friends suggested that perhaps they should leave. Burbidge agreed that it was probably a good idea. After carefully leaving money for the check and a tip they calmly exited the restaurant.

A few days later, I had heard the detailed description of the event from all of the witnesses at the table. I received a call from Bobby. He related the incident again and told me that he might be leaving town for a while. Since he was the only one that they recognized, the restaurant owners had tracked him down and were holding him responsible for thousands of dollars in damages.

It was a few weeks before I heard from Bob Burbidge again. Fortunately he had been between schools at the time the incident occurred. Always a gypsy/hippie, he was able to leave on a moment's notice. He had landed in Aspen, Colorado. It was April or May of the year. He was doing great, he said. He had started teaching in a park in Aspen. Already he had enough students to give him money for his simple needs. After initially being challenged by a couple of local "tough guy cowboys," he called them, he had quickly established a reputation for himself and people were coming to the "guy in the park" to learn to fight.

He was happy and believed that he had found a home. He was sleeping in a sleeping bag outside in the park; there was a YMCA just across the street for showers, a phone booth right next to where he taught. Life was beautiful. He even had a girl friend already.

As time passed and it changed from spring to summer to fall, things quieted down in Woodland Hills. The restaurant was repaired and the owners got on with their lives.

I heard from him about every two weeks, he loved it there.

Then one day in November or early December I received a collect call from Bobby at my office in Beverly Hills.

I could hear his teeth chattering as he spoke. He was calling from his phone booth in the park.

The weather in Aspen had changed abruptly a couple of weeks earlier. The days had turned cold; temperatures had dropped to around 30 in the daytime and

5 at night. There was either rain or snow almost every day. One by one his students had disappeared. He was still sleeping outside but now he was waking up with a layer of snow covering the sleeping bag.

"I'm in a little trouble here," he said. " My students are gone, I'm out of money, haven't been eating much." Then what must have been very hard for him: "Could you send me a plane ticket back to LA?"

Of course I told him it would be waiting for him at the airport. He returned the next day, stayed at my house for a couple of days and started his life up again. Bobby was no businessman. He was a pure *ronin*; his martial arts were never tainted by the quest for money. He spent a large part of his life staying in someone's spare room or garage, working out and writing music.

Sometime in mid 1987, I think it was, Bobby decided to move to Pacific Grove in Northern California, close to Santa Cruz. His sister Kim, a good black belt herself, and her husband, also a black belt, were living there.

Bobby found a place for a school. He called me and asked me to come up for his grand opening.

I agreed and combined it with a business trip to San Francisco, my favorite city in the world.

Because there was no commercial airport in Pacific Grove I decided to drive. I rented a car and left a little too late in the day. That was almost the worst mistake of my life. On the way up, after about 8 hours of driving, the last 3 hours at night, I went to sleep. I drove off the road and came within a few feet of running into someone's house! It was a very close call.

I pulled over somewhere and slept for a few hours in the car. Arriving in Pacific Grove about dawn, I found the dojo. Bobby had built a loft over the dojo floor and was sleeping up there with three dogs when I awakened him.

The grand opening went quite well, a few dozen people showed up and Bobby signed up quite a few students. We spent most of the day doing sparring demonstrations both with and without safety gear. I stayed all day and then went on my way to San Francisco.

Bobby kept that school for a number of years. He and his sister were very close, I'm sure it was a happy time in his life.

However, it was while he was there that he first discovered that he had a Malignant melanoma. One of the nastiest cancers that exist.

He had no insurance and had to go to County Hospital. After wasting too much time, they finally removed the melanoma, but only after it had spread and metastasized into his intestines.

The surgeons that removed the cancer from his intestines were butchers of the worst sort. They removed too much intestine in the first place, and then, while closing the surgical cavity, one of them dropped some adhering gauze into the open cavity. As weeks passed, Bobby suffered from increasing, agonizing pain. When they finally opened him up again they found that the adhering gauze had caused much of his remaining lower intestines to grow together, necessitating their removal as well.

Never completely recovered from the surgery, he was left with an abdomen that was nothing but skin over his internal organs. Most of the abdominal muscles had been removed. He continued to teach for 9 more years, knowing that just the right kick in the wrong spot could kill him. That was a constant source of concern to those of us who loved him. Of course we also knew that a melanoma can return at any time and when and if it does it is almost always fatal.

It was the melanoma that finally ended his life. He always knew it could. He made it for 9 years before it returned in his kidneys.

I can totally identify and understand what he went through. At the time of this writing it has been exactly 11 years since my own Malignant Melanoma was diagnosed and removed. They can return at any time. It gives you a different attitude about life. My doctor told me in no uncertain terms several years ago that I am "living on borrowed time."

At the time of this writing, I have been diagnosed with metastasized melanoma of the liver. There is no successful treatment for it at this time. I am starting a "clinical trial" drug program at the City of Hope cancer Center but the outlook isn't very hopeful.

I was with Bobby for several hours the day before he died. His hospital room saw a long procession of the old Martial Arts community pass through. During the time that I was there we talked about so many things. We were such very close friends. I loved him a lot! I will always miss him very much. That was on November the 24th, 2004.

It has been the same throughout time. One of the saddest things in life is to see those you hold dear pass away as you grow older. I miss them all.

Not long after attending the opening of Bobby's Pacific Grove school, another major change affected our lives.

SAN FRANCISCO

In early 1987, I had taken a position as the Western Area Vice President of another big commercial carpet manufacturing company. Lotus Carpets was headquartered in Dalton, Georgia, where most of the world's carpet is made. The Lotus division of Columbus mills was a newly formed commercial division. The man who put the new division together was Jerry Leifer, an old friend from CCC. He wanted me as Vice President of the company. I looked forward to working with Jerry again and immediately agreed.

I was responsible for developing the western half of the country. I had to hire about 25 sales people, oversee the opening of distributors, offices etc.

At that time most of the major carpet and furniture manufacturers in the world kept their western U.S. offices in the Merchandise Mart at 1355 Market Street in San Francisco. Lotus strongly suggested that I should move to San Francisco. Leslie and I agreed to go.

I grew up in San Francisco, living in the Bay Area until I was 23 years old. It has always been my favorite city in the world.

During my 14 years with CCC, I kept an office in San Francisco and used to spend at least 6 nights a month working there. I generally lived at the Mark Hopkins Hotel during those years. They kept a corner suite for me that I regularly stayed in. That suite became my home in the city. It was during that time period that I experienced San Francisco as an adult. I did a lot of business entertaining. I came to know all of the great restaurants and hang outs. I loved my time in San Francisco.

I have been fortunate to be able to travel extensively. I know Europe well, spent a lot of time in France, England and Scotland, also Italy, Portugal and Spain, as well as a great deal of time in Asia, Mexico and Canada. I speak French pretty well, thanks to 4 years of study in school. That makes a difference in Europe.

Of all my travels, which also include every part of the United States, I love San Francisco the most. In my opinion it is the most beautiful, cosmopolitan city in the world!

So with mixed emotions, not wanting to move 300 miles away from family and friends yet looking forward to being in the most beautiful City in the world, we made the move. Once again, it happened to be at a time in my life between karate schools so I didn't have that to deal with.

On December 1st 1987 we moved into a house on 22nd street in the heart of San Francisco. We had sold our house on Avenue San Luis in Woodland Hills and decided to lease a place for the first year in "The City," as San Franciscans refer to it.

Xian, whom I had really thought was going to come with us, had decided at the end, to remain in the San Fernando Valley with her school and friends. That was a blow to me. I might have decided differently about a lot of things if I had known she wasn't coming. She did visit but it certainly wasn't the same. John, of course went with us. He had just turned 13 and Xian 16. We also had our 2 Cairn Terriers, Rags and Riches, with us to lift our spirits.

Nevertheless, in spite of not having Xian with us, we had a wonderful year in the city. I was in Los Angeles 2 or 3 nights, every other week, so I was able to see her then.

I had to be gone at least 2 nights a week, developing the new company. Otherwise we were free to wander and explore the sights, sounds, the art and the great restaurants of that incredible place.

On Mondays and Fridays I worked from my office at home, phoning and writing. It still allowed free time for Leslie and me to take long lunches at fabulous restaurants around the city. Except for the travel, and Xian, it was a wonderful year.

At first I worked out every day that I was home, by myself or with Leslie and John in the garage of our house on 22nd street. Usually performing a one-hour routine of techniques, forms and weights, I stayed in good shape that way. I was in Southern California usually 6 or 8 days a month. I packed my gear and picked up sparring and workouts wherever I could, at Pohnel's, or David Torres', or Burbidge's schools, for example.

John missed the regular routine of the dojo, so, after looking around the city carefully I decided to enroll him in Rick Alemany's school close to where we lived. I knew Rick from the Internationals and knew he had a solid reputation as both a fighter and instructor. John was a good brown belt then, still I think he benefited by his 6 months with Alemany. John was the only 13-year-old kid in the adult class; it toughened him up a lot.

We stayed in the leased house in the city for only 8 months. The owners had come to us and, very nicely, asked us to either buy the house or move, as they needed to sell it. After pondering the matter, we decided that we wanted a little more space and started looking.

One day when we were looking at houses, something brought us across the Golden Gate Bridge into Marin County. As we drove past Sausalito and San Rafael, we stumbled onto the little community of San Anselmo.

We fell in love with it at once: beautiful homes, a nice little downtown area, and incredible views of San Francisco Bay from the hilltops. We walked into a local realtor's office and spent the rest of the day looking at houses.

We found the perfect place and bought it that afternoon. It was located high up above Butterfield Ave on a street called Woodside drive. Built into the hillside, it was a tri-level home with a big deck going completely around the front and sides of the top floor. The deck, living room and dining room windows afforded great views across San Anselmo, San Rafael and the San Francisco Bay beyond.

We moved into it in July of 1988. We loved it. We had all of the advantages of living in a small town, population 10,000. Yet we could cross the Golden Gate and be at lunch in San Francisco in 15 or 20 minutes!

We soon made some friends, something that we had not been able to do in the City. Leslie found a local "Women's Only" place to work out and I made a great space in the large garage for myself.

A few years earlier, at the Internationals, Leslie and I had befriended a woman who had won her black belt sparring division. Her married name was Eva Spencer. However she was divorcing and soon went back to her original Filipino name, Kalimaya Herrera.

Eva, as we continued to call her, was small and very pretty and owned a small martial arts school across the San Rafael/Richmond Bridge in Point Richmond, California. She had started training under me.

The proximity of her school was a Godsend; I could be there in 45 minutes when we were living in the City, and only 20 minutes from San Anselmo. I started working out there several times a week. Eva is a very talented black belt and presently holds a rank of 3rd degree black in the PUMA system.

The first thing I had to do was deal with a little problem she had there.

Eva is a very good fighter. She is usually the winner of the lightweight women's sparring division at any tournament that she enters. However, she is about 5 feet tall and weighs 100 lbs.

Two local black belt men had taken to inviting themselves to her school on sparring day. Each of them weighed in at about 200 lbs, and loved to use their superior size and strength to beat on her in front of her students. Usually leaving her bruised and sore for the ensuing period until the next sparing class. Eva has the heart of a lioness and never would complain about it. However, she told me.

Soon after we moved into the house on Woodside Drive in San Anselmo, I arranged to be there for the next sparring day. Leslie and John went with me. I told Eva to simply introduce me as her instructor, and leave it at that. I was 52 years old at that time and not that well known in Northern California.

Sure enough the local hot shots turned up that day. I had told Eva to just act normal, don't say any more about me other than being her "instructor from Southern California."

I put my gear on and sat back and let her start sparring with the first, most arrogant and aggressive of the visitors. I let it go on for a couple of minutes. Seeing that this creep was going as hard as he could to the body and obviously really "getting off" on it.

I stepped in the middle of them, without saying a word; I motioned for Eva to step out, and turned towards the jerk.

All I said to him was, "This is going to hurt."

Then I administered one of the worst and most humiliating beatings I have ever given anyone. In a couple of minutes he wanted to stop and bow out. I said, " No, not yet, I will tell you when we are through." I continued to beat him so badly that he had tears in his eyes. When I finally stopped and turned to do the same to his friend I found that at some time during those 10 minutes or so, his friend had packed up and left the dojo. They were never seen there again.

For the next year and a half I worked out on a regular several times a week, basis with Eva (Kalimaya). She was a very good fighter and an expert with kali sticks. Eva instructed Leslie in the use of the sticks and Leslie became quite proficient.

She moved her school to a room above the "Richmond Plunge," a public swimming pool. It was nice enough but because of the humidity it was a sweatbox! Still I continued to work out there regularly.

Sometimes John or Leslie joined me. John was usually in school as it was our custom to train in the mornings. I continued to work out in my space at home with them as well.

We lived in that house in San Anselmo for about a year and a half. It was a nice time in our lives.

I was still traveling about 2 nights a week. What we usually did was that Leslie would drive me down the hill to the bus station at about 5:00 AM on Tuesday morning. Notice I did not say " wake up and drive me down the hill." I don't think she ever remembered doing it.

I would then go to the San Francisco airport and from there I would fly all over the country as required by my job.

TRAVEL

My TRAVELS MADE up a huge part of my life. For many years starting in 1963, I traveled by commercial airlines, by my closest calculations, close to three million miles!

When I was with CCC, I averaged over four flights a week, all over the country and the world. Many of them were thousands of miles long.

I made many trips to Europe and Asia, both for business and pleasure.

When I was National Sales manager for Patrick Carpet Mills, I had national sales responsibility with dozens of salespeople under me, and we had ties with a factory in Glasgow that required frequent trips to Scotland. Almost all of my carpet positions required frequent trips to Georgia and South Carolina.

More about some of that later, but the result was thousands and thousands of hours in jets, airports and hotel rooms.

As you may imagine, I have had almost every kind of flying experience that you can think of, short of crashing and burning!

For example, one time early in my career I was in a DC10 flying from LA to Sacramento Calif. Our landing gear wouldn't come down and we had to make a forced landing on Foam at the Fresno airport. Very scary!

Another time I was flying from Boise, Idaho to Salt Lake City, and our 727 suffered a direct hit by lightning during a ferocious hailstorm. For about one minute that seemed like an hour, we lost all power. We were in a huge black metal coffin hurtling towards earth at hundreds of miles per hour. Then, somehow, by the grace of God, our power came back on and we managed to land safely.

On a night flight from LA to New York City about 1976 aboard a 727, we were hit by a tremendous storm. It covered the Eastern Seaboard, there was nowhere to divert to and we were low on fuel, so we had to attempt a landing at Kennedy or LaGuardia (don't remember which). As we were coming down, the winds were so fierce that first we would be looking at the ground from the left side of the plane and a few seconds later we would see the ground from the right side. Our biggest fear was that one of the wing tips would hit the ground first, cart wheeling us into a ball of flames. We finally landed on our wheels, but the pilot literally had no control over the 3-engine jet and as the 100 mph winds hit us the plane began to turn sideways. We did a complete 360-degree ground loop, just missing a large fuel storage tank before coming to rest at the end of the airstrip.

At Seattle airport, Seatac, one night in 1989, I boarded a plane about 7:00PM to take me home to San Francisco. There was a huge snowstorm in progress. It was decided by the control tower and the pilot that we could make a take off. We boarded at the Gate and taxied to our take off position far out on the runway. Then the force of the storm doubled. We were in the midst of a total "whiteout."

Stuck there at the end of the runway, we could neither take off nor return to the gate. We sat there for nine hours. The engines continued to run providing us with light and heat. However, after the first three or four hours, the smell of the jet fumes began to leak into the cabin. After five or six hours, almost everyone inside was sick. At the end of nine hours, it was now about 4:00 AM, the storm continued unabated. A bus loomed out of the white and pulled up along side the aircraft. We managed to leave the jet and board the bus. We were then, to our surprise, not returned to the Seattle Airport but instead taken for a two-hour ride through the storm to Boeing field, about 20 miles away. There, where visibility was about a half mile or so, we boarded another Northwest Airlines 707 and, taking off in the storm, flew to San Francisco. Since our flight was unscheduled we couldn't land immediately and had to fly a holding pattern around SFO for almost an hour. It was about 9:00 AM. Then I had to wait an hour for a bus for the one-hour trip to San Anselmo. I arrived home finally at about noon. It had taken a total of 17 or 18 hours, during which I had maybe slept an hour and been very nauseated the entire time. Ah, the joys of travel!

I can't remember how many times my flights have been cancelled, diverted, and delayed (usually meaning that you missed a connecting flight).

I have spent countless nights sleeping somewhere I didn't ever anticipate. For example I have spent 4 or 5 nights over the years, sleeping in a chair at Chicago's O'Hare Airport because of bad weather.

Some of the worst ever flights have been across Texas and Oklahoma's "Tornado Alley."

In the mid and late 1970's, CCC was carpeting many of the large Corporate High Rise buildings in Houston (such as the huge Pennzoil Building and the 55-story Shell Building), and in Dallas as well.

I would, several times a month, fly from LAX to Houston to Dallas to Denver and back to LAX in 3 days.

At certain times of the year, flying from Houston to Dallas we would encounter vast storms, with tornadoes under us. The pilots would try to fly over them, but the ferocity of the storm could still be felt even at 40,000 feet. Everyone, including the entire crew, would be vomiting for an hour before reaching the safety of the Dallas/Fort Worth airport.

One time, flying in a small, twin-prop "commuter" plane of an airline that I think was called "Southern Express Air" from Chattanooga to Atlanta, I was sitting by a window where I could see the left engine. About half way through the trip I began to notice a large bolt that was holding the cowling on the engine was slowly working itself loose. As I watched, the bolt was slowly protruding farther out of its place.

There were only about six or seven passengers on board and no flight attendant. I became more and more concerned and finally decided that I had to alert the crew. Slipping out of my seat belt and without saying anything to alarm the other passengers, I made my way to the front and knocked on the cockpit door. "Whadda ya want?" I heard.

"I need to speak to you", I said.

"Gotta wait till we land," the voice replied. "That's what I need to speak to you about," I said, trying to keep my voice low.

"OK. What?" and the door opened a crack. To my surprise there was no copilot, only one wizened old man in civilian clothes sitting at the controls.

I proceeded to tell him about the large bolt working out of the engine cowling. He listened with out turning around, and then simply said, "Holy Shit." Not a comment to inspire confidence.

I asked, "What can we do"? He replied, "Nothing I can do now, better go back, put your seat belt on and hang onto your Ass."

As I turned to return to my seat to wait out the 20 minutes or so before we either landed or crashed, he called out after me, "Might be a good idea to change seats!"

We landed safely; by the time we deplaned the bolt was hanging, literally "by a thread." I suppose they just tightened it up and went on their way.

In 1972, I had taken my family on a two-week vacation to England, France and Italy. In the Rome airport, we had boarded an Air Italia flight to make our return trip home. As is frequently the case in Italy, there was a labor strike in progress. I believe it was the garbage workers. Being a Socialist country, if one workers group went on strike most others supported it. We had boarded the plane and settled in when we were surprised to see the entire crew walk off the plane and shut the doors. Consternation reigned!

It was late August; it was probably close to 100 degrees on the Tarmac. It quickly began to grow hot in the plane, the doors were closed and the engines had not been started to run the air conditioning, of course none of the windows can open.

After about 45 minutes or so the interior had probably reached close to 100 degrees. The plane was full; people were beginning to panic. Cries of "Aria, Aria!" filled the plane.

We sat like that for close to an hour, then without explanation or apology, as if nothing had happened, the Italian crew re-boarded the aircraft and proceeded to prepare for take off. There was really nothing we could do about it but write a strong letter of protest upon our return home, which was, I'm sure, duly ignored.

Once on a daytime flight to New York City, I was sitting in the First Class section, as usual. (Those were the days, long gone.) CCC was making so much money and Jim Marcus was never stingy!

About halfway across the continent, the people on the left side of the airplane began to look out the window, talking and gesticulating. It aroused my curiosity and I moved to a vacant seat on that side of the plane. There on that side was a clearly visible, silver, disc shaped object pacing us at the same speed and direction. The cabin attendants were as excited as the passengers.

Everyone on the plane was watching, it was impossible to tell how far away it was because the size of the object was not known. My guess would be maybe 100 yards. It was more a feeling than anything else.

Speculation was rampant. It was not a shadow or reflection, sometimes it seemed to alter its course slightly up or down or a little faster or slower. Sometimes it disappeared briefly behind a cloud.

One of the flight attendants, more excited perhaps than the rest went forward and entered the cockpit to talk to the flight officers. She returned in a few minutes to tell us that they were very aware of the object and were watching it closely.

This went on for another 15 minutes or so, and then an announcement came over the PA system. It was the Captain.

In words to this effect, he said, "We have been watching this object for close to a half an hour. We have checked our radar, the ground radar from all the near by facilities. We have checked with all affected Air Traffic controllers and the nearest U.S. Air force base. It is not a weather balloon, a flock of birds or any known aircraft. Ladies and Gentlemen, what we have here is a truly, bonafide, Unidentified Flying Object."

Needless to say there were different emotions and reactions flooding through the plane. I was personally more excited than anything else. Whatever or whoever it was it didn't seem to mean us any harm.

After a total of about 40 or 45 minutes, the object came closer to us by about half its distance. From here we could see the classic "inverted cup on a saucer" shape. It did a maneuver somewhat like "wagging it wings" (if it would have had any) and with an unbelievable 90-degree course change, accelerated and sped out of sight at incredible speed!

When we landed at New York's Kennedy airport, everyone on board was still "up in the air" about the experience. We expected news cameras, reporters, and Air Force generals etc. to meet us at the gate. Not So! It was just "business as usual." With no one to tell our story to, we just all went on our various ways; nothing was ever heard of the incident again as far as I know. I saw no mention anywhere in the news.

My other UFO experience is even more odd!

This goes way back. It was 1961. I was living in the outskirts of Sacramento, California in a little town called Orangevale. I had bought a brand new,

3-bedroom house on a quarter of an acre for $5000. Yes, five thousand dollars. That was quite a bit of money then. I imagine that today, in 2007, it would sell for around $350,000 or more. Things have a way of changing.

It was the year that Kirk, my second son, was born. Scott was 5 years old.

We had lived in the house about a year. We were close friends with a couple about our age who lived a few houses away, named, Jack and Geniene Greenhalg. Jack was a young but successful landscape contractor; Geniene had been Miss Sacramento a few years earlier and was a bright, funny and beautiful woman.

When I say a few houses away I have to explain. There were only a handful of houses in the entire neighborhood. Our next-door neighbors, Van and Pauline Walker, had 50 acres and raised Appaloosa horses. There were no houses across the street; it was a vast orange grove. So the Greenhalg's home and a couple of other houses were our only neighbors.

Hold that picture. Flash forward 35 years, to about 1996.

I was, at that time, the Vice President of Contract Sales of a huge Floor covering Contracting Firm called Paul Singer Inc. I had made the decision that I had to stop traveling; I just couldn't stand it any more. All of the similar positions with big carpet manufacturers required extensive travel and I was totally burned out on it.

This new position kept me in southern California almost exclusively. I didn't like what I was doing nearly as much, but there was NO travel!

My secretary had taken a telephone call from a woman who was the VP of interiors of a big restaurant chain in LA. She wanted to speak to someone about a standardization purchase of floor coverings for a large number of restaurants. Normally I would have assigned the call to a salesman but because of the size of the order, the well-known name of the chain and because it was right on my way home, I decided to make the call myself.

The name of the VP meant nothing to me. I found the chain's corporate offices, parked, entered, and giving her secretary my card waited in the lobby to see her.

I was soon escorted into a well-appointed, private office. The woman introduced herself. She appeared to be, an attractive, well-preserved woman of about my age with a vaguely familiar face.

She sat behind her desk and stared hard at my business card for several moments. Then she looked up and said, "Does the J. on your card stand for Jerry, by any chance?"

I said, "Yes, and you look familiar to me we must have met somewhere quite a while ago."

I have trouble with names occasionally but never forget a face!

She said, "You knew me as Geniene Greenhalg." Then of course I knew her. We gave each other a friendly hug and sat down facing each other again across her desk. It had been almost 35 years but we had been such good friends.

We caught up for a few minutes on our separate divorces and life changes and what had brought us to where we presently were in our lives.

She sat silent for a moment and then said something that rocked my life.

She said, "It's so odd that I should see you now, I have been thinking of you a great deal for the past few months." She went on to explain.

"A few months ago I had a very strange, vivid dream. In it I remembered an event that took place all those years ago that I had completely and totally forgotten! We, just the two of us, were standing out in the street intersection between our houses; Louise and Jack had gone to bed and were sleeping. We were enjoying one of those warm, Sacramento nights. It was so dark out there in the country, no city lights to interfere with the incredible show of stars. We were talking and looking up at the sky when we saw it."

She continued, "At first we thought it was a plane, but it somehow looked different. We continued to watch as it approached us quite slowly, it couldn't have been a plane because of the way it was moving, more like a helicopter, but it was completely silent!" She paused. "We seemed transfixed, as it drew nearer it stopped and silently stood above us. It was perfectly round, there were red and white lights circling its outer rim, that and the outline of it against the background of stars made that fact obvious. We were incredulous, I remember saying things to each other, like, What the Hell is that, My God, etc. We were also more than a little frightened by it as well."

Then she said, "The weirdest thing about it was that I had never remembered this mind shattering event for over 35 years, not once! Until the dream a few months ago, I have been thinking I was losing my mind." Then, her voice broke a little as she asked me, "Please, do you remember it too, or have I made it up?"

I must have looked as if a hand grenade had gone off in my face.

I was dumbfounded, and didn't answer her for a minute or two as my mind processed and embraced what she had said.

It was if someone had turned on first a bright light and then started running a film in my mind! It all came back to me with vivid clarity!

I remembered everything. Besides what Geniene said, I recalled what we were wearing, the smell of the night, the sounds of crickets, even what it felt like to be in my twenties. It was if it had all just happened a few minutes ago.

It felt exactly like a fresh memory of an event that had just taken place.

I had totally forgotten it too. Until she told me of her memory of that night, it had been completely expunged from my mind!

We just at and stared at one another for a few minutes as we tried to fathom what had happened to us.

We discussed it then for about a half an hour in the privacy of her office, without interruption.

Try as we might, neither of us could remember past a certain point after we stood and stared at the object above us in the sky.

We couldn't remember going back to our houses, and we never thought of it or mentioned it again until today.

The memory of that night was completely hidden from us for 35 years.

I took my leave and drove home deep in thought, completely forgetting about the business that had take me there initially. The strange thing is, almost by unspoken agreement, we never saw or spoke to one another again after that day.

This has been one of the great mysteries of my life. I have never been able to bring closure to it.

I will let you draw your own conclusions.

Back to San Anselmo.

We were very attached to the house and our lives in Marin County. We had made a few good friends, particularly Rich and Leila Schmidt.

Not long after we settled in town, I thought, perhaps the local Police Department would be interested in my help somehow. I thought of offering free self-defense classes to the officers.

One afternoon I dropped by the San Anselmo police station. As luck would have it the Captain was in. His name was Rich Schmidt, a big, well-built, handsome man in his early forties. We hit it off at once. I explained to him about my life in the martial arts. I ended by offering my services in any way that would be useful to them. He said he would have to look into it and get back to me. We spent a pleasant hour or so together and I left.

True to his word, Rich called me back the next day; it was a Saturday and he asked if he could stop by my house to chat for a bit.

When he arrived we sat out on our deck to talk, drink coffee and enjoy the spectacular view. He explained to me that the by-laws of the San Anselmo PD precluded them from using any outside source for any kind of training. Although he was very appreciative of my offer, he couldn't avail himself of my services.

We became friends during that conversation. It turned out that he had recently met a beautiful Chinese woman named Leila. He told us he was in love with her and would like for us to meet her. Of course Leslie's first comment was, "So when are you going to ask her to marry you?" I think he felt quite comfortable with us when he discovered that we had an Asian daughter, enough so that we made a date for the four of us to go out to dinner that same night.

Leila turned out to be delightful. She was a typically hard-working, and very attractive, fully Americanized Chinese career woman of about 30. We all enjoyed each other's company very much. Our dinners and trips to the city became a regular thing. They became, by far, our best friends in Northern California, with the possible exception of Eva.

Soon after we met and became close friends they did become engaged. We were invited to their wedding. It was a great party and lots of fun.

Over the ensuing months the four of us became even closer friends; we would meet at least three or four times a month for dinner or breakfast or some kind of outing. This lasted for our entire stay in San Anselmo, for over a year.

Leila made frequent trips to Hawaii in her business, which was health-care related. Since Leslie and I were such Hawaiians at heart ourselves, we made plans to go together.

In May of 1989 we all left together for Honolulu. We stayed at the Ilikai Hotel. Leila had to work part of every day; I saw a few of my big clients as well. However most of the time was free and we roamed the island.

One morning Leslie, Rich and I decided to go to Hanauma Bay for some snorkeling. We rented equipment and spent a few hours meeting fish on a personal basis.

We were snorkeling pretty far out in the bay. We had split up and were a little too far apart, which is really a bad idea. It's easy to forget after a while that, after all, you are still in the ocean with all of its dangers.

Hanauma Bay was a volcano millions of years ago. It exploded and a third or so of it, on the ocean side, blew away and allowed the sea to come in. Consequently it is one of the most perfect semi-circular bays in the world. It is quite large and is a wildlife preserve that is filled with all types of exotic sea creatures. The outer area, where the sea enters, has a long coral reef stretching across the entrance. It is a few feet below the level of the sea.

Leslie was following a group of fish and had reached the reef. When she saw it she stood up on it with her head just below the surface. The reef, over the centuries, from time and tide has become extremely smooth and slippery. It was just at the time of tide movement over the reef. She suddenly found her self in a deadly situation. She couldn't stand and couldn't swim because of the combination of reef and current. I was about 100 yards away following some sea life.

For a minute it looked as though she would die there in one of the most beautiful places in the world. Then just as she was starting to take in water, Rich spotted her, swam to her aid and pulled her off the reef and back into the Bay. From there she swam back to the beach.

That was as close as you can get to death without it happening. Had Rich not spotted her and the situation she was in she would have surely drowned!

The rest of the trip was wonderful; it could have been tragic!

One other noteworthy story emerged from our time there on Woodside Drive.

Woodside ended a block past our corner in a cul-de-sac. John, who was 13 at the time, liked to skate board with some other kids in the cul-de-sac.

One day, about 4:30 PM, John returned to the house, minus his skateboard and obviously very upset. We asked what the problem was and he told us, "I was, minding my own business, skate boarding in the middle of the street, when a big man with a beard came out of a house and took my skate board away and back inside his house with him."

A skateboard thief, we thought! Knowing John as well as we did, we thought it better not to leap to any conclusions but to go and investigate the matter for ourselves.

We walked, with John, the half-block or so to the scene of the deed.

We went to the front door and, motioning John to wait at the street, we knocked on the door.

The door was opened by a large, disheveled looking man with wild hair and beard. I noticed at once that his pupils were dilated to different sizes. Not a good sign.

We introduced ourselves as John's parents and asked what was the problem.

He told us that John had been making a great deal of noise in the street in front of his home and using a great deal of profanity. The man had decided he had enough and went out and took the skateboard and told John to go away!

We knew John, and the story, we decided, was probably true. Nevertheless I explained that we would deal with John ourselves at home and could we please have his skateboard back?

Our antagonist said no.

I explained to him that he was therefore stealing the board and we would have to inform the police. With that he tossed the skateboard into the street and said. "OK but if I catch him out there again, I will strangle him."

Leslie was standing just behind me and to my right, somehow I sensed what was coming and raised my left hand just in time to catch her punch in my palm. It stopped about an inch short of the man's nose. I swear his pupils reversed, with the smaller one getting larger and vice a versa.

We returned to the house, a potential tragedy narrowly averted. I decided to call Rich and make a full report of the occurrence.

After listening to me he said, "We know him, he as always causing trouble, he is the Jewish Rabbi at San Quentin prison."

Leslie had almost broken the nose of the Rabbi from San Quentin.

LAGUNA BEACH

SHORTLY AFTER THAT, but totally unrelated to it, we decided for good reason to make another life-changing move.

My immediate superior, the resident of Lotus Carpets, Gerry Leifer, had suffered a mild heart attack, and while he was recuperating the owners of the parent company replaced him with one of their cronies. It was dirty, corporate politics at its worst. It made me very upset; Gerry was a good man, a friend and had done nothing but good things for the company. I didn't want any more to do with the owners after that! It was what I have learned to expect in large companies. Jim Marcus was one of the last of the generous, fair and enlightened owners of a big company. Most CEOs today are selfish, evil scum, interested only in lining their own pockets.

At the same time the owners of a major residential carpet manufacturing firm in Southern California had made the decision to invest heavily into the commercial carpet-manufacturing field. They were looking for someone to start up the new division from the beginning.

After meeting with them several times and working out a contract, I was hired as president of the new division. My new position would require me to live in Orange County, California where the factory was located. We listed and sold our house in San Anselmo, and quickly bought a home in Monarch Beach, California. Leslie cried for weeks, she truly loved Marin County and our house there.

However, she soon began to enjoy our new life at the Beach.

Monarch Beach is a very beautiful, upscale, security-gated development of homes surrounding the Monarch Beach Golf Course. It is located directly across the 101 Highway from the Ritz Carlton Hotel and Salt Creek Beach.

Halfway between Laguna Beach and a short walk to the Dana Point Harbor, it is located smack dab in the middle of the "California Riviera."

Our home was situated at the Monarch Beach Golf Course. Although neither of us ever played golf, it was still a great spot to live. It was a ten-minute walk to the Ritz Carlton Hotel. We had breakfast there, outside, at the ocean every Sunday morning. There was a special passage built under the Highway for residents of Monarch Beach to have access to Salt Creek without crossing over the 101. The homeowners association provided electric golf carts to the residents for use in going back and forth to the Ritz or the beach.

I was about 45 minutes from my new office and about the same to the John Wayne Airport. It was really a perfect spot.

I jumped into my work with great enthusiasm. It was exciting to be able to actually create a new company from the ground up. I started hiring the necessary people; designers, office staff, and key manufacturing personnel. We began to work on the concepts for a unique, new, product line. We selected a name for the new company, Westweave Carpet Mills.

Within a couple of months we had designed 8 or 10 products, selected colors, named them, and started sample production. At that point I was ready to hire sales people. For the following weeks, while samples and inventory were being produced I traveled extensively all over the country hiring sales people and agents to represent Westweave.

Within six months I had a new company completely formed and doing a great deal of business, almost a year ahead of schedule. It was very hard work, but a lot of fun too.

Corporate politics, always present, were the only negative issue I had to deal with. There was some serious resentment on the part of some of the executives with the parent company to this highly successful and profitable new division.

Our life in Monarch Beach took shape. Leslie made friends; she loved the beach and the life style. I was working too hard and too immersed in the business to make a personal life for myself there, unfortunately.

We had frequent, nasty, run-ins with the Homeowners Association. They were Nazis of the worst sort. Interfering with life in the community, acting well beyond their true scope.

Just a few examples, They had a woman on a committee whose job it was to measure the plants in your front yard and if they exceeded their "legal limit" by an inch or more, you were fined.

They had begun to look over the fences and were telling people what colors were acceptable for use in back yard furnishings and for children's play equipment.

The last straw for us was a parking issue. Each house had a 2-car garage and room in front for 1 or 2 more cars. Xian, 18 years old now, was still living and going to school in the San Fernando Valley. She frequently drove down and spent the weekends with us.

The 5-member association board decided that they didn't like the look of cars parked in front of the houses. Therefore they passed a new rule that there would be no more street parking. There was a parking lot at the rear gate, about a mile from our house. They told everyone that from now on they would have to park there.

We were furious, that meant that Xian, or any visitor would have to park and walk a mile to our house.

It was shortly before an election for a new board of directors. Leslie and I decided to run. We joined forces with one of our friends and a neighbor a young attorney (coincidentally, like Rich Schmidt, also married to a beautiful Chinese wife). We worked very hard. Clipboards in hand we walked every street and knocked on every one of the 200 or so doors in Monarch beach. We spoke personally to every resident. Most of them were as fed up as we were with the tyrannical policies of the existing Board.

When the Election Day came, the three of us were elected by a landslide!

Within a month after our election we had stopped the parking issue, and relaxed the rules for the Homeowners association, exactly as we had promised, to reasonable requirements. Consistent with beauty and safety of course, but within reasonable limits for a beach community.

Of course now that we were back in Southern California, the tournaments resumed. I had managed to keep my hand in even while we were in Northern California, participating in, of course the Internationals, and about one other Tournament per month.

Back where the action was I was soon doing 2 or 3 a month again. It felt good to see and work with all of my old friends on the circuit. Between Westweave, the Homeowners Association, and the tournaments I had a very busy life in Orange County. The natural beauty of the area was overwhelming.

We were so close to Disneyland that Leslie and I would frequently go and just spend hours sitting at a corner café in the park, drinking coffee and watching the people, and never get on a ride.

1989 closed as a very productive, exciting and busy year!

The following year began the same. Westweave had taken off like a rocket. My sales crew was assembled and functioning extremely well across the country. Sales were booming. My contract had included a 3-year clause assuring that, in addition to a large salary and expenses, I would also receive a percentage of all the total sales to be paid to me as a bonus at the end of each month.

No one had expected that Westweave would take off so quickly and so successfully. Our monthly sales were growing so fast that it was difficult for production to keep up with sales. Our profit percentages were higher than that of the parent company so that my large and growing monthly bonuses hurt no one. It was a great time, until September.

One day that month the two principals came into my office. I could tell the minute I saw their faces that something was up.

To make a long story short, they wanted to renegotiate my contract; I was making too much money!

To avoid any possibility of legal problems I will say only that it was a terrible blow, which resulted in my leaving, by the end of 1990, the company that I had given birth to and raised to adulthood in one short year.

After the loss of CCC, which had also failed me, this was another terrible blow. I lost all heart for the carpet business. The positions I held after that were just for the money. The enjoyment was gone forever.

What held me together at that time were, once again, the martial arts. I continued to work on two or three tournaments a month, plus producing one or two of my own tournaments a year.

We never know what awaits us around life's twists and turns. It can be something like the phone call that led me to the wonderful Karate Kid experience, or a visit from a couple of business associates that costs you years of hard work and pleasure.

I have learned this: that rising to success in anything is like climbing a rope. You have to keep letting go to reach higher.

We stayed on in Monarch Beach throughout 1991.

Looking through my calendars I see a note I wrote on the last day of December 1991. It says. "I hated 1991, it was the worst year of my life." (That held true until 2008.)

It was a year full of unusually big problems, legal, health, and more. Leslie had a brush with cancer, it turned out to be OK but it was very scary. I had a great many health issues, most of which were related to my Westweave experience. I had to do something, so in January, after leaving Westweave, I took a position as vice-president of a medium sized commercial carpet manufacturer out of Chattanooga, Tennessee. The name of the company was Hartford Carpet Mills.

It was much the same work as what I had been doing for Westweave, except that the product line was already established. I was traveling all over the country, working with sales representatives in most of the major cities. It required extensive travel. In the month of February that year, I was gone 17 of the 28 days. Average travel was 15 days a month. It was difficult and not very exciting.

The "special" nature of having a proprietary interest in the products and people wasn't there at Hartford. I did a good job for them but my heart wasn't in it. I was in Chattanooga a lot, too much. Usually I stayed at the Reed House Hotel downtown, about four nights a month.

I only stayed with Hartford for about eight or nine months. I truly disliked the people there. They had made it crystal clear to me from the start that I would always be considered an outsider. I wasn't a "good old boy," whose Great grandpa died fighting the Union at the battle of Cemetery Ridge.

That, along with the terrible travel schedule, was making me very unhappy. My old boss from CCC, Jim Marcus, had told me that I could come in with him any time; his new company was called CFA (Commercial Flooring Associates), and specialized in supplying carpet to the hotel industry.

I left Hartford and finished out the year running my hotel and other business through CFA where we split the profits. It kept me going.

So 1991 finally passed. There were some great tournaments that year that helped keep me going.

One of the few high points that year was the event at the Ritz Carlton Hotel.

One day I received a call from a martial arts friend, Terry Renaga. She and her son Gabe had a school in Oceanside, California. It was about 45 minutes south of my home. John and I sometimes went there to work out with them.

Terry knew some one in special events at the Ritz Carlton Hotel in Monarch Beach. This person had contacted her to say that they had booked a huge Sales Seminar for a National Corporation for about 1000 people. The seminar was going to last all week. As part of the activities that the Hotel wanted to offer, they had promised the clients a class in Tai Chi each morning at sunrise on the Beach.

Terry wanted to take the job but didn't know anything about Tai Chi and didn't have a clue about what she could offer them. Her style was a very "hard" form of Shorin Ryu. She asked me if I could help her do it. It was a very lucrative job, with plenty of money for me and Terry to split!

My son Scott and I had studied a little" Yang Style" Tai Chi through a program that Scott enrolled in at UCLA. I remembered the basic movements, but couldn't recall all of the forms. Nevertheless, I assured Terry that we could do it and we accepted the contract.

We had only a week or so to prepare so I came up with a very workable idea.

As far as I could find out the people attending the morning classes were made up of almost entirely of out of shape business people looking for a little "California Experience" that could tell the folks at home about when they got back to Cedar Rapids or wherever. That's exactly what we gave them.

On the appointed mornings, Terry, Gabe, Leslie and I were on the Beach first, well before dawn. I had a high collared black "Kung Fu" outfit that I had bought once in Chinatown to wear to a costume party. That was what I wore. The others wore black *gi* bottoms and matching t-shirts.

Each morning at dawn, about 100 or more people would drag themselves down to the sand and surf, many of them hung over, wanting and ready to learn Tai Chi (in one to four mornings.)

What I did was simple. Terry and Gabe also knew a form that we used in PUMA. It was a hard style Japanese Kata called "Pinan One." It was our required form for advancement from yellow to orange belt.

Each morning we introduced our beach students to "PUMA Tai Chi," a new, blended form of Tai Chi created and developed by the Grand Master of the PUMA system to meet the needs of American students.

Then we broke them into smaller groups and taught them to do Pinan One at the very slow Tai Chi speed on the beautiful Salt Creek beach as the sun slowly rose over the Hotel behind us.

The program was a great success and drew rave comments from the students.

PUMA Tai Chi!

My calendar for 1992 starts with "Thank God 1991 is over." Little did I know that one of my worst business experiences was still ahead of me.

The CFA connection had made money, but not nearly as much as I was used to. I was looking for something better.

I had been approached by two partners in the second largest commercial flooring contracting company in southern California. They wanted me to come in with them as Executive Vice President and help them run their organization. They were both entrepreneurial types, great salesmen but definitely lacking in management skills (how much I was to discover), and that was my forte.

After negotiating a very good compensation package I accepted their offer and started in mid-January. Everything seemed okay except for the commute.

We were still living in Monarch Beach; the housing market had fallen drastically and our large home equity had disappeared. We were reluctant to sell at that time and so I began the commute from Hell!

Leslie's mother lived in North Hollywood. So I worked out a schedule where I spent 2 nights a week there so that I could be in the office in the San Fernando Valley. The other days I commuted 1 ½ hours each way by leaving from Orange County at 5:30 in the morning and returning at 7:30 at night in horrible traffic. All of that turned out to be the best part of the time I spent with this awful company.

It turned out that the partners were, I want to say this very carefully, not right.

They fought constantly; they had differing views on everything. They reversed themselves on almost every decision. Each of them seemed to have their own private deals within the company. It was a nightmare!

Practically every week, one of them would have some kind of a tantrum or fit and fire someone that we couldn't afford to lose and it would be up to me to save the situation. About midway through the year, they started to do it to me too. One of them would say, "You make too much money, we are going to cut your salary by 25%." We would have a huge fight, then the other one would get involved and reverse the decision. Then they would have another huge fight. They came to blows several times. One of them actually shot at the other one once! Every day I went in ready to tear one or both of their heads off. It became unbearable. Never before or since have I seen anything like it.

When I finally left the company after 11 months, there was a huge fight over money; they never wanted to pay anyone, and you literally had to drag it out of them. We were in the conference room and I literally was chasing them around the gigantic marble conference table.

I could expand for 20 pages on the events at that place but don't want to at this time. It was horrible! It was just like working in a madhouse.

That year, mostly because of my commute schedule, I found time to only participate in 18 tournaments.

One of the lowest moments of 1992 occurred on Sept. 8th.

Leslie and I had a good friend, a woman named Judith Fernandez. Judith was an Interior Designer, who designed the interiors of major Hotels.

Judith, a single Mom, had moved into a new place in San Diego, with her 2 kids. Shortly after they got settled in they began to experience "break ins." Some actually occurred while they were at home sleeping. Judith had started bringing the kids into her room and bolting the door. She had called the police who had come to her home and investigated and had started extra patrolling in the area. Still, the intruders continued to come. Judith was in the middle of breaking her lease and looking for another place. However, she was actually in fear for her life and the lives of her kids.

Leslie and I had, a few years earlier, purchased two Colt .380 "Mustang" semiautomatic handguns. I also had other guns as well that I had acquired over the years. We went shooting from time to time and were both trained and proficient. We carried the Colts with us most of the time for protection. The Los Angeles area is like the Old Wild West in that respect.

Judith knew about our guns and asked Leslie if she could borrow hers until the danger passed. Leslie agreed and drove to San Diego to Judith's house. Leslie had to instruct her in how to use the weapon. She began by removing the clip and showing her how to empty and refill it. Then she showed her, without the clip, how to chamber and fire it. Next she was showing her how to insert the clip and cock a round into the firing chamber. At this point the first round failed to enter the chamber. Leslie had been taught that when that happened, to invert the position of the gun, so that the "stovepiped" round is facing down and away from your head and pull back on the slide. The round should then fall harmlessly to the ground.

When she followed the procedure, however, instead of falling to the ground, somehow the cartridge FIRED. The slug entered her leg, where it remains to this day, and the explosion of the round, while she had her hand over the slide, blew the entire palm of her left hand completely off.

Judith called 911, and Leslie managed to call me. I left work at once and drove to San Diego to the Emergency Hospital where she had been taken.

She had lost an important part of her hand. Some nerves were gone forever. Over the next two or more years, she went though skin grafts, reconstructive surgery and extensive hand therapy by one of the best specialists in the world.

We filed a big lawsuit against Colt that went on for three or four more years. Something had to have occurred that was a result of a flaw in the design or manufacturing of the handgun.

We ultimately went through four law firms, and ended up with a firm from Northern California purported to be the best in the world. They took our case on contingency, and proceeded to work on it. They hired a famous gun expert who wrote a thorough, and I'm sure expensive, treatise on what the flaw was in the gun that made it misfire in this way. We finally got a trial date. We were expecting a settlement of somewhere between $500,000 and $2,000,000.

On the eve of our trial the Colt attorneys contacted our attorneys and showed them that our "expert" had made a serious error in his explanation of the incident and all of his theory was flawed by a basic mistake he made in the gun's construction. We were screwed!

We had to drop the case, the time limit had run out. We could have sued the expert and maybe our law firm as well, but after four years we were sick of the whole thing and decided to drop it. What a sad discouraging comment on our "Judicial" system. We were RIGHT and we still lost. This is not the only time this has happened. I have no faith in the system whatsoever.

Leslie never recovered 100% from the injury. Her hand, after plastic surgery, still bears a very bad scar on the palm. She has no feeling in two of her fingers, and the bullet was so close to her femur that they recommended that we just leave it in there. It remains in her leg to this day.

At the end of 1992, there was yet another big change in our working lives. I quit the job I hated so much and went back to the commercial carpet manufacturing arena after the first part of 1993 as vice president of sales for an old established Southern California company named Patrick Carpets. At the same time, Leslie, who was now experienced in Contract flooring sales, having worked for me at the last place for a half a year, joined an Orange County flooring contractor called Wallichs.

I managed to remain active in the martial arts throughout the entire year, doing tournaments on the weekends and working out at least an hour every day.

In 1993, in part because of my new position with Patrick, and partly because of the way the housing market was still falling, we decided to move. We wanted to cut our losses and sold the Monarch beach house.

SHERMAN OAKS (AGAIN)

THE HOUSING MARKET was in a tailspin, so we decided to put our money (which was already considerably less than we put into the house originally), aside for a year and lease a place. We found a nice house on Benedict Canyon in Sherman Oaks, California. The five of us, including John, and Rags and Riches, our two Cairn terriers, established residency there for the next two years.

In March of that year, shortly after moving, I started with Patrick Carpet Mills. My position was that of National Sales Manager.

My tenure at Patrick was pleasant enough, especially after the nightmare I had just left. My responsibilities included the sales management of about 25 company-employed sales people and agents. I had to travel again and that was not good; by then I was so sick of it.

Most of their commercial carpeting items were made in the main Plant in Rancho Dominguez, California. However, Patrick had several products that were manufactured for us at a large, old Axminster Carpet Mill in Glasgow, Scotland. I used to travel there from time to time. I had made several vacation trips to England previously but never to Scotland. I learned to love Scotland and its, food, people, and whiskey.

Other than that it was a routine, rather boring job that afforded us a nice income. My true passion remained, as always, the martial arts.

Living back in the San Fernando Valley allowed me to renew my involvement in the tournament circuit. I participated, usually as director and MC, in about 25 or 30 that year.

We were also able to see old friends more often: Benny and Sarah Urquidez, Howard Jackson and his family, Ed and Leilani Parker, Johnny Gyro, Bobby

Burbidge, the Prouders, the Temples, Cecil Peoples, Mike Stone, Pat Johnson and many more were frequent guests at out home.

I resumed a heavy workout schedule and dropped the 10 extra pounds that I had gained in Orange County.

A few words about workouts.

I have exercised, religiously, all of my life! I believe that you can never stop. Especially after your 40th birthday. If you lay off for 6 months or more you can never get it back where it was.

I am, thank God, still in incredible shape now at 72 years old. I teach 5 days a week. I can still do every technique as well as ever. I still spar for at least an hour every week, sometimes much more. Any of my present students can verify this.

I don't claim to be "great," this is NOT my ego speaking! The purpose of writing this is only to pass on knowledge that I have acquired during a lifetime of training. I started working out and training on a regular, almost daily, basis at the age of 7 when I started boxing, and I have NEVER stopped!

When I hurt my right shoulder, I would kick more and develop my left side. When I broke a cartilage in my left knee, I taught myself to fight, right side forward. When I frequently suffered a broken bone in my insteps (as recently as 3 months ago) or knuckles, then I used the other side.

The point is, Never Stop! Keep on keeping on!

My old friend Bong Soo Han, the Grandmaster of Hapkido, and I used to speak at least monthly, for the past few years, up until his recent death in 2006 from cancer.

We shared this same belief. He too was teaching and still performing the same exact things that he had been doing for 60 years, at the age of 73. He would have been doing them at 83, I'm sure, had he not been attacked by cancer.

Don't stop! Adapt, change, alter, if you must, but don't stop!

A word about weights. I know that many of my fellow martial artists maintain weight lifting disciplines. I have mixed feelings about it.

My father lifted weights throughout most of his life. He started me on a program when I was 6 years old.

I have had a love/hate relationship with them for all of my life.

Like most people, I care about how I look. I was lifting a lot, when I was in my early 20's. I bought a "Life Membership" in a company called American Health Studios (they were out of business a year or two later). I was working on a rigorous lifting schedule four or five days a week, focusing on very heavy weights. I began to look like a body builder, my weight was up from 160 lbs to over 190 lbs, it was all muscle, and my right bicep was well over 16 inches. I was bench-pressing a very large amount of iron.

Then, after I had been doing this for a year or so, I had an opportunity to return to some regular boxing sparring. I found that I wasn't really hitting any harder and I was noticeably slower. It was eye opening. One of the trainers said, "You be too musclebound," or words to that effect.

I cut way back on the amount of heavy weight I was lifting and instead, worked with lower weights, and higher repetitions. Slowly my speed started to return, with a commensurate loss in muscle mass and weight.

My sparring improved accordingly. At 170 lbs with smaller chest and arms, my speed was considerably improved resulting in more actual hitting power.

I have continued with my on again/off again weight training throughout my life. Every year or so I decide that I don't like the way some part of me looks, so I will resume weights again. (Never, though, have I returned to heavy lifting.) I will use medium weight and ever increasing reps. then, after a while I realize that I am feeling tired, and losing hand speed, so I stop again.

It is my opinion that punching and kicking power is more related to a combination of speed and technique than to gross physical strength. My martial arts workouts keep me fast, and agile and strong enough to perform the locks and takedowns and the finishing holds that I need.

Throughout my life when I am not actually teaching several hours a day, I have a 1-hour routine that keeps me in peak condition. It consists of the following.

I start with about 7 or 8 minutes of calisthenics and stretching, including push ups (lots), crunches, leg raises, hurdle stretches and more.

Then techniques. I then do every hand and kick technique, 25 of each on each side, without stopping. That takes about 25 more minutes

After that I do all 13 of our *kata* (forms), doing each *kata* once with a 5lb "heavy hand" in each hand, then again with a 3lb in each hand and finally empty handed. That's about another 30 minutes. The whole thing takes almost exactly one hour; it is a great cardiovascular workout and makes me stronger and faster in just the right places.

Do that 5 or 6 times a week and I guarantee that you will remain in great shape.

In 1993, I was able to participate in more tournaments than the previous year, getting to spend a lot of good time with Dave Torres and my other martial arts friends

It was almost 20 years earlier, I believe, that I befriended "Little" Mike Stone. Not the Mike Stone of super star status who had been Priscilla Presley's companion. This Mike Stone was famous for two things: first, he had won the Congressional Medal of Honor in Vietnam and secondly he held several world records for breaking bricks and boards with his head!

I had seen Mike around the tournaments for a couple of years, sometimes competing in breaking, other times in fighting, or both. He was an average fighter, competing in the lightweight division (hence the nickname "little" Mike Stone.) I had refereed some of his matches and judged a couple of his breaking events.

We actually first became friends at one of the strangest tournaments ever held. It was some time in the mid '70s.

An unusual man named Hugh McDonald, sounding very Scottish but actually a black man from the Bahamas, had arrived on the scene in LA. He claimed to be the biggest martial arts promoter in the West Indies. (For whatever that was worth.) For several months he attended a number of local tournaments. He was very personable and made some good contacts in the martial arts community.

After a few months he began to enlist the aid of everyone he could to help him put together a large tournament. He was likeable enough, and before long had enough of us committed to do the job. I was to act as the Master of Ceremonies.

All of the preliminary work was done and the day of his event arrived. He had rented one of the larger venues in Los Angeles, a huge auditorium in downtown LA.

He had a very unusual method of hyping his event. He printed up numerous flyers and posters. He would splash the names of the world's most famous celebrities across the page: "The Beatles," "President Richard Nixon," "John Wayne," "Muhammad Ali," and so on. Underneath, in much smaller print it would say, "Special Invited Guests." Never saying that they were coming, just that they were "invited."

I had promised to act as director and MC. To my surprise and chagrin, as the day loomed I discovered that it was his plan to hold a combination, "Karate

Tournament and Disco Dance Contest." I asked him what ever possessed him
to do such a thing, he assured me that he had held similar events before in the
Bahamas and they were always quite successful.

The day of the event, the karate tournament was a disaster. He had split it up
to be held in various small rooms within the structure, there was no rhyme
or reason as to what was held where. The divisions were ridiculous, perhaps
combining, 6 through 10-year-olds, yellow through blue belt sparring, just as an
example, all in one division.

The breaking events were being held in a large room that had a raised stage.
Mike was competing. He was always a successful public relations man in his
own behalf. He had somehow gotten a representative of The Guinness Book of
World records to attend.

Mike was going to attempt to set a new world's record for breaking 24-inch long
bricks with his head.

The competition began; Mike quickly passed any and all competitors and was
going for the record. About 3/4s of the way to the record his forehead began
to bleed profusely. By the time that he had, perhaps, 10 more stacks of bricks
remaining to demolish, it was a river of gore.

I was announcing and was becoming very concerned; Mike was staggering from
one pile of bricks to the next and losing blood at an ever-increasing rate. We
were beginning to think that he might die.

At last it became extreme! He could barely walk; he was bleeding as if hemorrhaging.
David and I decided that he had to be stopped. We called for an end to it and went
to the stage where we had to physically restrain and remove Mike from the bricks,
his new world record unattained. He fought us every step of the way off the stage,
wanting to complete his head-breaking world's record attempt.

By that time the entire tournament was disintegrating. The disco dancers had
begun to arrive and were starting to turn on their music and to begin practicing
in the space where the karate people were still competing. It was pandemonium!
No one could find McDonald and there were pushing matches and fights
breaking out between the dancers and the fighters. Needless to say, the dancers
were getting the worst of it.

I decided I wanted no more to do with it. Somehow I ended up getting Mike
out of the building with me, head wrapped in bloody towels and still lamenting
that we shouldn't have stopped him until he had shattered the world's record
(along with his cranium).

It was a scene I shall never forget. Talk about total uncontrolled pandemonium. The police were finally called and the event closed down. I never saw Hugh McDonald again. I suppose he is back in the Bahamas.

Mike and I saw each other fairly often after that; he continued to compete and finally did break and hold the world's record for head-breaking. I don't know if his record still stands. He paid a price for it, his forehead is scarred and his eyes twitch.

I still recall his very first tournament. He called me one day and asked me if could come and help him that same weekend by MCing and directing a tournament for him. Three day's notice was typical of Mike, not known for his organizational abilities.

I happened to have the time free and, always a sucker for a fellow martial artist in need, I agreed to come. Then he told me it was being held in a Roller Skating Rink in Reseda, California! A roller skating rink? He assured me it was going to be fine. Out of curiosity as much as anything else, I agreed to go.

When we arrived it was already total chaos. Mike had somehow screwed the time up, telling different people different things. Many competitors were there already, there were no rings set up and the rink owners had just told him that there could be not tape on the floor to delineate the rings anyway. The trophy provider, whom Mike had only contacted a few days earlier, had called to say that they would be late. On top of it all he had just been informed of a misunderstanding about how long he had the rink for and he now had to be out three hours earlier than planned.

It had all of the makings already of a total disaster! I wanted to leave as soon as we arrived but Mike pleaded with me to stay and help. So I did. It was even worse than I had imagined it would be. The rink management were aghast at what they saw, they had no idea what a karate tournament was, when they saw all of the fighting and breaking etc. they wanted to have a dispute about everything.

The rings could not be marked off at all so the events spilled into one another. There were not enough, officials, timekeepers and scorekeepers to run even three or four rings. Another little detail that Mike had forgotten.

The trophies were not just a little late; they were very late, those that arrived at all. So the winners of the earlier divisions had to wait for their trophies. Some trophies never came at all!

I wanted to just run away but I stayed and tried to help as much as I could. Finally Mike made some kind of announcement, cancelled the remaining divisions and made lists of names and addresses of those winners who had not received their trophies to get them to them later. I finally slipped away, praying that somehow I wouldn't be associated with the event. I had nightmares about it for weeks afterwards.

Mike, who is an honorable man, was still carrying trophies with him to other tournaments for months afterwards trying to catch up to those people who earned them and failed to receive them at his debacle.

Years later Mike redeemed himself by giving a very successful, large tournament at the Hilton Hotel in Universal City. I was called in early that time and between us we organized a first rate event. It was shown on ESPN.

I have video of that Tournament. I was wearing a tuxedo and co hosting with Jeff Speakman. Jeff had just recently starred in his first movie, *The Perfect Weapon*, choreographed by Ed Parker, one of the last of Ed's works before his death. There were many Hollywood celebrities in attendance. As I remember, my great friend Ray Wizard won the black belt sparring. There was a hard-fought final with another friend, Tony "Satch" Williams.

A great story comes from that night.

One of the honorees for the evening was Lou Cassamassa, the Grandmaster and founder of the Red Dragons, after Ed Parker's Kenpo, probably the largest martial arts organization in Southern California.

Lou was also wearing a tux and had been presented with a plaque and a speech by little Mike Stone.

We had rented a club facility in the hotel for a private party, held at the close of the evening for those who contributed to the evening's success and some of the special guests.

The party was just getting started. Lou and I and my son John, who was about 14 at the time, were sitting at the bar. (John was allowed since it was a private party.)

The bartender was a very attractive woman of about 25 wearing a low-cut blouse that revealed a large and beautifully formed chest.

John was extremely awed by the presence of Grand Master Cassamassa. John had met, by then, almost all of the greatest martial artists in the world but something about Lou impressed him beyond words. Perhaps it was, in part, the tuxedo.

Someone came in to the room as we were talking and said, "Master Fisher, can you come for a moment to speak with Mr. Stone regarding a small matter?" Knowing this could be anything, I chose to go.

I said to John, "Stay here with Grandmaster, I will be back soon." John said, "Yes sir," and moved over to the seat I had vacated next to Lou.

John was very excited and awed by the opportunity to sit and engage in a one on one conversation with one of his martial arts heroes.

They sat in silence for a few moments, as John waited in anticipation for some secret martial Arts wisdom to be granted to him by the great man.

Lou Cassamassa finally cleared his throat, turned to John and said, "John."

Eagerly john replied, "Yes sir." here it was, perhaps a pearl of wisdom known to only but a few martial artists in the world.

"Look at the tits on that bartender," the great one uttered.

John, immediately stood, leaned over the bar and took a long hard look. His dream realized. "Yes SIR!" he said.

One of the great benefits of moving to Sherman Oaks was the accessibility to all of our old friends. We have always loved to entertain; Leslie is a wonderful cook so we made the most of living on Benedict Canyon in such close proximity to so many of our friends and relatives.

We were able to have Benny and Sarah (Eagle Woman) Urquidez as dinner guests. We enjoy each other's company very much.

I first met Benny Urquidez in about 1969. He was already famous on the Tournament circuit even then. He and my partner John Atkinson were frequent competitors for first place in the Black belt finals.

It was in that year that Benny, and his brothers, Smiley, and Ruben, came to visit us at our school on Ventura Blvd. in Tarzana. Benny had a recent cut on his shoulder; the stitches were just out, that he received in an altercation in a park. I didn't inquire about the "other guy," figuring that there are some things that you are better off not knowing.

I remember seeing them that year or the next, the entire clan, including Arnold and Lily too, fighting at the Internationals. I believe that 1973 was the year Benny took overall Grand Champion. The finals were held on stage, as always, on a Sunday night. Benny fought one of the best, tournament style fights I have ever seen against my friend John Natividad, another of the greatest fighters of all time. I was one of the corner judges that night.

During the early 70's I would see Benny frequently at tournaments. He was usually the Grand Champion. He displayed a ferocity that was practically unequalled.

Once we were at a tournament in Alhambra, California. I was acting as the rules Arbitrator for whoever was hosting the tournament. That gave me the freedom to roam where I wanted, and I wanted to watch Benny compete in his division. The event was being held in a high school gymnasium on a typical hardwood gym floor. The eight rings were about 20' x 20', marked off by tape as usual. I was standing in the center of rings 1 and 8 watching him fight in ring 8. I was standing just outside of the tape so I was within ten feet of the action.

The contact had escalated to somewhere between heavy and out-and-out mayhem, usually the result of there being a weak center official.

I can't remember whom Benny was fighting, but the crowd was really into the fight and no one was going to stop the match and tell them to go easier.

Just then there was a clash and I saw Benny foot-sweep the opponent and kick him in mid air resulting in the man's head hitting the gym floor with a sickening sound. The referee moved in and halted the action and as we all looked at the fallen fighter we saw that he wasn't moving. The ref and I got to his side at the same time; he wasn't breathing either, and no pulse was found. Quickly, without waiting to get to the microphone we started calling for the medics. Most tournaments provide only first-aid medical care, and frequently it is a volunteer who may or may not be there when you need him or her. In this case no one came. We started calling, "Is there a Doctor in the stands?"

Fortunately for everyone, there was. A man came down from the bleachers, identified himself as a physician and began to work on the fallen fighter. He resuscitated the man and brought him, literally, back to life; he had been dead for a minute or so.

Benny went on to be an internationally famous athlete. His fights were legendary. His record in the kick boxing ring was 62 wins, no losses, with 58 knockouts. He held three different World championships in many different weight divisions.

In 1977, Benny went to Japan for the first time. He became a national hero there. He fought and beat all of the best that Japan had, including their all-time-great undefeated champion who came out of retirement to defend the national honor of Japan. Benny knocked him out in the 4th round. After that, he was idolized in Japan. There were comic strips and films made about him there.

One of the closest fights I personally witnessed was between Benny and Howard Jackson. Howard was also a very close personal friend of mine. As a matter of fact they were both guests in my home on Benedict Canyon. Howard always thought that he should have been called the winner of that fight; I think it was his hardest loss. I thought Benny won.

Benny's sister Lily, a beautiful woman and a great fighter in her own right retired from the Tournament circuit to marry Blinky Rodriguez, the middle weight Worlds Champion, and raise their family. Sadly their son was killed in a senseless gang confrontation. Blinky went on after retiring from the ring to gain further world fame in his organization to fight gang violence. Lily herself died in 2007.

Benny married Sarah 27 or so years ago and they are a wonderful martial arts couple; they have a beautiful daughter, like her mother, Benny will say, and now a grandson. Sarah teaches at Benny's side at the "Jet Center" on Lankershim Blvd in North Hollywood. Known as "Eagle Woman" due to her Amerindian heritage, she is a formidable warrior herself.

We have several friends who are married martial arts couples; Johnny and Noel Gyro are another. As are Mark Zacharatos and his wife. Leslie and I taught together for 25 years. Leslie walked into my Tarzana school in 1979 when she was 26 and I was 43.

When we decided to move everything to Big Bear Lake, California, in 2002, Benny and Sarah came up to help us with the Grand Opening of our school. They stayed at our home for a few days. One morning, it was late October, we arose early and Sarah decided to take her early usual morning run.

We live a stone's throw from the lake and our boat dock. The temperature had dropped to about 15 degrees the night before and we are at 7000 feet. There was also a nice breeze blowing off the lake. The result was a temperature, with the wind chill factored in, of about zero degrees.

Benny and I were sitting at the dining room table discussing old friends and war wounds. Sarah put on her running outfit; a lightweight jogging suit and, saying, "See you in a little while," she took off down the street.

Benny and I were immersed in our reminiscences and continued to talk. I remember clearly, after about an hour, we were discussing the sad shape our hands are in. Benny was saying that sometimes he gets an eating utensil, like a spoon or fork in his hand and he can't let go of it. I was extolling the effectiveness of a prescription drug called "Salsalate" that I take for the traumatic arthritis that I have in my hands.

I got up to get some coffee, looked at my watch and remarked, "Sarah's sure been gone a long time." We realized that we had been lost in our discussion and over an hour had passed.

Getting a little concerned we decided that Benny would remain at the house, Leslie was still sleeping, and I would get in the car and go looking for Sarah.

I drove around Eagle Point, our neighborhood, and after 10 minutes or so I spotted Sarah. She was still running, as I pulled up next to her, I believe that she was extremely glad to see me. She had gotten turned around and being unfamiliar with the mountains had become lost! When she realized that she didn't know how to get back to our house, she had done the only thing she could do to keep from succumbing to hypothermia, keep running.

She was frozen, and in a bad state of exhaustion. I got her right back to the house where Benny got her in a hot shower and wrapped her in blankets.

She slept for a while and then they came over to our grand opening at the new school.

A typical Benny Urquidez story is about Frank Dux. Dux is the author of the fictional account of his supposed actual prowess as a kickboxer. He wrote a screenplay that resulted in Jean Claude VanDamme's portrayal in a famous film. In the film, Dux supposedly had gone to "China, exactly where is unknown, and fought in "death matches" in an event called "the Kumite" (which, incidentally is a Japanese word). Dux made the mistake of believing his own fiction. He had a school in North Hollywood on Moorpark.

The way I heard it was like this: Dux had begun to tell his students and others how he had beaten both Benny and our mutual good friend, for many years, and ex-World champion himself, Cecil Peoples, in various matches. Word had gotten back to them and finally they decided to do something about putting a stop to it.

One evening, Benny and Cecil arranged to go to Dux's school at closing time, one of them came in the back door and the other through the front and had a rather physical "discussion" with Dux that resulted in the end of those stories once and for all.

Since moving to the mountains, I go to LA every few weeks or months to stay with Beverly, Leslie's mother, for a weekend. Leslie usually goes every other weekend but sometimes I go instead. I always try to have breakfast with Benny on Monday morning when I am "Down the Hill".

Sadly, the last few times that I have seen Benny have been at funerals. First his brother Ruben, then Howard Jackson, and most recently his sister Lily.

We stayed for two years on Benedict Canyon, the same length of time that I remained with Patrick Carpet Mills. Leslie joined Patrick for part of the second year, 1994, as the architect and designer specialist. That enabled us to spend some good time together.

Speaking of good time together, 1994 was a good year for my kids and me. John was still living at home, and I was able to spend a lot of time with Scott, Kirk and Xian. Looking through my calendar I see Xian's name appearing very frequently. She was living in Woodland Hills, so we saw each other quite often.

Since then they have all spread over the map. Scott and his family live in Portland, Oregon, Kirk and his family in Idaho, and Xian and her husband in Hawaii. Of all my kids and grandkids, only John remains nearby. It has made my kids from the karate school, like Maxine, a black belt and my goddaughter, (just exactly like a real daughter to me), Russell Mannex, my godson and very good black belt, much more important in my life now.

It was that year, 1994, that Leslie had one of her many unusual birthday experiences.

She was approaching her 41st. It was bothering her some. One day a couple of weeks before, we were discussing what she might like to do on her birthday. She made a comment that I had heard her say before. She said, " I always expect more from a birthday, it seems like you should have something really special in your honor on your birthday, like a Parade."

As I thought about that it gave me an idea.

Why not?

This wasn't easy, but over a several day period, I called everyone I had phone numbers for. That was a LOT of people.

I told each one of them that I was giving a Parade for Leslie for her birthday. It was up to each person to decide who or what they wanted to be in the Parade. I asked each of them to call on April 22nd, and leave a descriptive message of their role and persona for the Parade.

On that day we left the house early in the morning, before leaving I installed a new extra long tape in the answering machine. Of course she had no inkling.

We drove up the coast and spent the whole day, lunch and dinner in Solvang, Santa Barbara and Ojai. It was a beautiful spring day.

When we arrived home that evening I went to check the messages, we had 90-some!

I sat her down at the dining room table and after giving her a glass of wine; I played her Parade for her. It was priceless!

Friends from all over the world had called. Each one had left a funny and/ or descriptive message describing their part in Leslies Birthday Parade. There were clowns, animals. Acrobats, freaks, you name it. I have never heard of any one else who actually was given a Parade of friends on her birthday! She still treasures the tape.

Patrick Carpet Mills abruptly ceased to exist, after 30 years in business, when it was purchased by Dixie Mills, an East Coast yarn manufacturing company, and then closed and sold off for its equipment and real estate holdings. It was a typical big-business move that hurt a lot of people and turned many lives upside down.

Within three months, every one of the 300 or 400 Patrick family were unemployed. Many had been there all of their working lives.

I took a little time off and looked for something I could do without travel, it was beginning to really bother me. By that time I had flown almost three million miles! I decided to try the contracting end of the business again and took a position with an old acquaintance, Paul Singer. He owned a huge West Coast flooring contracting firm. It was okay; I enjoyed very much being home every night, even though I preferred the manufacturing end of the business.

Being home every night also gave me an opportunity to spend much more time doing tournaments and working out with my friends. I didn't really need a school of my own then, in 1993 and 1994, because three of my top black belts, Ron Pohnel, Ken Firestone, and Johnny Gyro, all owned schools within a few minutes drive. John and I worked out at their places on a regular basis, sitting on their test panels and helping them out.

THE WOODRANCH SCHOOL

KEN FIRESTONE HAD a very nice school in Woodranch, California, located between Thousand Oaks and Simi Valley, across the street from the Ronald Reagan library. It was about a 50-minute drive (short by Southern California standards) from my home in Sherman Oaks. I started going there regularly. Ken was having some personal problems and was also developing a business in Hawaii.

He asked me if I would cover the school for him when he had to be gone. I liked the people and the place and agreed. I became a regular fixture at that school, and at Pohnel's school in Tarzana.

During 1995, I was very busy with teaching and the carpet business, and the number of tournaments I participated in dropped for the first time in many years to under 15.

That year, Leslie was hired by Shaw Carpets, the giant in the carpet manufacturing industry, and spent most of that year with them. She was in sales and specifications. She worked hard, enjoyed it, and made a lot of money. Towards the end of the year, Shaw made a big cutback in personnel to make their net look better and laid off 10% of their employees, starting with the most recently hired. Leslie just fell into that category.

In the middle of that year, we moved from Benedict Canyon to Woodcrest Drive in Sherman Oaks, a very nice place, bigger and with a pool, which the last place lacked. In the San Fernando Valley there are about five months of the year when, due to the extreme heat, a pool is almost a necessity.

Leslie went on her first of what came out to be 12 so far, annual rafting trips that summer. I never went, not the big fan of water that I was before my near death experience in Hawaii years before.

At the same time that I was covering classes for Kenny, and sparring at Pohnel's, I got involved in helping Robert Temple at his school in Santa Monica. Robert and Cynthia, the parents of our goddaughter She-ra, had been divorced. They were still friendly, both involved in the BKF, and Cynthia sometimes trained at Robert's school.

It was a great place for me to train. I got to work out not only with Robert and Cynthia but frequently ran into old friends like Lenny Ferguson training there as well.

Cynthia was just starting to break into full-contact kickboxing and boxing. She ultimately did pretty well; she had a featured part as one of Hillary Swank's opponents in *Million Dollar Baby*. I worked with her a lot at Robert's school helping her develop better boxing skills.

Shortly after we moved to Woodcrest, Benny called me to have lunch. He was, as always, traveling a great deal, but was working on a project in LA that he wanted to talk with me about.

He was involved in a plan to build a huge "Jet Center" in the Santa Monica area. He was looking at a piece of property that was almost a half of a square block. If he could acquire it, he wanted to develop a one of a kind martial arts center. It would have several rooms as big as most schools for teaching various martial arts, a weight room, boxing rings, and an area big enough to hold a good sized tournament. He wanted me to manage and run it. I was very interested. I would have left the flooring business in a second to do something like that. The plans and discussions went on for many months but it just wasn't meant to be.

A couple of interesting stories from 1995 follow here.

In August of that year, Ken Firestone, who was on a roll in the tournament circuit racking up dozens of impressive firsts, was invited to compete in a new "full contact" experiment.

A promoter was trying to develop a new fight league. It was to feature well-known fighters competing in what was essentially tournament style karate, in a ring, with gloves and footpads, at full contact.

The first big fights for the new league were to be held at an arena in Azusa, California. Kenny, who weighed about 175 lbs, was scheduled to fight for the heavyweight championship. Barry Gordon and I were to be his seconds.

When we arrived, you could smell trouble. The place held perhaps 500 spectators. A few were families who had come from Ken's school to support him, but 95% of the audience were drunk, local, gang bangers from the Azusa area. The venue was selling alcohol and the crowd was buying lots of it.

As the main event, we were scheduled to fight last that night. By the time the other five or six fights were over, the crowd was very drunk and unruly. The families from Ken's school were growing very anxious.

Finally we were called to the ring. As Ken stepped in, he, Barry and I looked across the ring. There facing us was a huge, local, black belt. He had to weigh 300 lbs. He stared insanely at Ken, baring his teeth that I swear appeared to be pointed!

We looked at each other. Barry said, "Do you have a gun?" I said, "Do you want to pretend you are sick?" We realized there was nothing to do but fight him.

Ken, like Bobby Burbidge, was an accomplished foot-sweeper. We agreed that a good strategy would be for Kenny to immediately foot-sweep him to the mat and try to establish some respect.

When the bell rang Kenny did just that. Or anyway he tried to. They moved to ring center. Kenny fired a powerful, perfectly executed rear leg sweep.

The opponent just stood there. Kens sweep made a loud noise and bounced back as if he had tried to foot sweep a fire hydrant. Barry and I looked at each other and said, "Uh oh."

For the next three 3-minute rounds, Ken used every trick he knew just to stay alive. He hit his opponent with everything in his arsenal but it had no affect on him whatsoever. When he hit Ken, it would lift him up off the mat.

Somehow Kenny survived. At the end of the match, we were pretty sure Ken had lost and we were praying that the judges saw it that way too. It had become obvious that his opponent was a local boy and a favorite of the gang members. We feared that we would be gunned down in the parking lot if the vote went Kenny's way. Fortunately we lost and were able to make it out of there with our lives.

There are a couple of other interesting stories from that time concerning those incidents that occur sometimes in the lives of real martial artists.

Leslie and I were at a tournament somewhere south of LA. I had a few students competing and for once we were a little late due to a scheduling conflict. When we arrived one of our guys was competing and winning the brown belt sparring division. We decided to sit in the stands and watch him before going to see if we could help the tournament promoter.

We found two seats, the action was furious on the floor and we were enjoying the anonymity and just being spectators for once.

Sitting next to us was a muscular young man wearing a muscle shirt with some kind of martial arts logo on it. He was being very vocal and demonstrative. There was a lull in the fighting as they called up two more brown belts to compete.

The young man started a conversation with us about the various fighters in the division, commenting on their good and bad points. We listened politely while he gave us his opinions.

One of us said, "Do you train?"

He replied, "Oh yes, I am a black belt." I asked, as I always do, thinking that I would know his teacher, "Who is your instructor?" He replied, without hesitation, "Jerry Fisher."

We looked at each other and I said, "Really? Is he pretty good?" The young man went on to tell us what a great instructor Jerry Fisher was. After listening for a while, and watching our student win the brown belt division, we excused ourselves.

We went to the announcing table to say hello to the promoter, he introduced us to the crowd and asked if I would take over the microphone.

We saw our "student" disappearing from the arena shortly after that. We never saw him again.

Another similar story concerns another type of occurrence, which many martial artists have experienced.

When I was with the Paul Singer organization, only a few people in the company knew about my martial arts.

I had helped a very good friend of Leslie's and mine, Rita King, a very pretty, high-ranking BKF black belt, find a job there as manager of the billing department at Singers. Rita and her 7-year-old son, Leonard, moved in to our house on Woodcrest and stayed with us for 6 months or more, until she could find a decent place of her own. She was a close friend and an excellent black belt. She also helped us with teaching in the early days at the Woodranch karate school.

At some point Rita had told a few people in the company about my martial arts background, and word got around.

Paul Singer was one of the two largest flooring contractors in the west. Annual sales, with about 200 employees, were in the neighborhood of about $200 million dollars. They were the biggest user of most of the large carpet manufacturers' products.

Paul Singer's number one supplier had a vice president of sales whom I will not name. This man had created a legend in the carpet industry about his black belt and his history as a famous fighter. It was talked about around the business. There was even a rumor; started by him I am certain, that he had killed a man with his "bare hands." His exploits were well promulgated throughout the flooring industry. He was described as "the man who defeated Chuck Norris AND Bruce Lee in the same day."

I thought it was very odd that I had never heard of him.

One day, Paul Singer Company and this mans' company held a joint sales meeting at a very large, prestigious hotel in Beverly Hills.

I found myself coming down from my room in the elevator alone with the "famous" martial artist. I was seriously interested in his training and where and with whom he had studied.

We turned out to be the first two down for breakfast so there was no way that he could avoid sitting at a table with me. As our conversation progressed it became very evident to both of us that he was a total fake and a liar!

He was forced to admit to me that he had trained as a child and received a blue belt in Tae Kwon Do. All the rest was pure fabrication.

I decided not to say anything for the time being. I watched over the next two days of the meeting. He seemed to shrink in size and his overbearing, bullying attitude disappeared.

I seldom saw him after that but I noticed that there seemed to be no new stories of his exploits making the rounds after that sales meeting.

A dead giveaway to a faker is this:

When someone begins to brag about his or her martial arts prowess, It frequently goes very much like this.

Jerk:	"Oh yeah, I'm a Black Belt in Karate."
Real thing;	"Really? What style?"
Jerk:	"Karate."
Real thing:	"Who was your instructor?"
Jerk	"I don't remember his name, some little oriental guy."

I can't remember how many times I have seen this scenario or a slight variation of it repeated.

Anyone who is a real martial artist can always name and expound upon their instructor and the style, or styles they have trained in. You don't forget! A bond develops between student and teacher over the three to five years it usually takes to earn your black belt that is unforgettable. Sometimes there may be a falling out or a prolonged absence but you NEVER forget!

As 1995 drew to a close, my involvement in the Woodranch school had become total. Ken was going to Hawaii more and more and finally, one time, he just didn't come back.

I was left with a real dilemma. I had become very attached to the 80-some students, many of whom had paid for a "Black Belt" course in advance. I didn't want to just see the school close and disappear. When I was certain that Ken was not returning, I decided to continue the school on my own, with Leslie's help.

The landlord had begun eviction proceedings against Kenny, so I negotiated a new lease with the owners and took over the school. We carried the 20-some people who had paid in advance at no charge for a year to help them recoup their losses.

It was a nice, big school in an affluent very upscale neighborhood. Our reputation grew and spread and within a year we had many more students. I was still in the carpet business as well, so I was working very hard!

Not long after the school started to occupy us full time, I changed carpet businesses. I left Paul Singer when they merged with the other major player in the industry, MSA, out of San Francisco. The merger made them the biggest flooring contractor in the world. I had enough of big corporations by that time and left to become vice president of sales and to run the flooring division for the largest Herman Miller office furniture dealer in Southern California, T.W. McAllister Inc.

McAllister was located in Calabasas, California. At the same time as I started there, we moved to a very nice part of the north end of the San Fernando Valley, called Porter Ranch. We had a lovely home there which was 20 minute to either PUMA Karate in Woodranch, or to my office in Calabasas.

1996 saw a further decrease in my tournament participation. Like David Torres, I was by then getting really burned out. With the aid of my records in my calendars, I computed that, including the Karate Kid Tournaments, over the years from 1970 until 1996 I had been heavily involved, either as the Promoter, the Director, the Head Official, or Master of Ceremonies, in more than 1200 Tournaments. Except for maybe, David Torres, I have never heard of any one else coming close to that number.

I could do them with my eyes closed; I had my big red footlocker that many people were quite familiar with. Inside of it was everything you need to do a karate tournament except a venue and trophies.

Clipboards, elimination sheets, line-up sheets, stopwatches, walkie-talkies, first aid kit, pencils and sharpeners, sponges for the timekeepers to throw into the ring when time is called. Tape for marking the rings, a tape measure. A bullhorn in case the sound system was inadequate. Everything! If someone said, "I have rented a location and have the trophies and some helpers to tape and keep score and time," I could show up with my big red box and do all the rest.

I just did it too many times. I could do them in my sleep, and did, in dreams. I realized that the time had come to phase out. Once in a great while after that, as a special favor to an old friend, I would do one but they became few and far between.

For the next few years the only regular tournament activity for us was the once or twice a year we would have an intramural tournament with Johnny and Noel Gyro for our two schools and a few others. For example, Jodi Sasaki would always bring some students, as would Joey Escobar and Roger Lacombe.

Johnny Gyro is one of my "sons" and we always looked forward to the camaraderie and friendship that we shared with him and Noel at our joint tournaments. Of course we trust them implicitly, which is essential when you partner on any kind of a business venture.

The year that Johnny won the Internationals I was, as always, the center referee for the finals. As usual it was Sunday night at the Long Beach Arena. There was a crowd of 5 or 6 thousand assembled.

The eliminations had been hard fought and the two remaining fighters were Johnny Gyro and Billy Blanks.

The rules were clear and the same as they had been all day: moderate to hard contact to the body and light, controlled contact to the head and face. The same as it always has been at the Internationals, and especially in my ring!

The finals consisted of 3 rounds of 2 minutes each, with a running total of all the points selecting the winner.

For the first two rounds it was very close; Billy was slightly ahead.

Then in the third and final round something strange happened. I was right in the middle of the action and to this day I can't say what caused it. The two were in a heated exchange of punches and kicks when I saw a look come over Billy's face, a look of pure anger. He brought a punch from his right side with full and deadly intent and it connected with Johnny's jaw.

They told me later that you could hear Johnny's jaw break in the top rows of the arena. It was a terrifically loud, sharp crack!

Of course I stopped the match immediately! A doctor was called into the ring; Johnny's jaw was badly broken!

Remember the gloves that were used in those days had almost no padding; they were intended only to protect the hands of the puncher. They were not meant to protect the opponent. That, and the entire history of tournament karate, prohibited heavy, full contact to the face and head. Every black belt knows that!

I disqualified Billy Blanks.

To say he didn't take it well is a gross understatement. He was livid! He loudly and vehemently, challenged my decision. I motioned for him to return to his mark and in front of all of the assemblage I made the rounds to the four corner judges, some of the best in the world, every one of them both fighters and instructors. It was unanimous! All of them indicated, with their flags, for all to see, that they voted for disqualification.

Billy was still furiously disagreeing. Then…

Mr. Parker, the man himself, walked up onto the stage. Out of the purest respect, everyone in the arena, including Billy, fell quiet. Mr. Parker stood silently for a few seconds then loudly announced, as he pointed his forefinger directly at Billy Blanks, "Disqualified."

Billy and I had been friendly before that, we used to joke with each other about the fact that his daughter was White and mine was Asian.

He never forgave me for that night; we saw each other a few times after that. Even though my wife and our good friend, and another BKF black belt, Johanna Williams, attended some of his very early "Tae Bo" classes, however it was never the same between us.

Johnny and I have remained close throughout the 27 years we have known each other. It took a long time for his jaw to fully recover.

One thing that Leslie and I have done for many years is to have a "New Years Day Brunch" at our home.

January 1st, 1997 was no exception. Our plan is simple. We invite a great many people in mid December. We ask for an RSVP. Once we have a pretty firm fix on the guest list, we order the food and drink. Almost all of our homes have been "party houses" since we do a great deal of entertaining. The house in Porter Ranch was perfect.

We schedule the brunch from 10:00 AM until 3:00 PM. Even if you were out very late the night before, you probably have to eat within that time frame. Our normal fare is croissants, quiche, strawberries, bacon, sausage, coffee, tea, juice and champagne and wine. It is usually a big success. We have been doing it for 25 years.

That year, 1997, we had 120 people in and out of the house. It was a great one!

We had a housekeeper for quite a few years named Sonia Ramirez. She was a nice woman and a trusted housekeeper. She loved our dogs, which is a key element for us.

That year we found out that for years, Sonia had been taking credit for making all of the food for the New Years day brunches. She would always come to help serve and clean up. We heard from several guests that year that we were so lucky to have her, not only did she keep the house immaculately but she could also bake croissants and quiche. Very funny!

DOGS

I LOVE DOGS. I think that if there such things as angels, dogs are they.

One of the only times I ever really hurt anyone outside of a mat or a ring or a tournament was over a dog. I was present when a biker type was seriously mistreating a dog. I wound up injuring him severely. Fortunately the two witnesses hated him as much as I did and told me to get away and they would give the paramedics and police a false description of me. I guess they did. That was a number of years ago and I never heard any more about it.

I have never in my life been without a dog, usually two. They are my best friends, and constant, loving companions. They offer true unconditional love, which is what I give them in return.

For 17 years, from the early/mid '80s to the turn of the century, we lived with two Cairn terriers. (Like "Toto" in the Wizard of Oz). They were multicolored, gray and brown and weighed about 20 lbs each.

Rags and Riches were their names. We loved them as our own children. Rags came first and Riches a year later. Rags was my special love. They went with us from Encino to Woodland Hills, San Francisco, San Anselmo, Monarch Beach, Sherman Oaks, Porter Ranch, and Woodranch.

They ate with us, slept with us and went wherever they could with us. At night I always fell asleep holding on to Rags' tail or foot.

When Rags was 15, he was getting so old. He had cataract surgery when he was 11. That had given him 4 more years of sight but it was fading again and this time there was nothing that could be done about it.

Leslie heard about the famous "Pet Psychic," Lydia Hibby. She is world-famous. She has written several books and has treated thousands of animals throughout her career. She is famous for having been called in when all else has failed, to consult with multi-million dollar race horses who are ill and can not be diagnosed by conventional means. She has a verified, almost 100% success rate. She communicates with them telepathically and is then able to tell the owners and vets precisely what is wrong with them. Big zoos around the world make use of her services regularly as well. She is the real thing!

As a birthday present for me, Leslie arranged for Rags and me to meet with Hibby for a session. We drove out to where she was working; it was on our way to our cabin in Big Bear. We were ushered into her presence, Leslie, Rags, Riches and me, for a half an hour.

What happened profoundly affected my thinking on several subjects.

Lydia sat facing the dogs and us. After we introduced everyone she sat quietly for a minute looking at Rags.

She proceeded to tell us things that Rags was "saying" to her. We were totally dumbfounded!

The things she told us were SO specific to just Rags and us. It wasn't some generalized gobbledygook like "He likes a bone," "He likes a ride or a ball." It was SPECIFIC!

She said things like this; "He wants me to tell you that the reason he doesn't want to sleep on the bed with you anymore is that he can't see the edge of the bed and is afraid of falling off. That's why he started sleeping under your side of the bed lately." Then, "He wants you to know that the reason he doesn't want his peanut butter at bedtime any more is because it is getting too hard for him to swallow," and "He still likes to walk around the edges of the patio for exercise, he knows the area and doesn't run into things," and on and on. Specific things that would only apply to us and not to anyone else. Who else gives their dog a bite of peanut butter every night? Rags had just started 2 or 3 weeks earlier sleeping under my side of the bed. Everything she said for a half an hour was right on the money!

We were astounded and amazed to say the least. As we were about to leave at the end of our session, she said, "You know he has been with you before?" I was surprised and asked for clarification. She said, "Sometimes they are with you 2 or more times in your lifetime." She "listened" to Rags for a minute more and said, " It has always bothered him quite a bit that the last time he was with you he was huge, like 150 lbs or more and had stripes. This time he is so small."

My last best friend for 10 years, Garm, was a 160 lb, brindle-striped Great Dane. There was NO way she could have known that!

That was too much. I asked her if Rags and I might meet again, she said "It's very likely that, if you look for one another, you may be together again."

We had taped the interview; we went over it again and again. We were shocked to say the least. For the $100 we paid her it is not possible that someone could have spied us out and even then they wouldn't have known all of the dozens of things that she talked about that were private between our dogs and us.

From then on I would frequently say to Rags, "We will meet again in the next life, you and I. No matter what or how."

He died 2 years later at 17 years old. I grieved horribly. It was one of the worst-ever experiences of my life. I took some consolation in the hope that we might meet again.

Rags died in August. The following October of 2000, we were making our regular, every other weekend, trip to our house in Big Bear. We had bought this cute little house as an investment, and get away place, with a half an idea that we might want to live in Big Bear some day.

As we were driving through the desert just west of Victorville, we saw a sign that said "Cairn Terrier Puppies." I slammed on the brakes and turned onto a dirt road. After a couple of minutes we came to a house and kennel in the desert. We pulled up to a gate in a fence around the house and heard a lot of Cairns barking. A pleasant woman in her fifties came out of the house and greeted us. We explained that we might be looking for a cairn puppy; she asked us in.

As we entered and sat down in the house, she explained that she had been breeding Cairn terriers for many years, both as pets and for show. We asked if she had any we could see now.

She said, "Sorry but I don't have any available at the moment. I have a litter in the next room but they are only 2 weeks old." I asked, "Can we see them?" She agreed and showed us to them.

There in the corner of the dining room was a whelping box. In it was a pretty, blonde, Cairn mommy named "Tootsie" and six tiny puppies.

I knelt down to see them better, and one of the males SAT UP. We were all three struck dumb for a few seconds. She said, "I've never seen anything like that in all my years of breeding dogs!" Then the tiny guy half walked and half crawled to where Leslie and I were sitting on the floor. He came right to us; we picked him up and held him. He covered us with kisses.

The breeder said, "My God I've never seen a puppy that age KISS any one that way either."

I explained, although perhaps she thought I was crazy, about Lydia Hibby and Rags.

Leslie and I KNEW it was Rags back again. Rags sat up ALL the time, more than any dog I have ever known. Any time he wanted anything or was interested in anything he sat up!

We knew that this was Rags, back again!

We marked his toenail with nail polish to be able to always recognize him on our frequent visits. Then, finally, we picked him up about 4 weeks later. We wanted a Scottish name for him to honor his heritage. (We had decided against "Rags" again.)

We named him DUNCAN after the king of Scotland best known in "Macbeth." He looks and acts exactly as he did as Rags.

Duncan is 8 years old at the time I am writing this. He has proven to be Rags again in a hundred different ways. Including where he sleeps and his love for Peanut Butter, his favorite toys, and games too. Leslie and I frequently say to him "When you were Rags you used to do that same thing!"

Six years ago I felt that Duncan needed a companion. Since we live in the mountains now, at 7000 feet in a forest beside a lake we have lots of wild animals.

My concern was that Duncan, being a terrier, would try to fight anything! I have a large, 60-foot long cyclone fenced dog run that can be accessed through a "doggie door" in my den. The coyotes, some of them more than 50 lbs, would come up to the cyclone fence wanting to eat him and Duncan wanted to fight them. Not good!

I decided to do some serious research on dogs as a companion for Duncan. After a great deal of study I decided on an Airedale. They were bred in Scotland and northern England specifically to kill predators, including wolves.

One of my good friends from the MMA, Irv Bounds, told me that his father, many years ago, bred pit bulls for fighting (he has since seen the evil of it and stopped.) However, his father told him the ONE dog he would never let his pits fight was an Airedale. They killed his dogs every time.

When I went to pick up my Airedale puppy, she was 6 weeks old and I drove to Northern California to get her. The breeder advertised "Big, Calm Airedales." Just what I wanted.

I met her and her mother, a 65-lb beauty named Molly. Molly's ear was all taped up. I asked the breeder why and she told me the story.

The night before they heard a pack of coyotes very close to the house. (They lived on 20 acres in the hills.) Molly took off in the dark and came back later with her ear torn up. The next morning they went out for a look and found three dead coyotes.

I wanted a good name for my puppy, something to go with Duncan. I, as usual, called my son Scott. I asked "Did Duncan, the real life person made famous in Macbeth, have a wife? Scott replied without hesitation, Yes, "Sybil Fitz-Seward." So SYBIL it was.

She has proved to be everything I wanted and more.

She weighs 90 lbs of muscle; she is sweet, loving and brave. On our walks in the mountains over the last five years, we have been attacked several times by stray dogs. They always go after 20-lb. Duncan. Sybil won't stand for that and has dispatched the following adversaries: a German Shepherd, a pit bull, a Dalmatian, a chow and a big mixed breed. I never let her kill or badly injure any of them but they have all departed the worse for the experience and in considerable pain.

Duncan and Sybil are my constant companions. They sleep with me and are full of unconditional love. They are like my children.

INJURIES

IN JANUARY OF 1997 I broke my left thumb at the joint nearest the palm. Either a left hook or ridgehand that inadvertently struck an elbow. One of the dangers of going fast with inadequate hand protection. It is still crooked.

You can't spend a life fighting and escape injury. Most of my injuries came during the early, bare-knuckle days. However some came from sparring and doing breaking. I still spar for hours every week but have stopped doing breaking. The old-style training contributed to the injuries as well. For example, in the '60s we used to slam full force punches for hours into *makiwara* boards to toughen and kill the nerve endings in our knuckles. I have no feeling in the knuckles of my right hand. They are huge and hard and when I hit something with them, it's like hitting with a hammer.

I have, broken, cracked, dislocated or badly bruised my hands and feet countless times. Sometime around my 68th birthday, my hands began to hurt more than usual. I saw a doctor, who after examining and X-raying my hands told me that I have traumatic arthritis, and prescribed a drug called "Salsalate" that helps considerably. About two years later I started having persistent pains in my feet and ankles, saw a podiatrist, same thing. The X-rays are full of areas showing healed breaks.

My weakest point and where I suffered frequent injuries are my ribs. I have broken over 20 broken ribs in my career. In the '80s I had a number of them; at that time I sought medical advice to see it there was a reason that I had so many. After seeing several medical people the majority opinion was that my ribs are a tiny bit thinner than that of the average person. That's why they break a little easier.

Bobby Burbidge broke two at once one night at his school with a, jumping spinning back kick.

Bill Wallace cracked my cheekbone. I had my coccyx (tailbone) broken from a badly-aimed kick. Numerous cracks in my shins. Nose broken twice: once from boxing and the other time in a bare-knuckle tournament.

My shoulders have also suffered a number of injuries and a dislocation or two over the years. Chong Lee cracked a bone in my right shoulder with an ax kick. I take glucosamine with MSM and chondroitin for that; it helps. I think I have also just worn out my rotator cuffs from almost 65 years of punching millions of times.

I tore the Y-shaped ligament in my left hip at the top of the femur. That was 25 years ago and it never healed completely. I tore the meniscus in one knee and broke the cartilage in the other. They have both healed nicely due to my following Bill Wallace's advice in training the muscles to compensate for the injuries. No knee surgery for me.

I was hit once directly in the throat by an elbow that resulted in a near death experience and a fractured larynx. The only reason I didn't die then and there is that I had lungs full of air and I forced out a *kiai* that reopened my closed air passage. The emergency room doctor said it looked as though I had been in a bad automobile accident. It changed my voice permanently. I had at one time been a good singer but as a result of this incident I lost all of the higher ranges.

I suffer from a disorder called BPPV (Benign Paroxysmal Positional Vertigo) from blows to the head. It means you get dizzy if you lay your head flat or look up. A common name for it is "top shelf" syndrome. It is caused from damage to the inner ear: boxing, most likely. No doubt from the same cause I also have tinnitus, a constant buzzing, like the sound of high tension electric wires, in my ears. Probably from boxing.

Every morning when I get up and every night when I go to bed, I ingest what I call a "slammer." It consists of one extra strength Tylenol, three 200mg ibuprofens, and an aspirin. Several doctors, including a pain management specialist, have written me prescriptions for extra-strength Vicodin, but I don't take it. I have presently, a box full of bottles of it; God knows what the street value would be. I just, even at my age, don't want to take heavy-duty drugs.

I have one only false tooth, in the lower front, a result of a bare-knuckle punch that split my tooth down the middle.

I had a number of cuts over my eyes and eyelids that gave me a good excuse to have my eyes done a few years back. The scar tissue and muscle cuts were causing the outsides of my eyelids to droop. Consequently, I was losing my peripheral vision so my health insurance paid for a blethoplasty.

Maybe the worst injuries of all were to my retinas. When I was about 63 or 64, I had to have both retinas reattached by laser surgery. Within a few months, they were detaching and I was starting to go blind. I had both of them fixed. Recently I saw an ophthalmologist for a check up and, thank God, they seem to be fine. I do have some occasional slightly blurred vision, which is apparently due the very early stages of cataracts. This may require surgery in 5 or so years. It is, however, probably not injury related.

A doctor told me a few years ago that my X-rays looked like those of a man who had been an abused child and grew up to be a rodeo cowboy.

On the other hand, although I am 72 years old, my musculature, blood pressure, athletic ability, flexibility, speed, reflexes and endurance are that of a 40 year old. (I only wish my face was).

So the reason for my writing all of this is to make a point.

I would do it all over again!

I have paid a high price with traumatic injuries. However, I think it has been worth every single one of them to be in the kind of condition that I am now.

I teach five days a week, still kick better and stronger that any of my young black belts, can spar for an hour at a time non-stop, and almost never be hit. Can still handle anyone that steps on the mat with me.

I'm not bragging! The point is this.

Don't ever stop! Keep working out, every day do something! If you hurt your left hand, punch with your right. If you hurt your right knee, kick with your left. Keep going, no matter what. Don't ever stop! Don't quit!

MORE STORIES

In March of 1997 Leslie was involved in a bad car accident on the 101 Freeway on her way to teach at the Woodranch school. A passerby called me on Leslie's cell phone and I was on the scene in minutes. Her car was seriously damaged and her injuries resulted in permanent TMJ damage to her jaw. The other driver was woman who had just had a face-lift and was going to see her doctor for a one-week check up and was loaded on painkillers. Traveling in the same direction, she came across the line and hit Leslie's Eclipse behind the back right fender and knocked her into a solid cement divider at 65 miles per hour.

We sued of course, and of course we lost. I have no faith whatsoever in our judicial system!

Speaking of pigeons, or was I?

In any case, I have some weird pigeon stories.

Once when Leslie and I were staying at the Sheraton Waikiki in Honolulu, we had a wonderful room with an incredible view of Waikiki Beach and Diamond Head from our lanai on the 20th floor. We were sitting, early one evening, on two chaise lounges watching the sun sinking in the west over the yacht Harbor.

One of us had been eating a banana and a small piece of it had somehow fallen and remained on the railing around the edge of the lanai. As we looked on, a white and tan pigeon landed on the railing and began walking towards the banana. As we watched he strutted towards it, stepped on it with one foot and, as it slipped out from underneath him he fell backwards, flapping and squawking in total disarray and very embarrassed.

On another occasion we were driving into the old Sherman Oaks Galleria Mall. We were going up to the entry, there were several pigeons walking around. I had come to a complete stop and just as I took my parking pass, the gate lifted and as I started to move forward one of the pigeons walked right in front of and under my right rear tire and exploded with a loud Pop as we rolled over him.

We decided that it was a suicide.

Lastly, while we were living in Porter Ranch, it was my habit, every morning, to take my coffee out onto our covered patio and feed a huge assemblage of creatures. It was like a scene from Bambi!

I would have, squirrels, chipmunks, mice, rabbits and usually about 30 or 40 birds there for breakfast.

One morning, it was cold and the sun was just coming up. I was feeding my friends and drinking coffee.

I heard a loud fluttering and a tan and white pigeon (again) flew down, under the patio cover where I was sitting and landed ON my head. I sat very still, after a while he showed no sign of leaving. I could hear Leslie in the house. I began quietly and without moving to call her. Somehow she heard me and came to see what I wanted.

She saw my guest, went back into the den and brought the video camera. She taped the event for several minutes.

Finally, my friend, I think, having warmed himself up sufficiently, flew away. We have the whole thing on tape. Weird!

I mentioned earlier about going to our house in Big Bear.

I had owned a house at Big Bear Lake for a few years starting in about 1972. I loved it there but circumstances changed, Scott and Kirk lost interest in it, and I sold it.

Leslie loved the mountains, so in our early years together we would sometimes take Xian and John and rent a house in Big Bear for long weekends.

In 1997 we decided to buy a place for ourselves. After looking for a while we found a nice little 3-bedroom, 2-bath house in the nicest neighborhood in town, Eagle Point, and in September of that year, we bought it.

We tried to go up at least 2 weekends a month. We kept it for several years. During that time we continued to fall more in love with the mountains and Big

Bear. It seemed more and more like the place we would like to settle. Less than 2 hours to Los Angeles, it is a resort community, so that although only having 18,000 year round residents it had facilities, restaurants etc. to accommodate the 100,000 who are sometimes there.

1998 brought new challenges.

The school was going very well, we now had about 150 students and were growing. My work at McCallister was OK except for the fact that Tom McCallister was the living embodiment of the unrepentant Ebenezer Scrooge, in every way. Never have I personally known any one so like that fictional character, as is Tom McCallister!

I had always been a sun worshiper. Most of my homes had swimming pools. Between that and the great amount of time I spent in Hawaii, all of my life I was always very Tan. I loved to lie out in the sun, and never used a sunscreen. Further I am cursed with blue eyes and blonde hair.

By the time I was 40 I had started to suffer from skin cancers, the basal cell kind that don't spread or metastasize. I averaged one or two a year, which I would have burned, or cut off. Because of that I had semi-annual check ups with a dermatologist.

Then in late 1996 I had noticed a new brown spot about the size of your little fingernail on my cheek below my left eye. I went to see a dermatologist who said "Keep an eye on it, okay?"

About four or five months passed and one morning, shaving, I saw a small bump in the center of the spot. I scheduled an appointment with him and he looked at it.

"He said, "Let's biopsy it," and used what is called a "punch biopsy" tool to take a plug out of the center, including the bump.

Several weeks went by; I thought, I guess no news is good news. Having had, by then, twenty or more basal cell cancers, I assumed that was what I had again.

One day, after about six weeks, I thought I would just call and confirm the results. The doctor wasn't in. I spoke with a nurse with a heavy Hispanic accent. She put me on hold and then returned and said, "You got a malignant melanoma."

I was devastated.

I knew that in most cases that is a death sentence.

I kept calling back until I could speak to the doctor himself. He verified the report. He seemed understandably upset, asking, "Didn't anyone on my staff call you"? I said "NO! Weeks have passed, important weeks."

I said to him, "Don't blame your staff! What is the worst thing you, as a dermatologist ever sees? A malignant melanoma! You should have called me yourself immediately!" It's a very good thing that it was on the phone; I would have beaten the hell out of him for sure.

I contacted my family doctor at once, who directed me to an oncologist who was anything but encouraging. He gave me all the statistics; basically I had a (good, he thought) 30% chance of surviving for a year or more IF he operated immediately, removing a big part of my face and all of my Lymph glands.

I wasn't ready for that. I started making phone calls to every doctor I knew to discover whom I could see and feel confident in.

I found a surgeon who specialized in face and neck cancer surgery, a Doctor Vener, who, it turned out, was also a black belt. I felt I could trust him. He said, " Let's not go that drastically, first we do surgery to clear the margins. Only then IF you have evidence of cancer cells in your Lymph system will we start cutting them out." That made more sense to me.

Within nine days of hearing the results of the biopsy, I was out of surgery with a piece of my face bigger than a 50-cent piece gone. However, the result were that they had cleared all of the margins. That's good.

Now the bad news. Melanomas are one of the most vicious, insidious forms of cancer. They are known to hide and lurk in your body and reappear later. There is no way to track them. If just one cell from the original site has gotten into your blood or lymph systems, they will come back at some future date. Usually they come back to brain, lungs or kidneys. By then it is too late.

When I first had the surgery the Doctors told me that IF I lived for five years I would be "out of the Woods."

I went in to see my family doctor at the end of the five years and told him I was celebrating. He said, " Sorry, now we figure 8 years." Great!

Then after nine years since his malignant melanoma was removed, my dear friend Bobby Burbidge died after his melanoma reappeared in his kidneys.

After that I went to an internist who told me, "The longest I've ever seen them come back is after eleven years." That will be 2008.

So, I waited. It's impossible not to think about it. However, it gives you a different attitude about life. Knowing at any time a symptom can appear that marks the beginning of the end.

The facial scar was a bad one! I hated it. After a little over a year I had a plastic surgeon repair it. It is still visible but not quite so ugly. (That's all I needed, more ugly.)

Now in December of 2008, I have been diagnosed with metastasized melanoma cancer in my liver. Almost 11 years after the original melanoma.

As always I will meet this latest opponent head on and fight with all my might. I am presently undergoing treatment at City Of Hope Cancer hospital in Duarte, California. Since this kind of cancer is not responsive to most of the usual treatments, I am participating in a clinical trial of some new drugs developed for this purpose.

WHAT NEXT

Since we are on the subject of death and dying, this is as good a time as any to tell a true Ghost Story.

The first house that Leslie and I lived in together was in Sherman Oaks in 1980. It was on Hortense Street. It was an older house, probably built in the early Thirties. It had the appearance of an English cottage, with diamond-shaped windowpanes and wooden shutters. The house was painted a medium gray with dark red accents. It had a high roof but no upstairs. There was a big living room, a separate dining room, three bedrooms and a swimming pool. The double garage was detached and set back from the street. The master bedroom had its own fireplace, as did the living room. The master bedroom also had double doors opening out to the pool. It was very nice, unusual and roomy.

We moved in and settled, with a room for John, and a room for Xian, who spent three nights every week with us. There was a large bathroom in the center of a hall directly between Xian and John's rooms.

We had a Great Dane named Mongo and a sweet kitty whom we called Tabby. It was the start of our life together. We were both in the middle of difficult divorces, but other than that things were good.

We had signed a one-year lease on the house. It was only two or three blocks from Sherman Oaks Karate, which was very convenient. I was in the carpet business and it was close to the freeway and not that far from either the LAX or Hollywood/Burbank airports.

Our first inkling that something might not be quite right with the house came just a couple of weeks after we were all settled in.

261

John was in bed asleep; Xian was not there, it was one of her nights with my ex-wife.

Leslie, Mongo, Tabby and I were lying on the carpet in front of the fire. It was about 11:00 PM. Tabby was doing one of those weird feline things that make some people uncomfortable. She had been lying on Leslie's back kneading her paws into her hair, when she stopped and began staring into a corner of the ceiling above the fireplace. She kept staring at the same place; we commented on it but didn't place any special significance in it, until we both began to hear a sound like crying. It was faint and sounded like a woman or a girl, crying sadly. It seemed to be coming from the exact spot where Tabby's gaze was fixed! We were mystified and more than a little spooked. It went on for about 15 minutes then stopped. Over the next few days we began to forget about it in the preoccupation of our busy daily lives.

However, this was just going to be the first of many eerie experiences in that house.

John's bedroom was directly on the other side of the wall where the headboard of our bed stood.

A few nights later, when we were almost asleep, we heard John, who was five years old at the time, get up. We heard his feet hit the floor, and then we heard him walk down the hall to the bathroom. We didn't think too much of it and went to sleep.

Over the next few nights the pattern repeated itself several times.

We discussed it one morning over coffee. John said he didn't remember getting up. We wondered if he was sleepwalking.

I decided to see what was up the next time it happened.

A night or so later there was another repeat of the event. We heard John's feet hit the floor; we heard his footsteps going down the hall. This time I leaped out of bed rounded the corner to the hall while we were still hearing the sound of the footsteps. I jumped into the hall and there was no one there. I could see John, through the open door of his room, 20 feet away in bed covered up and sound asleep!

So whose footsteps were we hearing?

At this point this was beginning to gain our full attention.

The footsteps continued to occur after that from time to time. We also occasionally heard the crying coming from various other areas of the house as well as that corner of the living room.

One night, again, as we were almost asleep, we heard a sound as of something falling in the other part of the house. Our bedroom was just off the large living room. The dining room was about 30 feet away from the door into our bedroom. The sound seemed to come from the direction of the dining room. We were instantly alert. I picked up the hand gun I kept by my side of the bed thinking it could be an intruder. We sat up in the dim light coming through our door from the lighted pool beyond.

We heard a sound as if something was rolling across the living room floor towards our open bedroom door.

Thinking it could be John fooling around I waited a few seconds before reacting. Just then, an apple rolled from the living room into our bedroom.

At that point I jumped out of bed, turned on the lights and, gun in hand, stepped into the living room. No one was there.

The apple was one of several that had been sitting in a fruit bowl in the center of the dining room table over 30 feet away. It had to have somehow, fallen out of the fruit bowl, rolled off the table, made a left turn, rolled 30 feet across the living room floor, made another left turn and rolled into our open door and into the bedroom!

By now we knew we were haunted.

Another night, we had just turned off the lights to go to sleep. I mentioned that there was a fireplace in the master bedroom. We kept a few items, collectables and art objects, on the fireplace mantle. We were still wide-awake, our eyes not yet adjusted to the relative darkness, when we heard a very loud cat's cry! It was definitely the prolonged scream of a cat that sounded either injured or very angry. It was coming from the direction of the fireplace.

Apparently Leslie must have raised her open hands, palms facing outwards towards the frightening sound. Then, as the sound ceased, we heard in the resulting silence a very audible clinking sound as something hit Leslie's outstretched palm.

I immediately turned on the light and there in Leslie's hand was a small pewter cat that had been sitting on the mantle a few seconds ago. It had flown through the air, about 20 feet, from the mantle and landed in her palm. The clinking we had heard was the sound of the pewter cat hitting her engagement ring.

That really got our attention. We were, for the first time, very disturbed by one of these mysterious happenings. We left the lights on that night while we slept.

Xian, as I said earlier, spent three nights a week at our house, the other four with my ex-wife. She was about eight and half years old at that time. She spent Friday, Saturday and Sunday with us. She had a nice room. It was at the opposite end of the hall from John's room, past the bathroom that was in between, at the front of the house closest to the street. We had made a nice 8 ½ year old girls room for her with white furniture and lots of toys and dolls.

We began to detect "disturbances" in Xian's room when she wasn't there. Noises, for which when we investigated we could find no cause. Little things seemed to be out of place.

Then one night, Leslie, John and I were the only people in the house. We were sitting at the dining room table, reviewing the events of the day prior to putting John to bed.

Suddenly we heard a loud crash from behind Xian's closed bedroom door. I quickly went to investigate.

As I opened the door, I saw a strange sight. Xian kept one of her favorite dolls, about 18 inches high, on a stand in the middle of a table close to her bed. It was normally centered in the table about 24 inches from any side. When I opened the door, the doll was on the floor, half way, about 2 feet, between the table and Xian's bed. It had obviously just landed there, as it was still moving slightly. Finding its balance on the floor.

There was no way, first of all, that the doll could have fallen over by itself; the stand holding it was meant for that doll and sturdy and well-balanced. Secondly, if it did somehow tip over all by itself, it couldn't have landed almost four feet away from the center of the table where it had been.

Strange things continued to happen; objects were always going missing. Things would be moved or seemingly hidden. We watched John carefully but we were able to determine over and over that he was not the cause. Xian obviously wasn't doing it either, because almost everything happened while she was gone.

Leslie and I are both meticulous housekeepers. Our house was always immaculate, ready for guests. Never any clutter. This house, no matter how often we cleaned, was always dusty. The dust seemed to reappear almost magically. No sooner had we dusted than 5 minutes later another layer of dust had replaced the last one.

We weren't the only ones to experience events in the house. Thank God, because that kept us from believing that maybe we were both crazy.

One day, in midsummer, we had a pool party; we had invited about a dozen people for food and swimming. Among the guests was our good friend Ron Chapel; Ron was one of Ed Parker's earliest disciples. Ron was a sergeant with the LAPD. He was one of the original founders of the BKF, a fine martial artist and a no-nonsense kind of guy.

We were all at the pool, settling an argument as to whether or not black people can float. Tommy Chavies, one of Ron's best black belts was proving that it he tried to float he would immediately sink to the bottom. Which, by the way is true.

Ron decided to go into the house to the kitchen to check on the food.

For some reason that I don't recall, a minute later I followed Ron into the house.

As I walked into the kitchen I saw Ron standing a ways back from the sink with his back to the stove. His usual color had changed to a pale gray brown.

I guessed that he had had an "experience" with our spirit. I was right.

Mind you, we had never told any one about our ghostly occupant, least of all Ron.

I asked what was the matter.

He said, "I was standing facing the sink; I used the salt and pepper on the meat and set them down on the edge of the stove. I turned to the sink and suddenly they were sitting on the sink to my right, I SWEAR I saw them move there by themselves!"

He was obviously very upset so I decided to tell him about what was going on in the house. Shortly after that, he left. We remained close friends forever but he never came to that house again.

One of the most eerie experiences occurred one night when my son Kirk was visiting us. We had dinner and talked for hours. He was getting ready to leave; it was about 11:00 PM.

Our living room was carpeted in light beige, thick cut-pile carpet. On top of that we had placed one of the beautiful hand-made rugs that I had brought back from China. The rug left about a three-foot border of the carpet showing all around it.

We were standing by the front door when one of us noticed something in the beige carpet. Partly under the rug was a design that looked as though it had been traced in the cut pile with a finger. We pulled the corner of the rug back so that we could see the entire thing.

Everyone is probably familiar with the "hangman" game. You draw a picture of a gallows and then pieces by piece you add a rope, a noose and then a person hanging from the end, one part at a time, until you have drawn the entire picture of a man being hanged.

There on the carpet, perfectly drawn, was the gallows part of the drawing. We at first thought, what an odd coincidence. We kept talking and then Kirk looked down and, paling slightly, he said, "Look—now the rope and noose are there!"

Needless to say, we were all three baffled and a little spooked. We stood around talking about it and then one of us pointed out that now the head and body were clearly evident. We were now getting really excited.

Little by little, as we stood there, the drawing was completed. It all took place over about an hour. Never did we actually see it happening. We would all be looking away at the same time for some reason and when we looked back another part would be compete.

As I think back, 27 years later, this was one of the oddest and somehow most frightening of the many experiences we had in that house.

Other things continued to happen at intervals of a week or two.

A pattern emerged. It seemed to us that the occurrences were somehow childlike. Many surrounded Xian's toys and John, and silly jokes or games a child might play.

We decided to hold a séance.

Those in attendance were Leslie, Kirk, Leslie's friends Nancy Stillwell and Elisa Garland (a psychic), Kirk's girl friend at the time, Laura Roberts, and me.

We had told only these people about the whole thing. I think we were afraid that people would tease us or make light of it. A few others, like Ron Chapel, had experienced occurrences on a one-time-only basis.

The night of the séance, all six of us sat around the dining room table and held hands. Elisa, as the medium, conducted the proceedings. After about 20 minutes or so, in the darkened room most of us became aware of a feeling or, in some cases a shape moving around the table. It just lasted a few moments and it was gone. Shortly after, that Elisa announced that it was over. We turned on a light and sat quietly for a minute, each absorbed in our own thoughts.

Then we began to talk and to exchange concepts of what we had experienced. With only one exception, we all felt that there had been the presence of a child in the room—more specifically, a little girl. Several of us remarked that she had been either very short or perhaps on her knees.

We discussed it for a long time, then one by one everyone left and Leslie and I were left alone to try to sort out what we had seen and heard from the others.

Certainly the idea of it being little girl made sense to us in light of the many kinds of events that we had witnessed. We had not shared our feelings of it being a child with any one but Kirk before the séance.

We were puzzled by the height of the child, so short. Then it occurred to us that perhaps there had been an earlier house on the same site that had lower floors. That would explain it.

More things continued to happen throughout our year in the house.

For me, the eeriest and most significant event took place shortly before we moved out. We had decided not to renew our lease. Surprisingly, the ghost was not the deciding factor. Actually, we have discussed this many times over the intervening years. We were never afraid there. At the time and now, 27 years later, we have never felt fear of the spirit. Some of the occurrences gave us a chill, more from the knowledge of facing the unknown than from fear. The spirit was that of a little girl who was sometimes playful, mischievous, or even sad, but never malevolent.

The last major occurrence in that house happened not long before we moved out.

Leslie and I were in the front of the house on the lawn. I had my Polaroid camera and was taking pictures. I asked her to stand in front of the house for a photo. The big, diamond shaped paned windows were behind her.

I snapped two pictures, and, if you remember Polaroid instant pictures, you removed them from the camera and waited one minute for them to develop.

As the second one developed and turned sharply into focus before us, there, looking out of the one of the diamond windowpanes, we could see the clear outline of a young girl's head. You could see her hair, the oval of her face and jaw and the vague features of her eyes, nose and mouth. There was absolutely no doubt whatsoever of what we were seeing!

The hair on the back of my neck stood up on that one.

We left that house after a year. Sometimes, after we moved out, and even occasionally today. I drive by it, wondering if the occupants since then have shared any of our experiences. I haven't been willing to knock on the door and ask.

For several years in the nineties and after 2000, our friends, Jerry and Jan Manpearl, both attorneys, had the greatest Halloween parties ever.

Halloween has always been a very special day for Leslie and me. We met on Halloween day of 1979, when Leslie came in to ask about lessons for John, who was not quite five years old at the time.

It was love at first sight. That was 27 years ago. She was 26, I was 43.

Jan and Jerry Manpearl had a big old two-story house in Venice, California, a block or two from the ocean. It was as if made for parties.

Every year, a day or two before Halloween, they would have a moving company take all of their furniture from the big downstairs portion of the house and put it in the garage. Then the entire inside and the big patio in the back would be set up for a HUGE costume party. Food, drink, a 5 or 6 piece LIVE blues and rock and roll band, and about 250 or more guests in full costume. It was a blast!

There were costume contests with great prizes. Leslie and I won a couple of times. She usually for the Sexiest. One time she went as a Devil in a skintight red, one piece, spandex, unitard. She had horns, a tail, red high-heel shoes and a pitchfork. It was a stimulating outfit.

Speaking of stimulating, another time she took first place was when I dressed her as a "Dominatrix." She wore a black leather teddy with silver studs, seamed stockingsand black high-heeled boots with a silver zipper up the back, chains hung from her body, and she carried a long black leather whip!

Another time we went with our good friend Rita King. Rita is a beautiful black woman with very dark skin. We made up a set of costumes and went together as one thing.

It's hard to describe, but I still have great photos. Leslie and Rita were dressed identically in a one-piece spandex out fit, to which they had added long streamers coming from their arms and legs and elsewhere. Atop their heads were exciting wigs.

However, the colors were different. Leslie's costume and wig were all in reds, oranges and yellows while Rita's were done in black, brown, gray and silver.

They were, "Where there is smoke there is fire." That's really what they looked like!

I was dressed as a Fireman! The three of us stayed together, danced together, ate and drank together all night.

We won the Grand First Place that year.

MORE WOODRANCH

As the later Nineties unfolded, our school in Woodranch continued to prosper and grow. Our original 70 or so students had reached about 150 by the end of 1998, finally peaking at about 225 in 2002. We had been blessed with a perfect location, some fine students who had reached their black belts and were a lot of help, and we enjoyed an impeccable reputation.

Part of the reason that I think our reputation was so good was that when we took over the school we made a decision. The previous owner had sold "black belt" courses to a large number of the students. This is a course, paid in full for at least 3 years ahead. Quite a lot of money.

When it was apparent that he was not going to be able to return, we had to either let the school close or take it over. We had become very attached to the students since we had started running the school months previously.

The rent was in arrears and the landlord was anxious. We made a deal with him, signed a new lease and started a new company to take over.

In the case of those students that had paid for three years in advance, we couldn't afford to carry them for nothing, but we did teach all of them for a year for just a few dollars a month. We had no obligation to do that but felt it was the right thing to do.

We put our heart and soul into the school. It was a labor of love. I was still doing very well in the carpet business so we didn't have to make money, we could teach the way we wanted without a serious financial motive. That is pretty much the way all my schools have been. Our curriculum and philosophy is directed by what is right as opposed to what is financially expedient.

Instead of advertising, we decided to put our money and effort back into the school. We had various, large successful events for our students.

There were several things, in particular, that we did every year.

First of all we had our birthday celebrations in April and June. We would bring in cake and ice cream and entertain the students and families.

Every summer there were two events that were very successful.

Every year, for 13 years, Leslie organized a river rafting trip. She has had as many as 40 students and family members on these excursions. It takes about four days and has always been a good, safe activity.

As an additional summer activity, we have always held a big, old fashioned picnic. We have had, with family members, well over 200 people at most of them.

It takes a lot of planning. We rent an area of a local park, well in advance. It has an area with tables enough to hold 200 people, all together and under a roof to protect everyone from the hot, Southern California, August sun.

There are barbeque pits at the table area. We provide all of the food and drinks and extras. We usually have a good core of our black belt students to help us with the duties.

The food is always fantastic, and the games help everyone work up a good appetite.

Leslie has the help of Black Belts like; Ryan Fowler, Kate Hansen, Meggie Tiffany, Edgar and Edward Villanuevas (father and son), Greg and Nichelle Megowan, (father and daughter), Lester Salvatiera, and always, our good black belt student and now owner of his own PUMA school in Solvang, California, Mr. Gates. His real name is Gates Foss. With all of them, the event is always a huge success.

As I said this is an "old fashioned" picnic. The activities include a sack race, a three-legged race, an egg toss, a water balloon fight, and a tug of war. With lots of prizes!

We rent a "Dunk Tank" and a blow up "Jolly Jump." The kids love those. Especially when one of their black belt Instructors is the "dunkee."

These picnics usually last from 10:00 AM until 4 or 5 PM. Everyone has so much fun!

Our Halloween party was probably the best event of all.

Every year at the Woodranch school, we hosted a huge Halloween costume party. By the time we sold that school in 2002, of our about 225 students, probably 170 or so were kids.

The school had two large mats separated by a wall with a big window in it. That way if we were teaching, as usual, on the front mat, we could still see what was going on in back. We had many good black belts so we could almost always split our oversized classes into two and send part of them on to the back mat with another instructor.

We also had two large dressing rooms, and an entry/waiting area in front of the office. Two bathrooms made up the rest of the 2200 or so square feet.

The entire area was decorated for Halloween. The dressing rooms became a fortuneteller's booth and a spook house.

Usually the back mat was made up for various Halloween related games. A fishing booth, a face painting table, a ring toss, and things like the "Ick Box," where the little ones had to reach in and feel around "eyeballs" and other slimy-feeling things to find a prize.

The front mat is where we played games for the kids. We would usually have 150 or so kids and adults in full, imaginative costumes, playing games for prizes and being judged for costume awards. The games went on for hours and included; Pin the tail on "something," a beanbag toss, relay races, and more.

Food was served outside in front of the school—great stuff, much of it prepared and brought by our families. There was always a big line-up for the food. We had a large parking lot and it would be full of dozens of costumed students and family members eating and talking.

Leslie organized and ran the games, with help from some of our great black belts. I was very busy keeping everything else under control, solving problems, directing kids to places, supervising the food and just hosting in general.

I love the kids. Some people are born to sing, others to run or nurse or perhaps they feel the call to God.

I was born to be a father. Especially after I turned 50. I have a capacity for love for these kids. Leslie and I have our own, four of them, plus five grandchildren and several godchildren. However, I think its safe to say that I have had hundreds of other kids who were just like my own.

Every other month I try to meet Kate Hansen and Meggie Tiffany for breakfast. They were 6 and 7 when they started training with us and now they are two of the most beautiful, good girls in the world, both 3rd degree black belts, who are now 22 and 23. Both will graduate from college in 2008 and have great lives ahead of them. I love them like my own daughters. I still think of them as 9 and 10 when they won the costume contest as a perfect Raggedy Ann and Andy.

The Halloween Party became one of the big annual social events for Woodranch. People talked about it for weeks before and after. Woodranch is a very upscale, exclusive neighborhood composed of affluent professional families. Consequently, many of the costumes were among the best I have ever seen.

Leslie and I were the biggest fans of our own party. It was, after Christmas, the major event of the year for us.

We had moved to Woodranch at the onset of 1999. From Porter Ranch with our 25-minute drive, we bought and moved into a beautiful townhouse directly across the street from the school. It now took less than a minute. It was a large 1700 sq. ft. 2 story home, on the golf course again and right at the pool. It couldn't have been a better place and location for that time in our lives.

We still had our other home in Big Bear Lake; we usually went up there, to 7000 feet, on the lake, every other weekend. We had furnished and equipped the Big Bear house with everything, duplicating the Woodranch home down to our toothbrushes. All we had to do was put the dogs in the car and make the 2-hour drive.

My son Kirk lived about 10 minutes from Woodranch, so that our two grandchildren Kelly and Claudia stayed with us very often; they also were students at the school. We saw them several times a week and loved them as our own. Then suddenly they moved to Idaho. A heartbreaking event.

Scott had, by then, moved to Portland, Oregon with our other three grandchildren, Torrey, Bronwen and Charlie. That was a heart-breaker for me. I understand, having had to make decisions like that in my own career. Nevertheless the loss is just as great even if you do understand the reasons.

Our years in Woodranch were wonderful. We loved the school, we loved the students, it was really like a big family and I, now in my sixties, was able to pursue my lifelong passion for martial arts almost exclusively. We had our families around us and I got to "father" hundreds of others.

I left the T.W. McCallister Company in early 2000 and joined another large national office furnishings company called BKM. My reasons were twofold. As

I said earlier, Tom McAllister was the epitome of Ebenezer Scrooge, and my headquarters for the new company would be in Santa Barbara. It also offered the prospect of considerably more money.

It also turned out that, although by now I hated the carpet business, I made a lot of money at BKM! I stayed there until the end of 2001. At that time I was finally able to leave the carpet business once and for all. It had been very good to me financially for 46 years. There had been ups and downs and I had grown to hate it. I really never got over the death of CCC and the terrible events at Westweave.

In 1999 my old friend and ex-business partner John Atkinson died. I have to say that I believe that John had a very unhappy life. His curse was alcohol. He was only about 52 or so when he died. Bob Ozman, Greg Zem, Bobby Burbidge, Dan Lipe and I were with him until the end.

My health, except for the Melanoma and a birth defect in my back called a spondylothesis, has always been excellent! I thank God and my grandfathers for that. I got the good genes! I don't count the injuries.

Other than those mentioned above my health issues have all been related to my life of martial arts. Earlier here I made a list my injuries.

In 1999 something new cropped up. I awakened one morning to find that I had a black spot in my vision. It wasn't dark; it was the black of outer space, total blackness. As the day progressed it seemed to be getting bigger. I knew that this was serious, I called my family doctor of 30 years, Ed O'Neill, and he sent me directly to an ophthalmologist that same day.

After examining me carefully the doctor told me that I had a tear in my retina that required immediate laser surgery or I would be blind for life in that eye. It was late in the day and he had an appointment, it was his wedding anniversary.

His office was less than a block from Northridge Hospital; he called over, scheduled the procedure and we walked to the hospital together.

The procedure only lasted about 15 or 20 minutes. It doesn't really hurt but it is very uncomfortable. You must sit completely still in a special chair while the doctor shoots a laser beam through the pupil and into the back of your eye and basically "welds" the retina back on. It feels as though someone is ramming a long blunt needle though your eye as hard as they can for 15 minutes.

He had put a solution in my eye to totally dilate the pupil. When he was finished he said, "It came out fine, you will be good by morning, I really have to run," and he took off.

I thanked him and started for home, it was raining, and I didn't realize how badly my vision was impaired until I started the 20 or so minute drive home. It was AWFUL! Combined with the rain I could hardly see a thing. I kept pulling to the side of the road, thinking my sight would clear up. It didn't. I called Leslie and told her what was going on; there was nothing she could do to help.

I finally made it home in about an hour and a half. The doctor should have told me what to expect, I could have left my car there and asked Leslie to come and pick me up. Idiot!

In a few days my vision was restored and except for a little blurriness I was better. I returned to normal activities except for a caveat to avoid sparring for six weeks.

Then, about three months later, it happened again, this time the other eye!

I was in my office in Santa Barbara when it started. I called Dr. O'Neill; he said, "Don't wait." He made a few phone calls and scheduled me to see an ophthalmologist in Ventura, about 25 minutes south on my way home.

By the time I got there it was getting worse. The black spot was bigger and moving faster than it had in the other eye.

The doctor took me in within 30 minutes of my arrival; it seemed like hours, I was going blind.

He did the same thing as the last doctor. This time I was prepared and made sure he only dilated the eye he was working on. When the procedure was complete, he placed a patch over the dilated eye and I drove the next hour to my home, again with the same instruction to avoid sparring for the next 5 or 6 weeks.

The consensus of opinion of the two ophthalmologists was that the cumulative effect over the years of repeated blows to the eyes and surrounding areas had caused first one and then the other retina to first tear and then start to detach.

It was very likely my early years of boxing that brought much of it about, exacerbated by blows to the head later in martial arts.

In the years since then, I have, fortunately, not experienced any return of the retinal issues. However, the two procedures left me with a lot of "floaters" in both eyes and frequent blurred vision. At the same time, and certainly no coincidence, I also started having occasional bouts of ocular migraines: migraines with all the symptoms except the headache. The main symptom is the flashing circular lights. My student, friend and nutritionist, Kat Blanc, suggested I take magnesium to alleviate them, and it works.

The reason for mentioning these "war stories" is to let the reader know that you can't mistreat and damage your body with impunity. At some point you have to pay the price.

I chose the road; I have to go where it takes me. Still I wouldn't do anything differently. If you are a warrior you have to follow your heart.

As the new millennium dawned we found ourselves in Big Bear. Leslie and I celebrated by drinking a bottle of 25-year-old Dom Perignon, and dancing at the lakeside at midnight in a snowstorm. Memorable.

The year 2000 at the Woodranch school was a good one. Our student base was high; we had some excellent students who had earned their black belts and who were now a great deal of help. We worked 6 days a week. Leslie liked teaching the little kids (so did I), and since I was still putting in a full day in my other business, from 7AM till 4PM, it worked better for her to take the early classes. I usually began at 5pm and taught until 9 or 9:30 PM.

We were tired at night, but it was a real labor of love.

Living across the street made it a little easier and more pleasant. At Christmas time we would have an open house a few days before and people from the school would come by all day for drinks and snacks. In the summer we frequently had kids over to swim. When we wanted to get away we would go to our Big Bear house for a day or two. It was a nice time. Only my continued involvement in the carpet business kept it from being ideal.

So many of the other schools I had seen over the years had been generally unorganized. I had begun years before to follow a more structured schedule. We always did certain things on certain nights.

Monday was "power night," Tuesday was "forms," Wednesday was "waza" (the term for all of our self-defense techniques), Thursday "sparring," Friday "techniques," kicks and punches. On Saturday we sparred again.

Of course all the classes were separated by age and belt level. Our classes were full and the school was a happy, productive place. We had so many incidents at the Woodranch that I wouldn't know where to begin telling them.

Like the time in the middle of a waza class an odd guy walked in to watch. He was a big, hairy man in his mid 40's. he started talking at the top of his voice about what we were doing. "That wouldn't work," and "You couldn't do that to me," and statements like that.

I have been through this so many times. Mostly at the old Tarzana school after they opened a Korean topless bar three doors away.

I always try to ignore them first in hopes that they will go away. I have always had a deathly fear of being sued.

However, this idiot showed no sign of going away, he just got louder and louder. I finally paused the class and walked off the mat to speak to him. As I approached him, I noticed that he reeked of alcohol and marijuana.

I said something like, "Please leave, you are disrupting my class." Of course he only grew more belligerent. Always thinking about the legalities, I remained in full view of my class (witnesses) and told him again that he had to leave.

He began to tell me that he was a veteran and a street fighter and he could "kick my ass" and so on.

So finally I said, in a low voice, so that it couldn't be heard on the mat. "Then why don't you? Go ahead, hit me." That was what I was hoping for, and he did, he started throwing punches, nothing got even close, I blocked them all, I started laughing at him, a sure way to make someone get more stupid.

Infuriated, he dived in for a double-leg take down, I sprawled back and brought my knee up into his face. Blood spurted form his nose and lips and as I stepped back he fell onto the floor.

He lay there for a minute, and then got to his feet. I was getting ready to really hurt him when he smiled and said, "That was fun," and turned and walked out, holding his bloody face with his hand.

Having made sure that everyone saw exactly what happened, I made a list of everyone who was witness to it, wrote it down and put it in my desk and resumed teaching.

That was about eight years ago and I never heard any more about it. I always think that some one is going to try to set me up for some kind of legal thing when that happens. At least, in part I'm sure, because of the He Il Cho episode.

Over the almost 40 years that I have had Martial Arts schools, things like that have happened probably, conservatively close to 100 times. At the Tarzana School we would have some drunk or another walk in from the neighboring bar at least twice a month wanting to show some one how tough he was.

One time, I recall, at the Woodland Hills School, again in the middle of a class, some weird guy came in. He looked like a movie star, handsome, bodybuilder frame (Benny Urquidez calls them "Beach Muscles"), wearing a little muscle shirt and shorts.

He walked right on to the mat and striking a kung fu like pose, standing on one leg in what appeared to be an exaggerated cat stance, he shouted, "I'm a New York street fighter and I'm going to kick your ass."

Our mat was open on the backside, as you stepped off you were in the area where the metal lockers and benches were situated.

This guy looked as though he knew a little about some martial art and he was very big and buff. Enough so that he appeared to pose a mild threat. So I acted accordingly.

I did a step across sidekick, he was still standing on one leg, the kick hit him in the midsection, it lifted him up and he flew about 10 feet through the air. He landed hard into the metal lockers and benches. I think the landing probably hurt more that the kick itself.

Some of my students helped him up, brought him a towel to staunch the flow of blood from where his head hit one of the lockers. As soon as he could walk we escorted him to the front door and sent him on his way.

BIG BEAR

ONE OF MY favorite "idiot" stories took place about a year ago in my Big Bear school. I was then 71 years old.

One day a tall (6 feet 6inches) blond man in his late thirties came into the school. He watched a class for a while. Afterwards he came up to me and introduced himself. He was a black belt in Tae Kwon do. He had trained somewhere in the San Diego area for five or six years.

We are the only real school in Big Bear; there is a nice guy, a student of my dear, old friend, Steve Fisher, teaching Shorin Ryu in the park, but he doesn't really like doing it and it shows. So people generally find their way to us.

This man, whose real name I will not mention, wanted to train with us. I told him what I tell any legitimate black belt who wants to pay to train. "You can certainly join, but you have to show us a good attitude, respect and follow our rules."

He agreed and signed up. I got my first tingle of doubt about him when he told me he liked to be called "Mr. Kicks." I agreed however, His real last name was hard to pronounce and I have known some great martial artists who went by some odd nicknames: Ray Wizard, Benny the Jet, Johnny Gyro, Wildman Baldwin, and many more.

He came to class about five times over the next two weeks. He wore his white Tae Kwon Do uniform and black belt. He performed his techniques like an adequate black belt, so I believed his credentials.

After about two weeks of general classes he came in for a Saturday sparring class. Our school here is smaller that Woodranch. Our adult sparring is held on Saturday between 1PM and 2PM. It is open to all belts, ages 13 and over. We

279

generally have about 20 to maybe 28 fighters on the mat. We spar for the entire hour, non-stop. I divide the class into two groups on the mat, the smaller and younger in one and the older and larger in the other. I rarely allow them to go from group to group except for my black and brown belts that I will allow to go with smaller younger people to help them.

My friend and 3rd degree black belt student Jim Ritenour helps me teach the sparring classes. He wasn't there that day.

"Mr. Kicks," since it was his first time on our mat, started with me. I never allow any one I don't know well to just walk in and fight my students until I have personally checked them out.

As I have always done, I gave him the short "rules of engagement" speech.

"Light touch to the head, no punching or kicking directly into the eyes, nose or mouth, Light to moderate contact to the body. You can go fast if you want but just watch your control. Especially with the lower belts and smaller people."

I started the class and I sparred with him for a few minutes. He was, as I said, an adequate black belt. His control seemed okay. My practice, for many years under these circumstances, is to hold back, go about half speed, with very light contact, mostly block and evaluate the new person.

He seemed okay, so calling "Switch," we all changed opponents to another in our group.

I soon heard some unusual sounds and looked over to see "Kicks" kicking one of my adult, male blue belts pretty hard. I went over to him and said "that's a little hard for a lower belt, save it for one of the black belts." He nodded but I detected something I didn't like in his eyes.

We switched again, this time "Kicks" paired off with another lower belt man. I was sparring but also keeping an eye on him. He started picking it up again even harder. He seemed to really be getting off on it now.

I stopped the matches, sent the lower belt that he had been pounding on over to my partner and took "Kicks" for myself. I said what I always do under circumstances like this. "Are you sure you want to go this hard?"

He said "I'm not going hard yet," and we started to spar. He started off okay, as before, but then the contact started to escalate. I will give just about anyone a few chances, but after that they are on their own.

He threw a very hard kick that could have broken a rib if it would have landed properly. I closed the distance inside of his reach and hit him very hard with a left hook and a right cross to the jaw followed by a strong right thrust kick. He went down into a corner landing sprawled out over a little table and the work out bags. He was pretty much out of it and certainly hurt. First making sure he wasn't going to resume the fight, I watched him for a while, and then I helped him up and into the office where he sat down in the chair opposite Mrs. Fisher's desk. I left him there to recuperate and went back onto the mat to resume the workout.

She said he sat there for a few minutes. Then when his eyes cleared and his color returned, he said to her "I think Mr. Fisher is mad at me." She replied, "Oh, no. If he was mad at you, he would have really hurt you."

He never came back.

As a follow up to this story, I volunteer for a weekly patrol with the sheriff's office and have done so for four years now. I was at the sheriff's station a week or two later, talking with a couple of the deputies, one of whom is a student.

I told them about the experience with "Mr. Kicks," then I described him and told him his real name. It turns out that they had been called out a couple of times to arrest him. He apparently is a "tweaker" who, when he gets high, beats up his wife, who is about 5 feet tall. They had been wishing that he would give them an excuse to arrest him a little "harder."

Another of the several Big Bear experiences involved a martial artist from Romania. He was a Shotokan brown belt, who had trained for seven years in Romania. His name was John "Something-escu." He was in town with a group of Romanian framing contractors who were working on some houses here. His English was terrible.

He trained with us for about 3 months. He never did get it about contact. I tried everything, I asked him to bring a translator, and we looked up Romanian/ English on the computer and wrote him letters. Nothing worked, he would always go very hard in sparring, and every Saturday he would get the hell beat out of him.

I have some very tough students here. Mr. Jim Ritenour, for one: he is a 200 lb, third degree black belt student, he has been with me for 12 years, is a Lieutenant of Detectives with the LA Sheriff's Dept., and spent 25 years on LA Sheriff's SWAT. He helps me run the sparring classes on Saturday. There is Mr. Jay Obernolte, a black belt student of mine; Mr. Jay is a 6 ft 2 inch 255 lb linebacker and a formidable fighter. We have many other tough fighters as well.

Every Saturday, no matter what I tried, John would come in and go as hard as he could and every Saturday we would take turns beating the hell out of him. I guess maybe he just liked it. He finally, I suppose, got enough and disappeared.

I could, literally fill a book with just stories like this but I'm going to stop here.

One more note. It seems like I am only talking about men here. I want to make it very clear that many of my best black belts are women. Of the well over 100 black belts that I have taught and trained in my life about 30 % of them are women. Starting with Leslie (Mrs. Fisher), who is presently, after 27 years of consistent training and teaching, a 7th degree master, and the highest-ranking woman in the PUMA system. Right up to the last few teen-age girls, Ali Pagan, Randi Cavalier, Devon Brown and McKenzie Wolf. Teresa Ritenour, also a third degree black belt, helps me teach forms on Wednesday nights.

We make NO distinction in the training, requirements or testing for our females. By the time a woman, whether she is 14 or 40, gets a black belt from me, she has trained, competed and fought with the men and can defend herself against the best of them.

What they may lack in size and upper body strength they more than make up for with speed, kicking power, focus and ferocity.

SOME OF MY WONDERFUL STUDENTS

In the Woodranch school, we promoted a number of women black belts; most of them are still involved in the martial arts. That makes me happy.

It has always been a source of disappointment to me when anyone attains their black belt and then quits. What a waste! It happens quite often. Unless there is a VERY good reason, I consider it to be an insult and have very little use for the people who do it.

One reason that it is so distasteful to me is that it says that, this person now believes that they know it all! After 3 or 4 years.

I have spent a lifetime, over 65 years so far, studying, training, and teaching and I still am learning. I make discoveries frequently even at my advanced age. There are always new and better ways to do things.

The Woodranch school was a little like Camelot and a little like Brigadoon. That may sound like an exaggeration, but it was a little slice of wonder and enjoyment for the time it lasted.

We had a wonderful time there. Leslie and I enjoyed it all so much. We created some great black belts, we made some friends, we enjoyed the kids, many of whom are now adults, and we kept our reputation good and strong.

Some examples that come to mind are:

Kate Hansen, when we first met her, was a terribly uncoordinated child of seven or so. Her parents enrolled her in karate at least in part, in hopes that it would help her coordination.

She worked hard with her friend Meggie Tiffany; they were dedicated, constant students. After five years they earned their black belts together. They were 12 and 13 at that time.

They didn't quit, they continued to come and take advanced classes and help us teach. Both of them became very beautiful young women. Kate really took to teaching: she was a natural! The kids loved her and she was a born teacher.

Because, I believe, of the experiences she had at our school, she made the decision to become a teacher and is now in her senior year of college pursuing teaching as a career.

As far as the coordination problem is concerned, one of my favorite ever rewards as a teacher myself came when Kate was, I believe, a junior in high school.

Kate had developed a love for golf, and still today it is one of her driving passions. She is a tournament competitor. She started playing as a little girl and joined the golf team in high school. She began to excel at it.

One of the high points of my life occurred one evening when I received a call from Kate's mom. She had just left a dinner that was held at the high school for the members of the golf team. Kate had received an award for her performance that year.

The coach had made a short speech when he presented Kate with her award. In his speech he said, "Kate is becoming an outstanding golfer, she is a mainstay of the team. She can hit the ball straighter and farther than anyone else on the team, male or female. Of course, Kate is a natural-born athlete."

Her parents and I knew that nothing was farther from the truth, she was born with little or no athletic ability, and she had learned and earned it through years of dedicated study of the martial arts.

Kate continues to train when her schedule permits and spars whenever she has the chance. She is now a 3rd degree black belt in the PUMA system.

Some of my first students when we took over the Woodranch school were Gates Foss and the Megowan's.

Gates became one of our best ever black belts and is another who is like a son to me. He is the same age as Scott, my oldest.

Gates is now a 5th degree in PUMA and has owned his on school in Solvang, California for several years now. He is a credit to our system and I am very proud of him.

The Megowans, Greg the father, and Nichelle, his daughter, are still actively teaching on a regular basis at the Woodranch school. It is because of them that the system has survived there.

By the time anyone reads this, Greg and Gates will be 5th degree black belts and Nichelle will be elevated to 4th.

Nichelle is attending USC, majoring in Premedicine. I have said to her for years that she should hurry up and become a specialist in Geriatric Sports Medicine so she can take care of me.

She is forming a PUMA Karate club at USC. She is another one I am extremely proud of. She and her father come up from time to time to train and work out at the Big Bear PUMA headquarters. She is brilliant, beautiful and an excellent martial artist.

Todd "the Dojo Dominator" Whetsel (by his own definition) is a 4th degree black belt student of mine. He is a psychologist, now living in Oklahoma where he continues to compete and teach the PUMA system. Todd is a very bright, funny guy and another credit to the system.

There are SO many more, way over one hundred. I can't list or mention them all here. I love and respect all of them, especially those that have continued in the art!

2001 was a good year at PUMA Karate. Our enrollment grew to over 200 students and stayed there. We promoted more good black belts. Most of them continued to train.

We staged two tournaments that year with the Gyros. One of the best things about those events was the good time we got to spend with Johnny and Noel.

My BKM business held up very well. Although the flooring business had become anathema to me, I liked the money. Going to Santa Barbara to my office was pleasant too.

In February, Duncan came to live with us, he was 8 weeks old and weighed 3 lbs. He was and has been Rags all over again, with some additional characteristics of his own. He is my best friend.

On my calendar I have a notation on April 16th that Duncan killed his first mouse today. Duncan was only 4 months old at the time.

Cairn terriers were bred for killing small animals. A cairn is a large pile of stones, used in Scotland to mark the boundaries of property lines. The Scots,

200 or more years ago, started to breed these little terriers to kill the mice, rats and weasels that bred and lived in the Cairns. They are very good at it.

The Scots began to make a sport of it. They would go out for a day on horseback with two Cairn terriers in their saddlebags and see whose dogs could kill the most vermin.

Consequently they became very fast, efficient killers. Duncan can catch a mouse faster than a cat; he grabs it, gives it one shake, drops it and goes on his way. Our house in Woodranch was right on a big golf course, so we had plenty of visitors for Duncan to dispose of.

By now he has done his full share to control the rodent population in Woodranch and Big Bear as well. Recently I built him his own cairn in an area in the back yard. We are anxiously awaiting the move-in of some rodent residents.

Scott and his family moved from San Jose, California to Portland Oregon in February. It was a good move for him but for me, it took my best human friend even farther away.

That February was also the month of my second laser surgery on the other retina.

In March of that year, we had another of the bad floods that have plagued us in our schools. Our Woodranch building backed up to a hillside; there was a walkway about 3 feet wide between the back of the structure and the hillside retaining wall. Every winter that we were there, at least once, during a heavy rain, the gutters would plug up and the water would flood the school.

It was a nasty experience. In that school we had a canvas mat stretched over two layers of carpet padding. When the floodwaters came in the back and stood about three inches deep over the mat, it was bad!

We would have to close down for at least three days, each time. The mat would have to be taken up; the carpet padding was ruined so it would have to be taken away. Dryers were brought in for a day or so to dry the concrete, then new pad installed and the mat rest restretched. The school was over 2200 square feet, with two separated mats. There was a great deal of work to do.

Every time this happened, the turmoil was very unpleasant and the closure was stressful. The landlords would pay for the work but it didn't make us feel any better about the disruption.

In June of that year we held a tournament that was very well attended. Afterwards in honor of my 65th birthday and our 19th wedding anniversary,

Leslie surprised me with a dinner at our favorite Italian restaurant. There were over 200 students, their families and our friends in attendance. Leslie further surprised me by standing up and singing a love song to me in front of everyone. Kirk, Mimi, Kelly, Claudia, Xian and John were all there as well.

Later, the following weekend in Big Bear, Leslie gifted me with the Rolex wristwatch that I had wanted. It was a nice 65th.

That year we "adopted" yet another kid.: Sasha Boubion. She, her mom Kim, and sister Sarah had been students of ours for almost 6 years. Sasha was 12 years old in 2001; she had been working hard towards getting her black belt. She was tall and skinny and had been sparring with the adults for at least 6 months, so that she could go directly to ShoDan and not have to be awarded a ShoDan KoHai, or "young person's black belt."

Sasha's Dad, Michael, was in the Navy; at the time he was a door gunner on a helicopter with a group called the "Firehawks." He later saw action in many parts of the world.

Michael received news a few months before Sasha's test that he was being transferred to San Diego. None of us wanted Sasha to miss her black belt test. So Leslie and I volunteered to have her live with us until the test date. Her parents agreed. Sasha lived with us all that summer. We both fell even more in love with her during that time.

Sasha earned her black belt, with honor.

She has subsequently continued her training. She comes up to Big Bear whenever she can and stays with me and helps teach. She has received her 3rd degree black belt now. She will be 20 in August of 2009. She will have been with me for 13 years by then.

Like so many of "my kids," I couldn't love her any more if she was my very own biological daughter. I am in constant touch with her, we text message each other daily. I would love to be able to see her more often but our daily messages keep me feeling close.

In August of 2001 we found out that my other son, Kirk, was also taking his family away and moving out of State to Idaho. This, soon after Scott moved to Portland. We had been extremely close to Kirk's children, our grandson Kelly and granddaughter Claudia. They stayed with us quite frequently, and spent a lot of time at the school as well. It was a very hard blow for us. We were devastated!

It was that, more than anything else that finally decided us to move to Big Bear Lake, our other home in the mountains, full time. We already loved it there and now we felt might be the time to go.

Therein lies a tale.

In order for us to move to Big Bear a great many difficult things had to occur. Some were harder than others.

I am a deeply believing Christian. As I mentioned earlier, it has been a long path that brought me here. I don't preach to anyone else, after all, maybe the "getting there" is one of the key elements. I, however have strong beliefs in that area.

I believe that sometimes we are directed in our path and we have to know when that is the case.

In order for us to move to Big Bear, once we had made the decision, a great many things, some quite difficult, had to happen.

We would have to do the following, in order and within the same, short, time frame.

Sell our house in Woodranch for a good price.

Sell the Woodranch School. (A huge undertaking since it had to be to a student who knew our system.)

Sell our existing house in Big Bear.

Find and buy a new, bigger, home in Big Bear (Leslie further wanted to be on the same street if at all possible).

Find and lease a place for a new school in Big Bear.

All of the details had to be timed right; it was a daunting task.

As soon as we made the decision to try to make it happen, everything fell right into place within a few weeks. It really was "meant to be."

The most difficult thing was to find a buyer for the school. You can't just sell a successful, ongoing school with 225 students to just anyone. The person who buys it must meet the following criteria.

First of all, they must be a good black belt in your own system. Otherwise how will they continue to teach students who range from white to black belt rank? They need to know and be proficient in your forms.

The new owner has to be a good, decent person. I would not turn my students over to anyone who was not. They are like an extended family to me.

They must want to be a school owner; not many people do.

Lastly they must have the money. No easy thing.

We had the perfect person. Mel Abraham was a 3rd degree black belt in Buge Ju Jitsu and karate. He had come to train with us a few years earlier and was ready for his 3rd degree in PUMA. He was a very successful accounting executive who traveled worldwide teaching accounting practice. He was well liked at the school. He was good at our forms and really wanted a school of his own.

Mel bought the school. We had about 20 good, proficient black belts who were ready and willing to help him with the workload. That was an added bonus; because of his travel schedule he needed capable people to cover for him in his absence. The Megowans have been particularly great in that regard.

Our old house in Big Bear sold within 2 or 3 weeks AND we found a perfect, larger house, with a boat dock, 3 houses down the street at an incredibly low price. We sold and bought at the same time.

The new house came with some furniture, most of which we sold off in a garage sale. There were two sofas that were particularly ugly. I left them in the driveway with a big sign on them that said, " Free." There were no takers. After 2 or 3 days I had an idea. I replaced the "Free" sign with a sign saying "$200.) After the first day someone stole them.

As soon as we were ready for the next step, we listed our house in Woodranch for a good price and it sold in three days for more than we were asking, before it even came out in the multiple listing sheets.

The escrows, monies, and move all went so smoothly that it didn't seem real.

As soon as we were ready, we looked for and found a perfect location for the new Big Bear School. (We know now what a miracle that was.)

Talk about something that was "meant to be." There is absolutely no doubt in my mind that this was the case here!

I truly believe that I am up in Big Bear for a reason. I have less than 100 students, that's as big as we want to be. When it gets too big we go to a waiting list.

When we run into a difficult or challenging student we say to each other, "This is why we are here."

Therefore late 2001 and early 2002 were a time of great change for us.

It was very difficult for us to say goodbye to the students at the Woodranch School.

Our students truly become "family" to us. When someone enrolls with me, I accept him or her into the family. It becomes my responsibility to not only teach them self-defense, but to help them in every way that I can to become the best person that they can be. I believe this whole-heartedly, I think that any of my higher belts will attest to it.

I am in touch with dozens of my black belts on a regular basis. I am more like a second father to them than a teacher.

One way that a real martial artist always spots the phonies is like this.

A phony will claim to be a "black belt", when you ask them, "What style?" they give you a blank look or say "karate." The real giveaway is when you ask them who their instructor was and they reply with something like " I don't remember his name, some little Asian guy." That is ALWAYS a lie!

You never forget the name of the person who brought you to black belt. Four or so years of blood, sweat and tears, 4 or 5 times a week under the direct tutelage of someone whom you have developed great trust and respect for is not something that you forget!

We moved to Big Bear full time in July of 2002, after doing some renovations and upgrades to our new home. One of the unexpected benefits from the acquisition of the new home was that it came with a boat dock.

The people we bought the house from were in a huge hurry to sell, he was a brain surgeon from Orange county, and the house had been their "getaway" place, as our previous, smaller house had been for us. He had become very ill suddenly and they just wanted out. Consequently we paid well below market value because we had cash.

Boat docks are at a premium on Big Bear Lake. Years ago restrictions were passed limiting the number of docks that are allowed. Almost at the last minute, the sellers, who could have sold the dock to someone else separately, for a lot of money, just said, "Oh, take it, we don't want to take the time to mess with it"

It was an unexpected development for us. I have never been the slightest bit interested in boats, but Leslie was. We talked about selling the dock, but decided to wait. A year or two later we acquired a 22 foot pontoon boat and now enjoy it very much in the summers.

I couldn't wait to get the new school opened. We hired a contractor to remodel the newly leased school space to suit our needs and began to learn about small town life!

The first thing we learned is what I call "the Big Bear Way."

The contractors here all seem to follow the same policy. It is something like this.

First of all, act like you don't want the work. When you do agree to do it, always underestimate the price, wait until you have started and then demand more money to finish! Do NOT show up on time on the appointed day! Never finish anything! Never do a good job if you can get away with a poor one!

It isn't just us, they do it to everyone, and here are a couple of examples.

We wanted to have a ton of gravel put into our 10 by 60 foot dog run. I bought the gravel and had it delivered to an area just at the front of the chain link fence where the gate to the run is located.

I asked a young man who had expressed interest in doing the work to come and look at it. Being used to doing business in a certain way all my life, I asked him, "How much will you charge me to use my wheel barrow and tools and bring the gravel in to the run and spread it?" He walked around, looked at the run, looked at and felt the gravel, tried out the wheelbarrow, and finally said "$125." I said, "Okay, go ahead." A few hours went by, Leslie made lunch for him, and he stopped and rested then returned to work. That afternoon when he was finished I went out, approved the work and gave him $125 in cash. He said, "It's going to be $175." I looked at him and said, "We agreed on $125." He replied, "It got hotter than I thought it was going to be." That is typical!

Some students of ours were building a spec house close to the lake for resale. They had hired a local contractor whom they knew personally.

They started the work and as it grew near to completion, the construction loan was coming due and they wanted to finish construction so that they could list the house for sale.

The house was due to be completed in March. By May it was still not done, it was obvious that the problem was that the contractor was taking men off the job and sending them on other projects. My student had a meeting and said "We have to finish the job." The contractor said, "You will have to pay me extra to put more men on it." Finally, reluctantly, it was agreed that they would pay extra and for a few weeks it moved along, then the work slowed down again. When my student confronted the contractor with the fact that there were once again to few men working on the house his reply was, "Well, this is our busy season!"

Furthermore the city and especially the Fire Department believe that their *raison d'etre* is for the sole purpose of trying to discourage business people from opening a new business, moving, expanding or in any other way improving their business in Big Bear Lake.

When we had leased the space for the new school, the various inspectors who perform inspections for the fire department did everything they could to keep us from opening. It was so bad that I finally had to have a meeting with the city manager. When he saw how foolish and arbitrary the demands being place upon us were, he stepped in and got us open.

We held a Grand Opening in October of 2002. It was a lot of fun and, I think, quite successful by small-town standards.

We had received a very nice, big, write up in the local paper. It helped bring us a good turnout. We had invited several guests, among them were our old friends Benny and Sarah Urquidez, they stayed with us for a few days.

Many of my black belt students were there.

Kate Hansen, Greg and Nichelle Megowan, Edgar and Edward Villanueva, Ryan and Scott Fowler, Whitney Love, Burnis White, Scott Snyder and Daniel Sallus were all there.

The grand opening was a real success for such a small town. We had signed up 22 students by the end of the two days of demonstrations.

By the end of our first month we had over 40 students. It was interesting starting new again after so long our students were all white belts, with Leslie and I doing all the teaching.

The people in Big Bear are, for the most part, very nice. A large percentage of those first 40 or so made it to black. After five years, five so far with two others getting close.

It has been a wonderful experience.

I will always teach, as long as my health permits. I love it, especially the kids and young people. There is a lot of good that we can do with those ages. They also keep your outlook young and enthusiastic.

Shortly after we moved up full time an interesting thing occurred.

In Woodranch, we had signed up an entire family for lessons. A father, Jim Ritenour, his wife Teresa and their two daughters Britney and Michelle. I have mentioned them earlier.

At the time they signed up in 1997, Jim was with the LA Sheriff's SWAT team, Teresa was a very pretty, retired LA Sheriff's deputy, Michele was 6 and Britney 11.

Michelle started first; she was so shy (like Whitney Love, another of our shy black belts) that she wouldn't speak. We finally had to tell her that we wouldn't test her for blue belt until she started talking to us.

Then Britney started, followed by the parents. By 2001 they were all black Belts. Michelle was awarded our "young person's" Shodan. We use the Japanese term *Shodan Ko Hai* for any one who has earned the rank but has not been training and fighting with the adults. (The sight of 8 or 9 year olds wearing full black belt ranks, sometimes even 2nd or 3rd degrees, has always disturbed me.) Later, as in Michelle's case, if they continue to train and spar and work out with the adults we will drop the "Ko Hai" from their rank.

Jim had grown up in Big Bear and it had a special place for him. Less than a year after we opened the Big Bear school, he bought a house and moved his family up here. So we had suddenly 4 black Belts with whom we had a very close relationship. At present they are all 3rd degree black belts and are all involved in the school.

Britney still works out and is a very fine martial artist. She, however, is 21 now and pursing future career interests. She became very involved in beauty pageants while in Woodranch. She won several titles in Ventura County and a year ago placed 3rd in the California Miss USA contest.

Jim is now a Captain of Detectives with the LA Sheriff's Dept and still commutes from Big Bear to LA, two hours each way, every week.

Teresa teaches forms classes for us every Wednesday. Jim frequently runs the adult sparring class for me on Saturdays. Michelle is usually there with him. That gives me time to do more teaching instead of just sparring.

They are now all 3rd degree black belts.

I also have several more active black belts in the school.

Jay Obernolte joined us over 4 years ago. He was a good Shotokan, green belt at the time. Jay is a big, strong guy, about 6ft 2 and 255 lbs. He is a successful, married with kids, local businessman in his mid thirties. Now a third-degree black belt, Jay teaches technique classes for me several nights a week. He has been a real asset to our school; we have complete confidence in him and trust him totally.

We have three young, first degree, women, black belts. All of them very good.

Randi Cavalier. Is 15, tall, slim, pretty, and a good fighter. She is one of the strongest females I have taught since Kate Hansen. She is teaching regularly and is becoming one of our best. We can count on Randi to step in at almost any level. She was terribly shy at first, four years ago. Martial arts have been very important in helping her overcome it. She now feels, because of her training and success with us, that she is ready and able to take on anything.

McKenzie Wolf is 14, looks 18. Tall, blonde, pretty, she looks like an ad for milk but is a very good fighter and teacher. She has a very "take-charge" personality and is very good with the juniors.

Tabby Ojean and Maxine Wong (my goddaughter) are the most recent. Tabby is 14, and is an excellent forms technician. She never misses a thing. We are working her into a teaching schedule.

All three of them are a big help and we are very proud of them. Randi is another sometime overnight guest; we are quite close to her.

Russell Mannex is an 18 year old who has been training with me for 5 years. Russell is one of our best fighters. Like SO many of our students he is like my own kid. He lives with his grandparents, who, when they need to go away, leave him to stay with us. Our guest room usually has a kid in it. Russell is bright and funny and loves to watch classic movies with me.

Russell is one whom will generally "get" the jokes I make about old movies such as *Young Frankenstein*, or *The Great Race*. He and I have watched them together and he has a wonderful sense of humor. In 2008 at a religious service held in a mountain retreat at Big Bear, my dear friend and Minister, John Dunn held the service to make Russell my godson. Russell subsequently joined the Marines and will report for duty at the end of his senior year. He continues to be an invaluable teacher at the school. He will make 2nd degree before he leaves for the Marines.

Stacey Crumpler is also a 1st degree black Belt who is a natural athlete and a great fighter. He does some teaching for me as well.

I have two "Ko Hai" black belts; both have trained for 6 years and are 11 and 12 years old: Max Schweitzer and Andrew Lopresti. They help me with forms and the junior sparring class.

Maxine Wang, a pretty, very bright, 17 year old who was just promoted to my 100th black belt! Maxine started with us five years ago and displayed an incredible talent for martial arts. She is one of only 4 in the last 5 years that we have skipped for a belt rank.

We both fell in love with Max; her mother, Emily, owns a large successful restaurant and has to go out of town a lot. Max started to stay with us on a regular basis. After a year and a half or so, we became her "official" godparents in April of 2006. We love her as our own daughter.

In 2006, Max stayed at our house over 90 nights. It's like having our own girl. That year Leslie went to China with Max for two weeks. She and Max have also gone river rafting every summer, to LA many times, Balboa Island, and Newport. And more.

For me, Max has been just like a real daughter who came into my life when I needed one very badly.

Xian married and moved to Hawaii and I rarely see or hear from her. I am hoping to rectify that situation in the near future.

Max is a very talented martial artist, her forms and techniques are as good or better that anyone that I have trained in years and she is one of the best female fighters of all the students in the school as well. I hope to have her in my life forever.

Another word about Stacey.

Stacy is about 6 ft tall and weighs 200 lbs. He is a very good fighter with excellent control. His forms and self-defense are excellent as well. He is an outstanding black belt. Stacey, like all of the people who stay with us all the way to black ,is a good person as well.

There will soon be two more black belts in Big Bear, Tyler Greenberg and Steve LoPresti.

Over the last 40 plus years, since I opened my first school, the system has continued to develop and change. It has never been my desire or intention for me or the system to remain static.

As I mentioned a couple of hundred pages ago, I truly believe that PUMA was one of the first true "Mixed Martial Arts." I still remember in 1959 being 23 or 24 years old living in Sacramento, California, working out at a boxing gym and mixing kicks into my heavy bag workouts. Much to the amusement of the other boxers, who had never seen any thing like that before.

As we learned more from the traditional systems, they too became assimilated and included in the overall movement.

I have continued the use of forms, (or *kata*; I use the words interchangeably) because I believe that they are important in perfecting power, balance, technique and self-discipline. We have 12 to be learned to attain black belt, with one more advanced form after black.

We spend a great deal of time on techniques as well, working on proper stances, breathing, focus, and the theory of power. Mostly with hand held bags rather than those suspended on chains. The hand held bags can be moved, adjusted and are "alive." They also offer a benefit to those holding them.

Where we have made the greatest strides and development is in the area of what I have come to call *waza*, a word used by Tatsuo Shimabuku to describe self-defense techniques and combinations.

Based on my experience in the real world, in the street and during the time that I worked with the LAPD, it is my belief that, in a "real" fight, you should always strive to remain on your feet.

Faced with bad odds you don't want to go to the ground. You can't run away if you are on the ground. If you are faced with multiple attackers, you want to remain standing so that you can utilize all of your weapons effectively. Also you don't face the risk, as we found to be true in actual LAPD statistics, to be held in place on the ground by one assailant while another stomps on your head.

When I first started as a Defensive Tactic Consultant for the LAPD, the prevailing theory of the combined panel members was to stay on your feet. Then with the advent of the Gracie brothers on TV it became "in" to go to the ground.

The panel was made up of about half "strikers" and half "grapplers," and a couple of us who favored a mix.

The popularity of the Brazilian Ju Jitsu people tipped the panel towards going to the ground. For a while that opinion prevailed, until the reports started coming back from the field.

In actuality it turned out to be a bad idea, for the reasons given above. The officers were too vulnerable once they went to the ground, unless they were positive that they outnumbered their opponents.

If a single officer went to the ground with one suspect, any other suspects could have their way with him while the man on the ground with him tied up his defenses.

Early on, in fight leagues like the UFC, the grapplers again held sway, until we learned defenses like the "sprawl" and the "guillotine choke" to counter the take downs. That changed it back again, giving the stand up fighters the edge.

Presently, most of the UFC fights seem to be won by punches and kicks to the head.

If you are familiar with traditional systems you know that there are defenses against grapplers included in most classical systems.

As an example, in Isshinryu, there is form called Seisan. In that *kata* there is a move at the end where the practitioner slides his right foot back into a Cat Stance and makes a grab, left hand over right, followed by a sharp twisting movement of the hands.

When I was first taught this form, initially by Gerry Finney in 1955 and again by Bob Ozman in 1968, I was told that it was an ankle break, grabbing a kick with a sharp twist to break the opponents kicking ankle.

However, when Ezu Shimabuku made a trip to the US, about 1977, he came to my school in Tarzana. We worked on the Isshinryu *katas* together prior to him promoting me to 3rd degree. While performing Seisan, with him I made mention of the ankle break.

He looked at me and shook his head vehemently.

"Oh no, Not ankle break," he said. "Neck Break!"

He then illustrated that, when an opponent goes for a "shooting" leg take down, you step back into a cat stance, give him your relaxed left leg and grabbing him under the chin with your right hand and by the hair or head with your left hand, you execute a sharp, snapping twist, breaking his cervical vertebrae.

"Neck Break!" he repeated.

The old traditional, styles are full of these techniques, many of them obscured by time or intentionally hidden from the casual student.

This brings us back to our present "state of the art" in *waza*.

Building upon the traditional methods and techniques from Isshinryu, Kenpo and Hapkido, I began to add new things in the '80s. What we call *waza* is now a wide-ranging system of self-defense. It is serious self-defense, not sport-directed.

For the past 2 years I have begun to incorporate more Ju Jitsu into the system. I have had the experience of having many mixed martial arts fighters train with me at my school. Some of the top fighters such as Joe Stevenson, Cub Swanson and Josh Burkman train with us.

Throughout a lifetime in the martial arts and 40 years of school ownership and teaching, I have had occasion to teach people from all walks of life.

Bouncers, bodyguards, all kinds of law enforcement people; police officers, deputies, FBI agents, CIA agents, DEA agents, Highway Patrolmen, undercover narcs, military personnel from every branch of the service, mercenaries and people whose profession I didn't want to know.

Not to mention dads, moms, doctors, lawyers, and every other day-to-day occupation.

I gear the teaching to the students. I don't teach other than a very basic "Tiger Mouth" to kids, whereas with the military we spend a great deal of time and practice on a variety of those deadly throat strikes.

A year or two ago I was teaching some of the bouncers from the local "biker bar" in Big Bear. I was teaching them some defenses against bladed or pointed weapons. One of the techniques was as the attacker thrusts straight at you with a weapon in his right hand, you step to your left, perform an open hand block with your right hand on the back of the assailants weapon hand, knocking his weapon downwards and away from you, then you immediately slide your hand upwards and, making a "tiger mouth", strike the attacker hard in the throat. I explained to them that I would only use this against someone who was attacking with deadly force because this can be a killing blow.

Unbelievably, about 3 nights later, one of the bouncers that I had taught, was attacked by a young drunk who had broken a beer bottle and thrust it at his midsection. He did exactly as we had practiced. The attacker, when struck, fell to the floor and couldn't breathe.

The paramedics were there in minutes and saved the attackers life on the way to the hospital.

It turned out that this idiot was the son of an attorney from "down the hill" as we call it. The father was going to sue the bouncer, the bar and ME!

Fortunately the owners and other bouncers had gathered a large number of witnesses who gave statements of the fact that this was a deadly attack and that the bouncer acted in fear for his life. The suit was dropped.

This is just one incident, there have been many, many others, some involving myself that I do not want to put into print. Suffice it to say that I KNOW that what I teach works.

We concentrate on effective blocks, powerful counter attacks featuring, ridge hands, elbows, joint locks, throat, groin, knee, and eye strikes and hard throws and take downs. Again, modified and diluted for the kids.

I also teach knife. Here I am even more selective in my choice of students as I fear the legal responsibility. Our knife fighting system is one of the best I have ever seen, tested in actual use and practice by my military students.

Our sparring is basically kick boxing, when ever I have tried to mix the kick boxing with the *waza* it has resulted in an unacceptable student injury rate, so I teach them on separate nights in separate classes. Of course, as training continues, the higher belts and all the black belts become adept at mixing the two and combining the kickboxing and *waza* as might be required for a given situation.

I also stopped doing breaking some years back. I was really into it at one time. My hands are a mess from boxing, bare-knuckle tournament competition and breaking most of all. I have to take a prescription drug called "Salsalate" for the traumatic arthritis in my hands. Otherwise they don't want to open and close very well.

A good part of the condition is from doing breaking in my earlier years. We also, at the Tarzana school and even earlier when I was practicing on my own in Sacramento, had *makiwara* posts to punch and strike.

These beauties were the brainchild of some of the old Okinawan Masters. Picture this: a pair of 2-inch by 6-inch boards, set into the ground solidly, preferably with a cement base, about 5 feet from floor level to the top, held together at the very top by heavy rope tied tightly around both boards for about 12 inches from the top down.

The idea was that you would practice, every day, punching the *makiwara* as hard as you could. Always striking with the first two knuckles of the punching hand.

The purpose was to strengthen your hands and to kill the nerve endings of the striking area. Believe me, it works. My students can testify that I have no feeling in the first two knuckles of my fists.

The old masters knew that when that happens you lose your fear of striking full power and when you do strike it is like being hit with an unyielding object such as a hammer.

The downside is that you will eventually do irreparable damage to your hands.

The classic example of what I am describing here are the hands of Grand master Hee Il Cho. If you know him or ever get to meet him you will see that his hands, especially the right hand, are misshapen to the extent that they look like hooves. He is, in my opinion, one of the, premier "breakers" in martial arts. He has however, paid a dear price for it.

I have gotten away from breaking for the past 10 years or so.

The injury level to my students is unacceptable to me. Over the years I have seen SO many hand injuries. Not only to the strikers themselves but also to those holding the boards as well. Broken knuckles, fingers, even wrists. I have seen a 10-inch long wood splinter go through a holder's arm almost severing a nerve that could have cost him the use of his hand.

There are a lot of tricks that are used in some demonstrations. I always felt that they were dishonest. Such as baking the pine boards the night before to remove all moisture and making them quite easy to break. Or starting a crack at the end of each board with a chisel or screw driver prior to striking. Another favorite is, if the boards are not square, instead of being 12 x 12 if they are 12 x 10, they are much easier to break.

If you are breaking ice or long bricks, the size of the spacer between the objects struck can greatly increase the success of the resultant break. The bigger the spacer, the easier the break.

One of my favorite stories about breaking involves my old friend Chong Lee.

It was about 30 years ago. Lee had arranged to do a demonstration for a local high school. He asked me to come along. When we arrived, we found that the demo was being held on the football field for the football team. It was a tough audience.

Lee began by demonstrating some of his kicking techniques. He was quite well known in martial arts circles at the time, he had just published his first book *Dynamic Kicks*, and it was becoming well known.

The football players, although I'm sure they were impressed, wanted to act cool and tough for their peers so some of them acted as if "any one could do that."

Then Lee began the breaking demo, using 12x12 pine boards. We both broke some with punches and kicks. Still some of the members of the audience continued to act unimpressed.

Finally, Lee broke three boards with a punch, very difficult to do. The biggest and most vocal and rudest member of the audience stood and, walking to where Lee was standing, towering over him at about 6 ft 4 he said, "I can do that."

Lee said, "Be my guest," and we held the boards for him. I felt that there was a good chance this 18-year-old giant could do it and I was afraid he was going to ruin Lee's demo.

The young man pulled his arm back and with all 250 lbs behind the blow, he struck the boards right in the center.

The sound we heard was not the boards but the breaking of several bones in his hand. He screamed and fell to one knee. In the resulting confusion I saw Lee doing something with the boards.

The demo was concluded, the remaining players were very impressed because the loudmouth was the strongest person on the team. I believe that Lee actually signed up a few of them as students.

Later on our way back to the car, I said, "Were you afraid that he was going to break the boards and show you up?"

Lee laughed and replied, "No I turn middle board the opposite direction than outside boards, no break that way!"

Chong Lee, my daughter's "Uncle Lee," was a funny guy.

Once at his Ventura Blvd School an incident occurred that I would always remember.

It was close to the end of the day, sometime in 1977. Lee was teaching his last class of the day. Two young men came in wearing karate uniforms under their jackets. They sat in the front and removed their jackets and put on what appeared to be new black belts. Lee saw them but paid no attention until one of them stood and in the middle of Lee's class said "We are here to see if you are as good as we hear you are." Lee said "Okay, you wait," and continued to teach.

He finished his class and said again, "You Wait." As the last member of the class left the studio Lee said again "You wait."

He then went around, locked the back door, turned out the lights and beat them to a bloody pulp with a chair.

I asked him later "A Chair?" His reply to me was:

"Sure, Koreans aren't stupid!"

In the time that we have been in Big Bear, we have come to have the same kind of "family" that we experienced in Woodranch and schools before that.

A lot of it has to do with the fact that when we take on a new student we treat them as family. The longer that they are with us the stronger the bond grows.

Many of my students are like sons and daughters or nieces and nephews to me. I truly mean that, I love them that much. A permanent, and extremely strong, bond develops when you spend 4 or more years 4 or 5 times a week, teaching and guiding young people. I think that is especially true in the martial arts.

My home is always open to those in our martial arts family. Its difficult to say how many nights that my guest rooms have been occupied with our students, from Big Bear, as well as the many students visiting me who trained with me in previous schools.

Probably well over 100 nights a year.

I feel extremely blessed by it. My kids and grandchildren have spread all over the map, most of them far enough away that I never get to see them. It's the saddest fact of my life. Two of my son Scott's children, Bronwen and Charlie are now training in martial arts. One of Bronwen's ambitions is to be a martial arts teacher herself. Needless to say that makes me very happy.

I was born to be a father. My first son, Scott, was born when I was only 19 years old. I haven't stopped "fathering" since. It makes me feel happy and complete.

I will continue to teach and "raise" kids until I die, on the mat hopefully, while sparring intensely with one of my many fine students. That would be perfect!

The martial arts have provided me with a "way of life" that I would not otherwise have had. The honor, respect, ethics, love and friendships that I have enjoyed through my involvement in martial arts have rewarded me with most of the best parts of my life.

At 72 years old, at the time of this writing, I look back across my life frequently. It all passes so quickly. It seems like no time at all since I had my first boxing lesson at the YMCA in San Francisco.

Life continues even now to change and mutate. My wife and partner, Leslie, with whom I spent the last 27 years, is now just my dear and loving friend. We divorced about a year ago. We are in frequent contact still and will stay friends for life.

After thinking that I was too old to ever find another woman in my life, I met a wonderful young woman, Wendy Meidt, who is my angel and companion. At this time I am battling a cancer that may or may not end my life. Only God knows. Wendy is here with me always, watching my diet, going to my medical appointments with me and keeping me as happy as I can be The latest great news is that a radical new radiation procedure called "Cyberknife" appears to have eradicated my cancer, thank God.

The most important and valuable lessons I learned about life came to me through my immersion in the martial arts.

Like all of us, I have made mistakes, errors in judgment, and done things that I later wished that I had done differently.

Sometimes I would have given anything to have a moment to live over again and made some change in my actions. That cannot be.

Still I have the knowledge that I always acted in accordance with my conscience and the ethical dictates that I began to form as a child watching John Wayne on the screen.

John Wayne's characters always tried to do the right thing; their honor was of the highest caliber. They never bullied anyone or took advantage. They were defenders of the weak. At the same time, no one was ever able to push them around or make them do anything that they didn't feel was right. They followed the dictates of their heart, their morals, and their ethics.

I was so fortunate to spend 14 years working directly under Jim Marcus, my boss at CCC. He was the finest, most ethical, fairest man I have ever known personally! He approached life with good humor and a true "Golden Rule" attitude. I never saw him treat anyone in a manner that he wouldn't want to have been treated himself.

I worked for Jim from the time I was 28 until I was 42. I went from being a young salesman to become the vice president of sales and marketing in that great company.

It was the real beginning of a long successful business career.

I was in daily touch with Jim, I usually in LA and he usually in New York City. Fortunately, we spent a great deal of time together, either in our individual offices or traveling together on the road. His mentoring, guidance and example was so much a part of my development that I cannot over state it.

At Jim's 100th birthday party, I was fortunate to be one of the 100 or so guests at a very posh Beverly Hills restaurant. His wife Helen, 20 years his junior, had done a wonderful job of creating this testimonial for Jim. The cross section of people included politicians, owners of other big companies, personal friends, and family.

Jim was honored with many things including a commemorative stamp issued by the postmaster of Los Angeles.

At the end of the day there were three speakers; I was one of them.

I spoke for about five minutes, sharing a few anecdotes about my life with Jim. Towards the end I discussed how my life had always included the martial arts. I mentioned that I had been fortunate to train under and with the best martial artists in the world. I said I had learned so much from all of them.

I also said that I learned as much or more from Jim Marcus than from any of my other teachers. I closed by saying:

"Jim didn't teach me how to punch or kick or how to make someone submit to a closing hold, what he taught me was more important, he taught me to be a better man."

In the last analysis, when you look back at your life, with all its mistakes and tragedies, successes and failures, its moments of glory and sorrow, highs and lows, if you can say, "I always lived by my conscience and ethics and always tried to live in a way that I don't have to ever be ashamed of my actions," then you have had a truly wonderful life.

The overriding drive of my life has been love! I have loved deeply and strongly, I am a strong Christian believer. I think that love is the greatest force in human nature. I love my "kids," biological or otherwise without reservation, I love my family, my friends, dogs, and good-hearted strangers.

If you strive throughout your life to do the right thing with honor, courage and a heart full of love, you will have No Regrets!

J. Fisher